PENGUIN PLAYS
THE JOURNALISTS/THE WEDDING FEAST/ SHYLOCK

ARNOLD WESKER (F.R.S.L., Litt.D.), born in Stepney in 1932, was taught at Upton House School in Hackney. His education came mainly from reading books and listening to BBC Radio. From 1948 to 1958 he pursued many trades from furniture maker to pastry cook. His career as a playwright began when Lindsay Anderson, who had read *The Kitchen* and *Chicken Soup with Barley*, brought Wesker to the attention of George Devine at the Royal Court Theatre; Devine, uncertain about *Chicken Soup with Barley*, sent it to the Belgrade Theatre in Coventry, where it was first produced in 1958 under the direction of John Dexter. A year later, having been turned down by the Royal Court, *Roots* was directed by Dexter, again at the Belgrade, Coventry, and in the following months he directed *The Kitchen* at the Court for two Sunday night experimental performances 'without decor'. Later in 1959 *I'm Talking about Jerusalem* was added to make up *The Wesker Trilogy*, which created an enormous impact when produced in its entirety at the Royal Court in 1960 and again at the Shaw Theatre in 1978. In 1979 the National Film Development Board commissioned a film script of the three plays, which, because Wesker made many cuts and additions, is a new work – *The Trilogy* twenty years on! Over 350,000 copies of the Penguin edition have been sold, and the hardback is in its fifth printing.

His other plays include *Chips with Everything* (1962, voted 'Play of the Year'), *Their Very Own and Golden City* (1965, winner of the Italian Premio Marzotto Drama Award in 1964), *The Four Seasons* (1965), *The Friends* (1970), *The Old Ones* (1972), *Love Letters ... Pl........ ...r* (1977), *One More Ride o........................* (1980), *Annie Wobbler* (1..........................982), *Yardsale* (1984), *Wha...........................*, *The Mistress* (1988); thes.......................Voman Plays*; *Bluey* (1984............................Sullied Hand* (1985), *Wha..........................., Badenheim 1939* (1987), *Lady Othello (1987), Beorhtel's Hill* (1988, community play commissioned for the 40th anniversary of Basildon).

In addition to plays for the stage Arnold Wesker has

written television and film scripts, poems, short stories and numerous essays and lectures. He has published two collections of essays, *Fears of Fragmentation* (1970) and *Distinctions* (1985), and three volumes of stories, *Six Sundays in January* (1971), *Love Letters on Blue Paper* (1974) and *Said the Old Man to the Young Man* (1978). In 1974 he wrote the text for a book of primitive paintings of the East End by John Allin, *Say Goodbye You May Never See Them Again*. In 1977, after a brief stay in the offices of *The Sunday Times* to gather material for *The Journalists*, he published an account of his visit called 'Journey into Journalism'. In 1978 came *Fatlips*, his only book for young people. Penguin have published six volumes of his plays and a collection of short stories under the title *Love Letters on Blue Paper*.

From 1961 to 1970 Arnold Wesker was artistic director of Centre 42, a cultural movement for popularizing the arts primarily through trade-union support and participation. From 1981 to 1983 he was President of the International Playwrights' Committee. He is a grandfather and lives with his wife and one of his three children in North London.

ARNOLD WESKER

THE JOURNALISTS
THE WEDDING
FEAST
SHYLOCK

VOLUME 4

PENGUIN BOOKS

PENGUIN BOOKS

Published by the Penguin Group
27 Wrights Lane, London W8 5TZ, England
Viking Penguin, a division of Penguin Books USA Inc., 375 Hudson Street, New York,
New York 100014
Penguin Books Australia Ltd, Ringwood, Victoria, Australia
Penguin Books Canada Ltd, 2801 John Street, Markham, Ontario, Canada L3R 1B4
Penguin Books (NZ) Ltd, 182–190 Wairau Road, Auckland 10, New Zealand

Penguin Books Ltd, Registered Offices: Harmondsworth, Middlesex, England

The Journalists first published in Poland by *Dialog* 1974
First published in Great Britain by Writers and Readers Publishing Cooperative 1975
Published in Penguin Books 1980
Reprinted with revisions 1990
Copyright © Arnold Wesker, 1975, 1990

The Wedding Feast first published by *Plays and Players* 1977
Published in Penguin Books 1980
Reprinted with revisions 1990
Copyright © Arnold Wesker, 1977, 1990

Shylock (formerly *The Merchant*) published in Penguin Books 1990
Copyright © Arnold Wesker, 1990

The Merchant first published in East Germany by Henschel Verlag 1977
Published in Penguin Books 1980
Copyright © Arnold Wesker, 1977

All performing rights of *The Journalists*, *The Wedding Feast* and *Shylock* are fully protected,
and permission to perform any of the plays, whether by amateurs or professionals, must
be obtained in advance from Ian Amos, Duncan Heath Associates, 162–170 Wardour
Street, London W1V 3AT who can furnish all particulars.
All rights reserved

Printed in England by Clays Ltd, St Ives plc

THE JOURNALISTS

This is the eighth version of the play, resulting from rehearsals for world première in Wilhelmshaven, 10 October 1981.

For
VERA ELYASHIV –
journalist and dear friend whose stubbornness
helped shape this play

QUOTATIONS

A journalist is stimulated by a deadline. He writes worse when he has time . . .

It is the mission of the press to disseminate intellect and at the same time destroy the receptivity to it . . .

The making of a journalist: no ideas and the ability to express them . . .

Truth is a clumsy servant that breaks the dishes while cleaning them . . .

KARL KRAUS, *German satirist* (1874–1936)

PUBLISHER'S NOTE

To obtain background material for this play, Arnold Wesker got permission to sit in on all the departments of *The Sunday Times*. An unplanned offshoot of his two-month research was a long essay called 'Journey into Journalism', written in December 1971. Jonathan Cape's offer to publish the essay lead to confrontation. Certain journalists on *The Sunday Times* objected strongly to its appearance, and after an embattled, acrimonious correspondence which added some 10,000 words to the original slim document, Wesker felt honour-bound to withdraw his essay from publication until five years later he was given the go-ahead. It was published by *Writers and Readers* under the title 'Journey Into Journalism'; and later, together with the play and his diary of writing the play by Jonathan Cape under the general title of *The Journalists*.

About this misadventure, Wesker stated at the time, 'My journey into journalism was an unhappy one – an affectionate excursion which went sour ... It's sad since I'd been very impressed with what I'd encountered in my eight weeks with them and thought I'd written a fair, serious and, though critical, yet affectionate piece. They didn't agree and so, since I'd obtained their co-operation for a play, I couldn't abuse it by publishing something they felt unfairly represented them.'

The Journalists is of course based on personal observation; but it is not a *pièce-à-clef* or simple documentary of *The Sunday Times* – nor is it the author's purpose that the play be misread as such.

Its scale of social and work relations and its elements of stage rhythm are in the best Wesker tradition already familiar to playgoers who applauded *The Kitchen* and the epic *Their Very Own and Golden City*.

INTRODUCTION

All drama is open to many interpretations. And they are made!

It *is* true that the writer doesn't perceive all the implications of his work, but equally true that the experience he's assembled in the order he's assembled it is intended to be evidence of one or a set of specific statements.

They may not be the only statements his work makes – it's in the nature of any assembled evidence that it will suggest the proof of different things to different men, but of all the possible statements a work makes – whether poetically or with a greater degree of prose – one will sound the loudest simply because the author has directed all the selection of his material into making it. One pattern will emerge the strongest because the author has delineated its shape with greater emphasis. What he has taken out in his various drafts he has taken out because he's said: that detracts from my theme, blurs my meaning.

When directors and actors interpret a play they are engaged in the act of discovering that one sound which is louder than the others, that one pattern which is stronger than the others.

Whatever sounds or patterns my audience will find in this work there is only one main one which I intended; may not have achieved but had hoped to.

The Kitchen is not about cooking, it's about man and his relationship to work. *The Journalists* is not about journalism, it is about the poisonous human need to cut better men down to our size, from which need we all suffer in varying degrees. To identify and isolate this need is important because it corrupts such necessary or serious human activities as government, love, revolution or journalism.

Swift wrote a novel which gave this cancerous need a name – Lilliputianism. The lilliputian lover competes with his (or her) loved one instead of complementing her. The lilliputian

9

journalist resents the interviewee's fame, influence or achievement rather than wishing to honour it or caution it or seriously question it. The lilliputian bureaucrat (involved in the same process, but in reverse) seeks to maintain his own size by not acknowledging the possibility of growth in those over whom he officiates; he doesn't *cut* down to size, he *keeps* down to size. The lilliputian revolutionary is more concerned to indulge resentments or pay off private scores than to arrive at real justice.

Thus government, love, revolution or journalism are time and time again betrayed. It is this with which my play is concerned.

ARNOLD WESKER

London, 24 January 1975

NOTES

THE SET

An impressionistic layout of the main offices of *The Sunday Paper*. There is a 'cut away' called The Centre Space where the action outside the offices is played.

In order that action and dialogue are evenly distributed over the stage area, the designer must pay careful attention as to which office is near which.

But however the rest is laid out, The News Room must occupy a large space, for most of the final activity goes on there.

To the rear is a screen upon which are projected the huge printing presses. At a point near the end of the play the projection is taken over by a film of the presses beginning to roll.

PRODUCTION

Activity must be continuous in all sections throughout the play while the plot weaves its way stopping here and there – sometimes for a lengthy exchange, sometimes for a few lines. Occasionally conversations will take place on the telephone between individuals from different offices.

While the audience focuses on one 'frame' (section) at a time, the orchestration of what happens *at the same time* in each remaining office is a director's problem. The following may help:

The rhythm of a Sunday newspaper office is one of a slow beginning at the start of the week (Tuesday) working up to an agitated flurry, which culminates at about six in the evening on the Saturday when the button is pushed to start the printing presses rolling for the first editions.

It is important, however, to remember this: it is a Sunday paper, not a daily one; therefore a lot of the pages will be laid out early on in the week. Many articles, indeed, have been set up weeks in advance. This means that not every department is hectic on the Saturday. For example the Arts Pages are well advanced, but Sport – which is waiting for stories of the Saturday matches – is frantic. The two real centres of Saturday's activity are The Stone – where the printers and journalists lay out the pages and make the last minute changes (this area is not shown); and The News Room – where the editor and his closest advisers shape up, on blank sheets, the final product (this area is shown).

I have not indicated every action, but certain routine movements are continuous throughout – growing in intensity towards the end of the play, and the following actions can be drawn from to help the director in his orchestration:

Messengers taking copy from 'The Stone' or from one department to another.

Reporters writing or subs correcting copy at their desks.

Journalists reading newspapers – endlessly! – or official documents.

Journalists in conversation in each other's departments.

Journalists shaving themselves with electric razors, women making up (could toilets be shown? they are constantly washing print off their hands).

A woman pushing a tea trolley is ever present; reporters flow to and from it for tea and sandwiches.

Reporters, secretaries at typewriters.

The constant making or receiving of telephone calls.

Individuals with special information being interviewed.

Clatter is continuous but, of course, volume of noise must be regulated or projection of dialogue will be a constant fight for the actors. Could it all be on tape? then actions could be mimed. I'm thinking particularly of typewriting.

Journalists are alert, fast-thinking and fast-talking individuals. The clue to achieving the right rhythm is to maintain a quick delivery of lines – but in the beginning to have long pauses *between departments* which become shorter as the play continues thus giving the impression of increasing activity.

When action takes place in The Centre Space the rest of the action and noise freezes.

TIME

This may be a problem since there are many assignments which are concertina-ed. It must be imagined that we are covering a week of five days *but* this week is also five weeks. That is to say we've taken our Tuesday from the first week, our Wednesday from the second week and so on. Time is therefore taking place on two planes, and some stories belong to the week, others to the five weeks.

The first professional presentation of *The Journalists* took place on 15 June 1978 on French radio under the auspices of Lucien Attoun's France-Culture. Jugoslav TV presented a television version of the play, setting it in a TV house instead of a Sunday newspaper. The first production in the UK was an amateur one given by the Criterion Theatre, Coventry, on 27 March 1977.

The world première for the professional stage took place in Wilhelmshaven, West Germany, 10 October 1981, directed by Klaus Hoser.

The only professional performance in the UK, has been a reading by professional actors to raise funds for the Jacksons Lane Community Centre in Highgate which took place in the Centre's theatre once in the afternoon and again in the evening of 13 July 1975. The following was the cast:

MARY MORTIMER	Sheila Allen
HARVEY WINTERS	Ian McKellen
CHRIS MACKINTOSH	Sebastian Graham Jones
JULIAN GALLAGHER	William Hoyland
PAUL MANNERING	Michael Mellinger
HARRY LAURISTON	Dave Hill
MARTIN CRUIKSHANK	David Bradley
ANTHONY SHARPLES	Gawn Grainger
MORTY COHEN	Oliver Cotton
DOMINIC FLETCHER	John Hug
JANE MERRYWEATHER	Katherine Fahy
ANGELA GOURNEY	Janet Key
SEBASTIAN HERBERT	Bernard Gallagher
JOHN PROSSER	Hugh Thomas
ERNST GUEST	Brian Badcoe
RONNIE SHAPIRO	Harry Landis
MARVIN McKEVIN	Jim Norton
GORDON FAIRCHILD	John Bennet
TAMARA DRAZIN	Lisa Harrow
NORMAN HARDCASTLE	Brian Cox
CYNTHIA TREVELYAN	Gillian Barge

SECRETARY	Liz Hughes
PAT STERLING	Jennie Stoller
SIR ROLAND SHAWCROSS	Robert Eddison
RT HON. GEORGE CARRON	Mark Dignam
SIR REGINALD MACINTYRE	Peter Jeffrey
OLIVER MASSINGHAM	John Gill
A FINK	Jonathan Pryce
AGNES	Cheryl Campbell
JONATHAN	David Yelland
DESMOND	Andrew Byatt
MAC SMITH	Fulton Mackay
MESSENGERS, SUBS, ETC.	Lindsay Joe Wesker
	Arnold Wesker

Directed by Michael Kustow
Designed by Hayden Griffin
Lighting by Rory Dempster

CHARACTERS

MARY MORTIMER, *a 'columnist'*
HARVEY WINTERS, *the editor*
CHRIS MACKINTOSH ⎫
JULIAN GALLAGHER ⎭ *journalists on In Depth*
PAUL MANNERING, *News editor*
MARTIN CRUIKSHANK, *News reporter*
ANTHONY SHARPLES, *Business News editor*
MORTY COHEN ⎫
DOMINIC FLETCHER ⎭ *Business News journalists*
JANE MERRYWEATHER, *Women's Pages journalist*
SEBASTIAN HERBERT, *Arts Pages editor*
ANGELA GOURNEY, *Assistant Arts Pages editor*
RONNIE SHAPIRO, *Sports editor*
MARVIN MCKEVIN, *Assistant Sports editor*
GORDON FAIRCHILD, *Foreign editor*
TAMARA DRAZIN, *a foreign correspondent*
NORMAN HARDCASTLE ⎫ *journalists working in*
CYNTHIA TREVELYAN ⎭ *Political and Features*
SECRETARY, *to the Editor*
SECRETARY, *in the News Room*
PAT STERLING, *a freelance journalist*
SIR ROLAND SHAWCROSS, *Minister for Social Services*
RT HON. GEORGE CARRON, *Minister for Science and Technology*
SIR REGINALD MACINTYRE, *Chancellor of the Exchequer*
OLIVER MASSINGHAM, *Under Secretary of State – Foreign Affairs*
A FINK, *a man with 'secret' information*
AGNES ⎫
JONATHAN ⎬ *sons and daughter of Mary Mortimer*
DESMOND ⎭
MAC SMITH, *a trade union official – Municipal and General*
MESSENGERS, SUBS, REPORTERS

ACT ONE

PART ONE

The Centre Space

[MARY MORTIMER *is interviewing* SIR ROLAND SHAWCROSS, *Minister for Social Services, in his office. There's a tape recorder on the desk.*]

SHAWCROSS: And that, Miss Mortimer, is precisely what democracy is: a risky balancing act. The delicate arrangement of laws in a way that enables the state to conduct its affairs freely without impinging upon the reasonable freedom of the individual. Tilt it too much one way or the other and either side, state or individual, seizes up, unable to act to its fullest capacity.

MARY: But surely, Minister, with respect, you must agree that the *quality* of democracy doesn't *only* depend on the balance of freedom which our laws create between the individual and society, does it?

SHAWCROSS: By which you mean?

MARY: By which I mean that you may give the letter to the law but ordinary men are forced, daily, to confront the depressing petty officials who interpret those laws.

SHAWCROSS: Go on.

MARY: I could go on endlessly, Sir Roland.

SHAWCROSS: Go on endlessly. I don't see your question yet.

MARY: Well, I'm rather intimidated about going on, you've said these things much better than ever I could.

SHAWCROSS: Be brave.

MARY: All right. Great wisdom and learning may be required to *conceive* statutes but who expects great wisdom and learning in officials? And the ordinary man meets *them* not *you*. He faces the policeman, the factory superintendent, the tax-collector, the traffic warden – in fact the whole gamut of middle men whose officious behaviour affects the temper and pleasure of everyday life.

SHAWCROSS: And your question is?

MARY: What concern do you have for that?

SHAWCROSS: For the gap between the law maker and the law receiver?

MARY: No, with respect, I'd put it another way. For the change in the *quality* of the law which takes place when mediocre men are left to interpret it.

SHAWCROSS: That sounds like a very arrogant view of your fellow creatures, Miss Mortimer.

MARY: Sir Roland, forgive me, I must say it, but that's evasive.

[*Intercom buzzer rings.*]

VOICE: Your car in fifteen minutes, Minister.

SHAWCROSS: Thank you. [*Pause.*] Miss Mortimer, our first hour is nearly up. Tomorrow you're dining with us at home – it is tomorrow, I think? We can continue then. But for the moment I'd like to speak off the record. You've created a very unique reputation in journalism. Rightly and properly you're investigating the minds and personalities of men who shape policy. And you're doing it in depth, in our offices, our homes and on social occasions. I'm surprised so many of us have agreed and perhaps it will prove a mistake. We'll see. But there are aspects of government which it's obviously foolish of us to discuss in public no matter how eager we are to be seen being open and frank. I'm not evasive but, to be blunt, some of my thoughts are so harsh they could be demoralizing. Ah! you will say, that is the part of the man I'm after. But I often wonder, how helpful *is* the truth? You're right, the ordinary man must face the numb and bureaucratic mind. Our best intentions are distorted by such petty minds. But that can't really be my area of concern, can it? I might then be forced to observe that the petty mind is a product of a petty education. Should I then go to complain to the Minister of Education? He might then say education is only *part* of the influence on a growing person – there's family environment to be considered. Should he then interfere in everyman's home? No, no, no! Only God knows where wisdom comes from, you can't legislate for it. Government can only legislate for the *common* good; the *individual* good is, I'm afraid, what men must iron out among themselves. But I don't *act* on those thoughts. My attempts at legislation are not less excellent because I doubt the excellence of men to interpret them. So, which truth will you tell? That I aspire to perfection of the law? That I mistrust the middle men who must exercise that law? Or will you combine the two? The first is pompous, the second abusive, the third confusing.

MARY: And you don't think people would respond to such honesty?

SHAWCROSS: No! Frankly. Most people can't cope with honesty.

MARY: With respect, Minister, but that sounds like a very arrogant view of your fellow creatures.

SHAWCROSS: Ha! [*Pause.*] We'll continue, we'll continue. I must leave.

[*Both go to door which he holds open.*]

And it's not necessary to keep saying 'with respect', Miss Mortimer. Do you enjoy saying it? Funny thing, but people enjoy saying things like 'your honour' 'your Majesty' 'with respect' 'your highness' . . .

Now the offices of *The Sunday Paper* burst into activity.

Editor's Office

[HARVEY WINTERS, *the Editor, dictating to secretary.*]

HARVEY: '. . . And so, you ask, "Where do the best minds go? Not into politics or the civil service", you say "there's no role for this country to perform – instead they go into journalism and the mass media". Journalism as an act of creating self-awareness in society! The best minds don't want to legislate or exercise power so, they comment! Good! And for that very reason I believe it matters intensely the way newspapers, radio and television report and comment on race relations. In Britain, Television News has been an offender – no, a *gross* offender; the interviewer asks people in the street what they think and the weirdest notions of reality are listened to with the respect accorded to truth, as if the electronic marvel of it all sanctified the instant communication of ignorance!' [*Phone rings.*] Bloody hell! I'll never finish those letters. No calls after this. Hello, Winters.

[*It's* ANTHONY SHARPLES, *editor of Business News Section.*]

ANTHONY: You rang?

HARVEY: Tony, yes. I want you to do something on women in the Stock Exchange.

ANTHONY: Love to.

HARVEY: I was thinking of a light-hearted leader, not an occasion for solemnity.

ANTHONY: Indeed not, no, indeed. Something about 'can the dirty joke still be told on the floor?' How many words?

HARVEY: About 450?

ANTHONY: Done.

In Depth

[*Two journalists:* CHRIS MACKINTOSH, JULIAN GALLAGHER.]

CHRIS [*tearing sheet from pad*]: Falling bloody bridges! This subject must have priority over something though God knows what.

JULIAN [*banging on phone receiver*]: Hello? Hello? Blast! Going through to someone else. [*To* CHRIS] Here's that couple of quid I owe you.

Business News

[*This is a large section, only part of which we see, the rest tails off stage. Three journalists:* ANTHONY SHARPLES, MORTY COHEN, DOMINIC FLETCHER.]

DOMINIC [*who's been listening on a phone, shouts, off-stage*]: There's a stringer here says that the Transport and General Workers' Union in the north have an eccentric official who's bored with head office contracts. He insists that every new contract *he* draws up has to have an original clause in it and this time he's insisted that every man get a day off on his birthday. Anybody interested?

VOICE [*off stage*]: Try Features.

DOMINIC [*into phone*]: An incredibly stupid suggestion from one of my colleagues to try Features.

Editor's Office

[MARY *knocks and enters.*]

SECRETARY: Good God! How triumphant she looks.

MARY: They're going to work.

HARVEY: What was he like?

MARY: Shrewd, evasive and charmingly civilized.

SECRETARY: She's obviously enjoying herself.

MARY: Loving it.

SECRETARY: Why, Mary Mortimer, you're even radiant.

MARY: Don't I deserve to be? I worked bloody hard to set up those interviews and they're all going to happen.

HARVEY: We all worked hard –

SECRETARY: – had to pull strings you know. The notorious side of your brilliance isn't the most helpful key for opening the doors of power.

MARY: He's got the best journalist on Fleet Street working for him, stop complaining.

SECRETARY: You'll not expect me to do that.

In Depth

CHRIS: I don't know why the bloody bridges fall down. I don't even know why they keep up.

JULIAN [*pointing to pile of documents while hanging on to a phone*]: By the time we read through this lot we'll be able to build them ourselves. Hello hello HELLO!

CHRIS: Have you got hold of anyone yet?

JULIAN: Going through to someone else now. Hello? Press office? At last. It took five people to get to you. Julian Gallagher, *The Sunday Paper* here. These bridges that keep falling down. Is your ministry making a statement yet?

Editor's Office

HARVEY: You getting your ministers to talk on the science versus politics issue?

MARY: I'm free ranging over everything.

HARVEY: Because I want us to build up a body of comment on that issue and your profiles will be central.

MARY: It's not easy. Not everyone sees the future as you do in terms of science versus politics.

HARVEY: We'll help them then.

MARY: And I trust you're planning to plaster the Saturday screen with the maximum spots?

HARVEY: Don't teach your granny to suck eggs.

MARY: Even granny's male pride is a little punctured, isn't it?

HARVEY: And don't draw me into your emancipation wars, love.

MARY: Confess. Liberated though you may be, Harvey Winters, women do not a paper make. Confess.

HARVEY: I'm not biting. Now be a good girl and go. Look! Letters!

MARY: I'm going. Got me laundry spinning round the corner.

Arts Pages/Women's Pages

[*An office with two journalists from Arts Pages,* SEBASTIAN
HERBERT, *editor, and* ANGELA GOURNEY; *shared with editor of
Women's Pages,* JANE MERRYWEATHER.]

JANE [*just entering with mocked-up sheets*]: Not a very inspir-
ing week's work, is it? An article about women's bums, one
about two awful designers who make men's suits for £150 each
and another about wild tea-drinking parties.

ANGELA: Women are only supposed to be able to write about
boys and knickers. Stop complaining or cross the frontiers to
us on the Arts Pages.

SEBASTIAN: Where she still might find the literature to be
about women's bums and knickers.

In Depth

CHRIS: Do I want a cigarette? Yes I do want a cigarette.
[*Reaching for packet.*] No I don't want a cigarette. Bridges!
Christ! What a come down for In Depth.

Political and Features

[*Two journalists:* NORMAN HARDCASTLE, CYNTHIA TREVELYAN.]

CYNTHIA: Look at these photographs. We've created a mon-
ster.

NORMAN: Aargh! The maimed, the dead, the diseased –

CYNTHIA: – and the starving. Look at them.

NORMAN: Someone must do them but I don't want to look at
them.

CYNTHIA: And I can't get him to snap anything else now.
'Where the violence is, send me there,' he says.

NORMAN: You've encouraged a morbid squint in his eye.

Editor's Office

HARVEY: What's on today?

SECRETARY: You mustn't forget to speak to Chris Mackintosh about the collapse of Atlantis Insurance.

HARVEY: After the eleven o'clock.

SECRETARY: After the eleven o'clock. Then lunch with Morgan King MP.

HARVEY: The new fiery socialist superstar.

SECRETARY: The very same. Then the boss wants you at five.

HARVEY: Can't see myself in a fit state for him after three hours of wine and fiery socialism.

Political and Features

CYNTHIA: When he first came here he could hardly talk. Just threw his photographs on the desk and asked could we use them. In those days I pretended ugliness had poetry. Look at them. Not even pity, is there? 'This is how it is!' And every time he comes in with a new batch of evidence about cruelty it shows in his own features. Bloody hell, they make me feel so wretched!

News Room

[A SECRETARY, *who spends most of her time answering the phone, taking down messages and handing them to the News Editor,* PAUL MANNERING. *A reporter,* MARTIN CRUIKSHANK.]

MARTIN [*waving newspaper*]: Another cutting to give to the honourable Miss Mary Mortimer for her Morgan King MP file.

SECRETARY: Where's he been speaking this time?

MARTIN: Humbermouth. Quote: 'Opening the town hall in the latest new town of Humbermouth, Mr Morgan King, the socialist MP for New Lanark, upset councillors by attacking what he called "the dead spirit of the place". In a speech which can't have endeared him to the town's architect he said: "But where is your town's spirit? This town hall? A building where functionaries meet to organize your rates and drainage problems? Surely," the fiery MP for New Lanark continued, "a town's heart is its concert hall, its swimming pool, libraries, meeting places, its gardens; where are they?"'

PAUL: Splendid. I've no doubt the bitch'll go to town on that one.

Political and Features

NORMAN: Jesus! I've got a lump in my throat.

CYNTHIA: Give up smoking.

NORMAN: It's all right for you to be flippant.

CYNTHIA: Who's flippant? You got a lump in your throat so stop smoking.

NORMAN: You also think it might be cancer?

CYNTHIA: Norman, for God's sake.

Business News

DOMINIC: So I charms into me lap the lovely tennis player, who's also rich, privileged and American, and says to her, 'Ho hum, you think that now you're in my arms I'll not put out that story?' 'But,' she says, 'I thought you were a business journalist not a sports reporter.' 'I am I am,' says I, 'but,' I pretend to her, 'the lesbian love affair of a famous Wimbledon player is too good for any kind of journalist to let slip.' With which she jumps out from the comfort of my ample thighs and cries, 'It's a terrible profession, terrible! Have you no standards?' 'Standards?' I say. 'Profession?' I say. 'I don't believe journalists have a profession. I don't know what that profession is anyway. And certainly they don't have any standards. It's the law of the jungle!' I cry, 'and not a very colourful one at that!' But, soft Irish nit that I am, I relent and in the end swop my silence for a night in the net – in a manner of speaking.

Editor's Office

[NORMAN *visiting*.]

NORMAN: How about letting me take a look at the guerrillas in the Middle East?

HARVEY: Climate's rotten. You know you catch whatever disease is in the air.

NORMAN: I'm serious, Harvey.

HARVEY: So am I.

NORMAN: You haven't got a better person in this paper to do it.

HARVEY: Bloody hell! The egos in this building.

Arts Pages/Women's Pages

JANE: I'm not used enough. I ought to be more provocative instead of practical. 'Down with children' not 'Cheap canvas chairs from Chelsea'. 'Down with children'. 'Must mothers of handicapped children be martyrs?' That sort of thing. Dammit! I'm paid well enough. I want to be stretched. [*With its double entendre*] I luuuuve being stretched.

Editor's Office

HARVEY [*on the phone to* CYNTHIA]: Cynthia, is Norman nearby?

CYNTHIA: No.

HARVEY: He having problems with his wife?

CYNTHIA: Afraid so. Why?

HARVEY: He's pressing me about going abroad again.

CYNTHIA: Guerrillas in the Middle East?

HARVEY: The same. What's his illness this week?
CYNTHIA: Cancer of the throat.
HARVEY: Bloody hell! I'll talk to Gordon.

Sports Pages

[RONNIE SHAPIRO, *Sports Editor*. MARVIN MCKEVIN, *his assistant*.]

RONNIE: Fascist! That's what it is. All sport is fascist activity. I've just realized.
MARVIN: Only just?
RONNIE: Governed by rules against which there's no appeal.
MARVIN: You've been talking to too many referees.
RONNIE: I mean apply them to a democratic society and they wouldn't hold up for ten seconds.
MARVIN: How about taking over the Arts Pages for six months?
RONNIE: And what's more fascist than all that crap about healthy body healthy mind?
MARVIN: And character being built on the playing fields of Eton?
RONNIE: All balls. *What* character, that's the point. The Arts Pages? I'd love to.

Arts Pages/Women's Pages

SEBASTIAN: It's 9000. Last year we received 9000 books to review of which we succeeded in covering roughly one fifth – nearly two thousand in fact.
JANE: Is that good or bad?
SEBASTIAN: Very good, my girl. What, 1900 books in 52 weeks? Work it out.
JANE: You work it out.
SEBASTIAN: I will, I will. That's let's see, 52 into 340, six – that's roughly 36 books a week which, although many are reviews in brief, is pretty good going. Yes, very good I'd say.

Editor's Office

[GORDON FAIRCHILD *of Foreign Department, visiting.*]

HARVEY: I'd like the research to begin now, Gordon. Go right back to the thirteenth century, who was Islamized, which minorities remained, the role of Imperial England in protecting them, why did they survive, how many guerrilla groups can be identified, and what part did the Secret Services play?

GORDON: What about the power of the priests?

HARVEY: Right! You can give a breakdown on the sects as well.

GORDON: I'm thinking of something more on the lines of linking the massacres to the religious rabble-rousers.

HARVEY: Too big. It's a separate piece.

GORDON: But central, don't you think?

HARVEY: I know that priests everywhere have a lot to answer for and one day we'll write it – something for Tamara perhaps – but not now. This massacre's enough. O.K.?

GORDON: As you say.

[*We watch* GORDON *move to Foreign Department and for the first time pause in dialogue to absorb the scene.*]

Foreign Department

[TAMARA DRAZIN, *foreign correspondent.* GORDON, *just entering.*]

GORDON: Harvey wants us to keep going at our Middle East war.

TAMARA [*with irony*]: He's not afraid of 'boring' our readers?

GORDON: Even if it does.

TAMARA: Small blessings.

GORDON: And I agree with him.

TAMARA: And I'm sick. Look at it. [*Indicating telex reports.*] For what? What in this world is worth such savage slaughter?

GORDON: Keep cuts to a minimum then.

TAMARA: Cut it? I want to weep on it.

Arts Pages/Women's Pages

JANE: Do you know what Mary said to me when I first came to work here? 'If you're young and in charge,' she said, 'and you want to deflate an old journalist, my advice to you is this: when she – or he – brings his piece to you, you flip through it and then throw it on the desk and say – well, honestly, I didn't expect you to show me something like this.'

ANGELA: That sounds like our Mary. What made you think of that?

JANE: Don't know. Remember the time I invited the politicos to our ideas luncheon and we ended up giving *them* ideas? Well, I gave the idea for those in-depth interviews of cabinet ministers to Norman and – well – oh, I don't know. Credit grabbing is one of the sicknesses of this profession. Takes it out of you.

Foreign Department

[TAMARA *is cutting out her clippings and pasting them in her book.*]

TAMARA: Look how full my scrap-book's getting.

GORDON: I've an idea which I put to Harvey and he likes.

TAMARA: Do you know why we all keep scrap-books of our little bits and pieces?

GORDON: It's a serious long term project for you, listen to me.

TAMARA: So that in twenty years time we can say 'Look! I was right. Here it is. In print!'

GORDON: An in-depth probe into the power of the priests. Something on the lines of linking massacres to the religious rabble-rousers. The priests have a lot to answer for, you know.

TAMARA: What priests? There are priests and priests.

GORDON: All dogma begins with the priesthood. And where there's dogma there's massacre.

TAMARA: I'm not fit, Gordon, believe me, I'm not fit.

News Room

[PAT STERLING, *a freelance, talking to* PAUL.]

PAUL: I don't think it's our story, Pat, not really. Aren't girls of twelve having abortions all the time?

PAT: But this one had been refused by a National Health Service gynaecologist. Some shrivelled-up old hag.

PAUL: We can't help being shrivelled-up old hags, you know, and isn't it all over anyhow?

PAT: That's why you can print the story.

PAUL: And the poor child's had her abortion privately?

PAT: If you play adult games says this gynaecologist, 'you must expect adult consequences'.

PAUL: Awful, yes, I know, terrible story. Have you tried the *News of the World*?

PAT: Don't you just *know* what they'd do with it?

SECRETARY: The eleven o'clock in five minutes, Paul.

PAUL [*assembling papers*]: I'm sorry. [*Leaves.*]

PAT [*to* SECRETARY]: Your paper *will* print this story. I'll find the right door. Sooner or later.

Foreign Department

GORDON: Perhaps you should see a psychiatrist.

TAMARA: Uch! They're so immodest. They imagine every distress is curable, everything can be explained!

GORDON: Did you know I was under one for three years?

TAMARA: 'The fault of the past!' Such awful presumptions. They're too arrogant to acknowledge there's such a thing as *endemic* despair and you can't *pay* to have *that* cut out. It's something you're born with.

GORDON: Or something you have if you can afford it.

TAMARA: That's a crude observation.

NORMAN: Really now? Crude to observe that the starving child can't afford to reflect on life's hopelessness?

TAMARA: Ah ha! The starving child. He had to be brought in.

GORDON: Don't sneer at the starving child, my dear. Without him you'd have no endemic despair to enjoy.

TAMARA: Demagogue!

GORDON: Scorn not the man who doth attempt alleviation of man's ills.

TAMARA: Scorn such a man I do not. But man's relentless and ugly stupidities are mine to despair of. You want to do good deeds? Do them. I will give you my cheque and God bless you. But do them silently and not heartily and give me leave to lament what I will.

GORDON: I'm even more convinced you need help.

TAMARA: And don't insult me.

> [*She leaves.* MARTIN *passes her, extending a greeting she ignores.*]

MARTIN: She's getting worse.

GORDON: She worries me. She's speaking louder, faster and, with her deep-throated Slavic accent, she's becoming like a Nöel Coward caricature.

MARTIN: A man just rang in, American, freelance. Says he's got a trunk load of documents that reveals the 'truth about Ethiopia'. [*Imitating*] 'Oh boy, man, is this big. Wait till you get a load of *this*. This is really big.'

GORDON: They're all big.

Sports Pages

[MARVIN *entering.*]

MARTIN: Bloody hell!

RONNIE: I'm not interested.

MARVIN: Those phoney sports stories in the *Daily Sun* I've been blasting?

RONNIE: What of them?

MARVIN: Harvey stopped me this morning and said lay off.

RONNIE: *That* he should've said to me.

MARVIN: 'Lay off,' he said, 'my opposite number is squealing.'

RONNIE: Are we trying to change sports reporting or are we not trying to change sports reporting?

[*Phone rings. It's* HARVEY *from the Editor's office.*]

HARVEY: Ronnie?

RONNIE: Yes, Harvey.

HARVEY: Yesterday's *Financial Times*. Page 12. Second column, three up from the bottom. Got it?

RONNIE [*who's been turning pages of the F.T.*]: Got it.

HARVEY: Aston Vale Football club is offering you, me and others shareholdings in the club. Might make a good story for 'Bullseye'. Who's selling them, how many, why, and who's buying. O.K.?

RONNIE: O.K. Thanks. [*Phone down.*]

Editor's Office

[*It has been slowly filling up with people for the 'eleven o'clock' editorial meeting.*

Present are ANTHONY SHARPLES, CHRIS MACKINTOSH, GORDON FAIRCHILD.]

HARVEY [*to* ANTHONY *and having just put down the phone*]: You going to stop reading that paper and listen to us?

ANTHONY: When *you've* stopped phoning.

HARVEY: Right, gentlemen. And what are we going to do about our beloved leader and his government this week?

GORDON: I think it's about time we tried a touch of irony in our political commentaries. 'Today poverty is your own fault, today you can stand on your own two feet. Anyone can become Prime Minister.'

CHRIS: 'Our beloved leader has proved it.'

GORDON: 'And our nasty chancellor has proved it. All of them self-made and nasty men saying you too can also be self-made and nasty men . . .'

CHRIS: Think they'll get the point? [*To* GORDON.] Here's that couple of quid I owe you.

Political and Features

[TAMARA *visiting.*]

CYNTHIA: 'Why so pale and wan, fond lover?'

TAMARA: I think what I'd like is a good, old-fashioned nervous breakdown.

CYNTHIA: That's a shocking thing to say, Tamara.

TAMARA: There's such honesty about going to pieces.

CYNTHIA: You mustn't be frivolous about such things.

TAMARA: Mornings. Wake up. A disc-jockey's forced jocularity.

CYNTHIA: Well, thank God for a little jocularity, I say.

TAMARA: These offices. Sour jealousies. Battles for space. Defeated journalists.

NORMAN: *Not* first day of the week, pleeease.

TAMARA [*picking up newspaper and turning pages*]: Then all this. The smug weariness of experienced politicians. The intimidations of bigoted minorities. The tortuous self-defence of money makers. The pomposity of knowledge-glutted academics. Genocide in the Middle East. And us, with our five or six hundred words, I feel so guilty being able to cope with it all.

CYNTHIA: Guilts! Guilts! Those sombre, Jewish guilts.

NORMAN: The price we pay for the pleasure of your company is the depressing effects of your conversation.

Arts Pages/Women's Pages

ANGELA [*who is checking proofs*]: Sebastian, is it your idea of a joke, a correction, or an improvement to change the words of my review from 'to put it mildly' to 'to put it wildly'?

SEBASTIAN: Oh, here's a much better printer's error. [*Reading from a proof.*] 'They become incredibly wound up; yet these is method in their madness for the unwinding is ceremonies and without a bitch.'

Political and Features

CYNTHIA: As a matter of fact I'm about to embark on a long eulogy of disc-jockeys.

TAMARA: Really.

CYNTHIA: All about the joy they bring to drab lives.

TAMARA: And how their constant stream of gaiety denies the existence of unhappiness and how there's nothing more gloomy than laughter at all costs?

CYNTHIA: It's not laughter at all costs, it's music at all costs.

TAMARA: *Music?* A spurious urgency, perhaps, to cover up for poverty of talent.

CYNTHIA: You're growing old and square.

TAMARA: What an easy vocabulary of insults we have these days. 'Square' presumably is the state you need to think others are in so that you can feel young? [*She leaves.*]

CYNTHIA: How complicated these central European ladies are.

Editor's Office

[*Editorial continuing.* PAUL *from News Desk entering.*]

HARVEY: Hello, Paul. Our problem is that we're all in agreement that government's wrong and we're right.

ANTHONY: Oh, I don't know. I'm more inflationary than you.

HARVEY: Are you? Well, you're wrong then. I think we're entitled to be absolutely critical of *all* aspects by now and it would be absolutely consistent with our policy to criticize the government's economic strategy.

ANTHONY: There *is* no economic strategy.

GORDON: But there *is* a philosophy. I mean 'let lame ducks go to the wall and stand on your own two feet' *is* a philosophy.

ANTHONY: Yes, but it's not a strategy.

HARVEY: Anyway, they're changing doctrines. State subsidy, for industries suffering from 'non-culpable decline'.

ANTHONY: From what?

HARVEY: 'Intervention in industry,' says the minister in today's

34

Times, 'is respectable in areas of non-culpable decline.' What do we say to that?

GORDON: Sounds like a very sad apology for dying. 'Please, everyone, forgive my non-culpable decline.'

Business News

MORTY: The great thing about Arnold Weinstock is – the man's so sane.

DOMINIC: What is there about shop keepers, d'you think, that mesmerizes the intelligent journalists of Business News?

MORTY: If he has to sack 5000 men because of waste he'll do it. And he'll justify it by saying it's better for the sacked ones because men get depressed hanging around doing nothing, lose self-respect.

DOMINIC: Compassionate man, Weinstock.

MORTY: And those that stay know that they're good because Weinstock has kept them and so they're men of confidence.

DOMINIC: A Solomon, no less!

MORTY: His prime task? To weed out a waste. He appeals to men's greed but, paradoxically –

DOMINIC: – paradoxically –

MORTY: – paradoxically he must elicit from them a high degree of *co-operation* in order to satisfy that greed.

DOMINIC: Paradoxically.

MORTY: His approach is precisely that of a good business journalist – determined to cut through half truths and vague generalizations.

DOMINIC: Really?

MORTY: 'Never believe anything,' he says, 'all information is suspect.'

DOMINIC: Arnold Weinstock's attitude is rather like that of the baron of whom it was asked: 'Why do you build your walls so high and strong?' To which the baron replied: 'In order to give the peasants' hovels something to lean upon.'

Editor's Office

[*Editorial continuing.*]

HARVEY: Where are we on the spaceship deaths?
PAUL: No further than any other newspaper.
GORDON: Anyone know why the monkey died last time?
ANTHONY: Boredom, I think.

Political and Features

[MARY *rushes in with her bag of laundry.*]

MARY: I'm late for the 'eleven o'clock'.
NORMAN: We've got another Morgan King quote for you. Cynthia?
CYNTHIA [*reading from a cutting*]: 'Addressing the annual Durham Miners' gala over the weekend, Mr Morgan King, the new fiery socialist superstar member for New Lanark, said: "I believe that before any legislation can be passed in parliament there must exist the machinery to communicate an understanding of that legislation."'
MARY: What the bloody hell does he think newspapers and television are for?
CYNTHIA: '"It is not enough to print our complex white papers which few understand, nor to leave their interpretation to the not-always-adequately-briefed and random intelligence of busy, information-drunk journalists who interpret according to bias or the quality of their minds."'
MARY: The impertinence! The incredible impertinence of the man. How dare he? 'The quality of their minds'. Who the bloody hell does he think he is. A jumped-up miner's son with exaggerated notions about the value of self-education!
NORMAN: Uh-uh-uh-uh!
MARY: Well *I'm* not intimidated by working-class haloes – the pain of poverty has never blinded me to its product of ignorance, and underprivilege was never a guarantee against char-

latanism and *that's* the function of journalism – to protect society from shabby little charlatans like him.

NORMAN [*leaving*]: And who will protect society from shabby little journalists?

MARY [*calling after him*]: I'll take you on some other time.

In Depth

[NORMAN *visiting*.]

NORMAN: Where's your master?

JULIAN: Don't have masters or deputies in our department. Some of us just get paid more.

NORMAN: Worthy, worthy.

JULIAN: Being someone's deputy is an invitation to assassination. He knows it, I know it, so we drop titles. Lovely life. Easy, civilized, just what I was born to. Scurrying across Europe to investigate this and that, pause for a love affair, a ballet, a bit of skiing. You ever go skiing, Norman?

NORMAN: Are you mad? Skiing? You can break legs and die of exposure and things.

JULIAN: Glad to see you can laugh at your fears.

NORMAN: I'm not laughing. That's the mistake everyone makes. I ceased laughing after Molière. Humour for me is an internal haemorrhage, otherwise it's contrived giggles.

Editor's Office

[*Editorial continuing*. MARY *entering*.]

HARVEY: Hello, Mary. I think we ought to have someone in the Middle East in case war breaks out.

ANTHONY: In *case* war breaks out? With six million refugees and every major power full of pious platitudes? War? *And* revolution, *and* famine, *and* cholera.

HARVEY: Any volunteers to go?

GORDON: Me please.

HARVEY: You'll bloody stay here and co-ordinate.

ANTHONY: No free trips this time, my lad.

HARVEY: I'm thinking of sending Norman to take a look at those Middle East guerrillas.

GORDON: You thinking or is he asking?

Sports Pages

[MAC SMITH, *a trade union official, visiting.*]

RONNIE: So it's settled then?

MAC: I can't be sure, Ronnie.

RONNIE: There's very little any of us can be sure of in this life, we know, but, Mac, we met six times last week. Management say they're not yet closing down the garage. Your men are safe, for the moment.

MAC: Ah, but are they? And has management said they're *not* closing down the garage? They've changed the *date* for closure, but *we* asked them to withdraw it.

RONNIE: And haven't they agreed on that?

MAC: The position's very ambiguous.

RONNIE: Industrial disputes usually are, old son.

MAC: Don't be frivolous, brother, the strike threat's not passed yet.

Editor's Office

[*Editorial continuing.*]

HARVEY: Right, now, science and politics.

ANTHONY: Morty's getting a good picture of investments in technology. Should have it by the end of the month.

CHRIS: Norman's pursuing the backbone: 'Has technology rearranged the genes of political issues?' or some such thing to do with futurology.

GORDON: That'll bring them in.

HARVEY: You remain sceptical?

GORDON: I remain sceptical.

MARY: We doing something more about this racist new book on race by the way?

CHRIS: What do you suggest?

MARY: Oh – something suggesting he's erring according to Hudson's law of selective attention to data?

PAUL: That might boomerang. Since the journalist's profession is given to just that: the selective attention to data.

Business News

DOMINIC: They want to take over the shipyards? Workers' control? Right, here's what I'll want to discover:

One: Can they produce workers who can manage and administer, can they overcome demarcation issues, can they double production?

Two: If they can, will it be allowed to work?

Three: If it's not allowed to work will this produce a chain reaction of protest from workers in other industries?

Four: If it is allowed to work will the example be followed in other industries?

Five: Most important – will it not produce hierarchy creating its own disenchantments.

As a good barrister by training my questions are already succinctly formulated.

MORTY: And as a good reporter the answers already written, I trust.

Editor's Office

[Editorial continuing.]

ANTHONY: And how's Mary's profiles? Coming along are they?

MARY: Four down three to go.

ANTHONY: Committing themselves on science versus politics?

MARY: Here and there. George Carron will, of course.

PAUL: I should hope so, being the Minister for Science and Technology.

GORDON: Do they actually let you come into their houses, fondle their dogs, tickle their grandchildren, pour wine for you and all that?

MARY: All that and more.

ANTHONY: More. Ah ha!

MARY: Harvey, I'd like, while we're talking about profiles, to pursue someone else I think we all should be keeping an eye on.

PAUL: Morgan King MP no doubt.

HARVEY: Oh, the superstar. I'm lunching with him today.

GORDON: You planning to rubbish him? Poor man. He's only just started his political career. I'd've thought small fry for you, Mary.

PAUL: She's actually been having a go at him for some time.

ANTHONY: Under cover of that 'witty, cool and deathly column' of hers.

HARVEY: They're heathens, Mary, ignore them. Tell us.

MARY: I don't know. He smells phoney. I'm just saying he needs to be kept an eye on and I'd like to know you'd be interested if I came up with anything.

HARVEY: Providing we don't get snarled up in any more litigations. Our libel insurance is running low.

GORDON: I actually get prickles on my skin every time I see Mary prepare to lunge for a kill. Thrilling. That's my word for it – thrilling.

MARY: Harvey, would you excuse me. I don't think you need me. [*She leaves.*]

HARVEY: You must stop getting at her or I'll begin to think it's professional jealousy, and you wouldn't want me to think that.

PAUL: I think she's lethal.

CHRIS: But a brilliant journalist.

PAUL: *You* all think so, I know.

Political and Features

CYNTHIA: Don't you ever feel uneasy, sometimes, as a journalist? We inundate people with depressing information and
they become concerned. Then we offer more information and
they become confused. And then we pile on more and more
until they feel impotent but we offer them no help. No way
out of their feelings of impotence. Don't you ever feel guilty?

NORMAN: Constantly.

PART TWO

The Centre Space

[*Part of the lounge in the home of the Rt Hon.* GEORGE CARRON,
Minister for Science and Technology. He's playing chess with MARY.]

CARRON: I'm a bachelor, Miss Mortimer. If I'd been married
– nice cultured woman and all that – I might be more interested
in literature, films, plays. But I'm not.

MARY: You don't mind me asking, Mr Carron?

CARRON: After three gruelling sessions with this old man? Ask
away. I'll tell you what I mind and don't mind. But art? Can't
help you there. You'll have to put me down as uncultured.
Science and politics, those are my passions.

MARY: And chess.

CARRON: Ah, chess. My only addiction.

MARY: So, it doesn't worry you that all those upstart writers
are required reading in the schools?

CARRON: Worry me?

MARY: After all, *their* values point to one kind of society while
you're legislating to shape another kind of society.

CARRON: Worry me? Strange question. Check. Look, I'm an
old man and, I'll confess, not a very happy one. I began my
career as a labour politician from a farm labourer's background, and half way changed my politics to Tory – a man's

driven by the profit motive, plain and simple, I soon found that out. But, it makes for a lonely life. To be despised. Not nice. You live with it but you never get used to it. Still, that's not the point. What I'm saying is that experience shaped me, not art. I didn't change roads because of what I read in books, but because of what I read in man. I'm tone-deaf, colour-blind and get very impatient with the convenient concoctions literary men make into novels. I saw a play once and I thought to myself, yes, well, them people can behave like that 'cos they got good scripts written for them. I prefer men who write their own scripts. They do it in 'The House' and they do it in the cabinet and they do it at international conferences and that's real. Art shaping society? I doubt it. Science, yes, not books. Still, I've got to believe that haven't I? Minister for Science and Technology and all that.

MARY: Can we talk about science then?

CARRON: You haven't moved out of check yet.

MARY: Sorry. [*She moves.*]

CARRON: Ah! You know what you're about, don't you?

MARY: I've got three children who kept calling me bourgeois for playing bridge so I pacified them by learning chess.

CARRON: My one regret – no children. Watch out for your queen.

MARY: The editor wants to focus on the science versus politics debate.

CARRON: Facile divisions. Journalese. Look, the argument goes like this, I know it: there develops, it is said, unnoticed by most of us, a whole range of scientific discovery which creeps up behind societies and suddenly – is there! And each time it happens, the argument goes, then all the political deliberations of decades are rendered useless and we have to begin to formulate our opinions all over again. Right? It's an attractive picture and I can see why newspapers choose it as a popular controversy, it's ripe for oversimplification! But how accurate is it? Look at the period between 1900 and 1913, 'La Belle Epoque' we call it. Worldwide economic growth, prosperity, scientific and technological advances. The lot!

MARY: Science made *possible* by politics, not in *conflict* with it.

CARRON: Exactly! But look what happened after 1913 – something neither science nor political philosophy could account for: an idiotic, soul-destroying world war!

MARY: Then who *should* account for it?

CARRON: Ah! Now you're asking a question which needs the kind of complex answers newspapers can't give and presumably didn't give in those early 1900s. Instead they oversimplified, as you're trying to do. Books! History! The interaction of ideas – that's where you'll find your answers and where I think you ought to guide your readers for their answers.

MARY: But, Minister, that's a contradiction. You said *experience* changed men, not ideas from books. Now you're saying certain *ideas* formed the basis for 'La Belle Epoque'!

CARRON: Contradictions? Well, you've got to live with them also. A Jewish MP once told me a story about an old rabbi who was asked to settle a dispute between two men. The first man tells his version and the rabbi listens, thinks, and says: 'You know, you're right.' Then the second man presents his side of the argument and the rabbi listens, thinks and says: 'You know, you're right,' At which the rabbi's pupil who was standing by waiting for wisdom says: 'But rabbi, first you said this man was right, then you said that man was right. How can that be?' And the rabbi listened and thought and said: 'You know what? You're also right.'

In Depth

JULIAN: We were at this party and this Tory bag came up to me and she asked me what I did, so I said, despite my extremely youthful looks, I said: 'I edit *The Sunday Paper*, ma'am.' And she, ignoring my youthful looks, believed me and whispered: 'Ah ha! Wanted to meet you. *I* think you've got three fully paid up members of the Communist Party on your In Depth team.' And quick as a flash I said: 'Oh no, ma'am, they're not as right-wing as all that!'

Arts Pages/Women's Pages

ANGELA: [*reading copy*] Good God! What a negative piece! Ever thought of asking a critic 'not to bother this week'?

SEBASTIAN: What, him give up his precious space? My dear girl, people opening their Sunday paper look forward to reading a critic's piece. Wouldn't miss it for the world. Even if it is only a bumbling on.

ANGELA: Funny creatures, critics.

JANE: Are they any good at taking criticism of their criticism?

SEBASTIAN: Most accommodating. The better they are the less they mind what you say. It's only the minor critics who go into tantrums.

Editor's Office

[PAUL *visiting*.]

PAUL: I'm not happy about our attitude to the government, Harvey. I know you feel we should be more vigorous in our comments but we do stand for something, you know.

HARVEY: Not uncritically, Paul. You can't say we're irresponsible in our condemnations of government policy. We've got a first-class team, Oxbridge firsts, good, hard analytical brains who understand the problems and –

PAUL: – and nothing, Harvey. They understand nothing. You know and I know and anyone who's an old hand knows that newspapers can't deal in truths but only in facts, and sometimes judgements. Not this lot though. They still believe in the sanctity of print!

HARVEY: I don't think that's fair, Paul. They're aware of limitations and careful of judgements. We'd do the same if the left were in power.

PAUL: I know that, Harvey. But not everyone else on the staff knows it. They're a bit cynical these youngsters you've gathered round you. They see *The Sunday Paper*, being an old conservative family newspaper and therefore commanding more credibility, as being the best journal through which to infiltrate radical views. True! The very words they use. 'Infiltrate radical views.'

HARVEY: Come now, Paul, don't let's get too portentous.

Business News

ANTHONY [*reading and laughing at a newspaper report*]: We're being told here by the illustrious *Telegraph* that – and I quote: 'The Business News section of *The Sunday Paper* is like the TV power game programmes, tending to see all business as a jungle and all business men as nasty, wrangling, grinning, smooth handshaking, back-stabbing villains . . .'

DOMINIC: Except Arnold Weinstock, of course.

News Room

MARTIN [*on the phone*]: Let's get this straight. They put a bomb in the boutique, gave them ten minutes to clear out and sent this note to *The Times*? O.K. let's have it. [*Writing down*.] 'If you are not busy being born you are busy buying.' Yes. 'In fashion as in everything else capitalists can only look backwards . . .' Jesus! This is school kid's stuff. O.K. go on. 'The future is ours.' *What*? Spend our wages on *what*? 'Nothing to do except spend our wages on the latest skirt or shirt.' They call this political analysis? Yes, all right, go on. [PAUL *enters*. MARTIN *explains*.] The Anarchists Brigade have struck again, a boutique. [*Into phone*.] 'Brothers, sisters, what are your real desires?' Yes. 'Sit in the drug store, look distant, empty, bored . . .' Yes, I've got it. Or *what*? 'Or blow it up or burn it down.' Yes. 'You cannot reform profit, capitalism and inhumanity, just kick it till it breaks.' *What*? Revolution? It just ends like that? Revolution? 're-vol-u-tion.' Got it. No, I don't write shorthand. I find most people so boring in what they say that my slow long-hand is fast enough to catch what's worthwhile. Thanks. [*Replaces receiver*.]

PAUL: A bomb in a boutique? My own particular problem is to distinguish between their outrage and their envy.

Foreign Department

[*Urgent sound of 'tick-tack'.* MARY *and* TAMARA *are reading what is coming through the telex machine.*]

MARY: Where the hell is our fiery socialist speaking from now?

TAMARA: Hamburg.

MARY: He's every bloody where.

[*Phone rings. It's* HARVEY.]

HARVEY: Mary? I want you to look after Peter's affairs for the month he's away.

MARY: And who'll look after mine?

HARVEY: Come on, love, you know you've always wanted to be special features editor and you've got the biggest shoulders of any of us.

MARY: Very flattering.

HARVEY: And the sharpest intellect. There! That better?

MARY: Isn't it about time Paul was pensioned off?

HARVEY: That question discredits you. I'll forget you asked it.

MARY: He's tired, sentimental and a third-rate mind.

HARVEY: He's efficient, dependable and knows the job from top to bottom. I don't like sacking old men.

MARY: If I'm to fill in for Pete he'll get in my way.

HARVEY: You're relentless, Mary.

MARY: A quality you not infrequently rely upon. Are you free?

HARVEY: No.

MARY: I want to hear your impressions of Morgan King.

HARVEY: Ten minutes. [*Phones down.*]

TAMARA: There's something unhealthy about your dislike of Morgan King.

MARY: I can't stand do-gooders.

TAMARA: Oh come now. Every politician is a do-gooder.

MARY: Please, read it, Tamara.

TAMARA [*Reading from long, white telex sheet*]: 'I tell you of these incidents in my private life because, if we're talking about the need for society to produce the whole man then let *us* be seen as whole men, imperfections and all, since it is an imperfect man for whom we must build a compassionate society.'

MARY: Really! Who does he think he is? Protesting his imperfections as though we wouldn't believe he had any in the first place. Don't you find something irritating about a good person?

TAMARA: Not just 'something'. It's perfectly easy to identify: their goodness, by comparison, reveals our shabbiness. Simple!

[MARY *exasperated, leaves.*]

Sports Pages

MARVIN: I've got eight brothers and they've all, all of them got funny names. Like Jack the Corporation, James the Jumper, Willie the Woodman. And why? Because my parents were publicans and each of us was born in a different pub. Solly the Dun Cow, Chris the Mortar and Pestle, Horace the Mulberry Bush. It was Jonah The Pig and Whistle who used to object most.

RONNIE: And you, Marvin. What were you called?

MARVIN: Don't laugh? Marvin the Mermaid.

News Room

MARTIN: And yet, you know, I've a sneaking sympathy for The Anarchists Brigade. There's something about ostentation makes you want to blow it up.

PAUL: It's their cosy world of small sabotage that irritates me, their weakness for simplified political platitudes.

SECRETARY: I mean they're just spit-and-run boys, aren't they?

MARTIN: Do you know I saw a Rolls Royce with a TV aerial on it today? Why should anyone want to watch TV while being driven through interesting streets? Pale blue it was. And I was confused between admiration for its mechanics and disgust for its opulence. Got this great urge to crash into it. Irrational really. Not an urge I was proud of. Bit mean.

PAUL: Their passion for destruction is inherited from the enemy they loathe.

SECRETARY: Relieves them of tiny angers.

MARTIN: I did *so* want to knock it down.

PAUL: And their little bombs are not the most persuasive argument for nuclear disarmament.

MARTIN: Still, they have tried everything else without much effect. Marches, sit-downs, teach-ins, civil disobedience.

Art Pages/Women's Pages

SEBASTIAN: I read your piece on Hughie Green, Jane. You actually think he's a genius?

JANE: Yes, I do – and I chose the word carefully.

SEBASTIAN: What an extraordinary misuse of the epithet!

JANE: His television parlour games have the highest ratings.

SEBASTIAN: Oh, I see. Impressed by numbers are you?

JANE: *And* he's a man of the people.

SEBASTIAN: Is that his claim or your conclusion?

ANGELA: Old ladies love him, it's true, but his gags are terrible.

JANE: Which is precisely what puts him on a level with 25 million viewers who are desperately relieved to hear a famous man only able to make jokes as awful as they would themselves.

SEBASTIAN: And *that's* genius?

JANE: 'The people count,' he says, 'and I am the people's servant.' And then he makes a brilliant volte face and defends the establishment. 'I sincerely believe,' he says, 'that there are certain of us who are better equipped to know what is good for us than others.' And double-thinking like that is real genius.

SEBASTIAN: Not in my dictionary it isn't.

Sports Page

RONNIE: We used to have a woman on the travel page who regularly, for two years, used to hand in stuff saying such and such a place was a lovely sunny beach until the Jews got there! Didn't care that it was never printed, she never seemed to get the message. And it took two years before management could bring themselves to sack her. She was a widow, you see. Lived alone. Cruelly abandoned by kith and kin. Acid personality – but a loner. You can't fling people on the dole just 'cos they're anti-semitic, can you?

MARVIN: No sense of revenge, that's what irritates me about you Jews. Understanding of everything and everyone. Not healthy, Ronnie boy. Bite! Gotta bite back.

RONNIE: That's our trouble. We're beginning to.

Business News

[CHRIS *visiting*.]

DOMINIC [*to* MORTY]: And who's your Arnold Weinstock for this month?

MORTY: Oh, he'll last, my son. Good for a reference every two months or so – at least.

ANTHONY [*to* CHRIS]: And what are our In-depth colleagues in-depthing this week?

CHRIS: The crash of boring old bridges I'm afraid.

ANTHONY: And what help can we offer you on that?

CHRIS: Not crashing bridges, old son, but crashing insurance companies.

ANTHONY: Ah! The ill-fated Atlantis company.

CHRIS: I've got a lead from a high-up on the Board of Trade.

DOMINIC [*mocking*]: 'At 08.00 hours the shrewd and enigmatic Mr Cruikshank –'

MORTY [*taking up the mockery*]: '– a clean-shaven, handsome man, greying attractively at the temples –'

DOMINIC: '– was seen by his cleaner to arrive an hour earlier than usual at the head office of Atlantis Insurance –'

MORTY: '– Meanwhile, back at the Board of Trade, Mr X –'

DOMINIC: '– who shall remain nameless –'

MORTY: '– was heard cracking his hard-boiled, mid-morning egg –'

DOMINIC: '– four minutes, of course –'

MORTY: '– with greater anxiety than usual –'

DOMINIC: '– At that moment, 800 miles away in the Bahamas, the beautiful wife of the Swiss ambassador was sun-bathing with the even more beautiful wife of the junior partner of Atlantis Insurance and discussing the latest wines of the little known but highly sought after Chateau de Montaigne –'

MORTY: '– At first sight all these far flung incidents have no connection –'

CHRIS: Care to take over the column, boys?

ANTHONY: Oh, we're much too flippant for your serious investigations, Chris. Now –

CHRIS: Now. What's the percentage an insurance company must set aside to cover claims?

ANTHONY: Well, let's see. The big boys arrange that sort of thing amongst themselves, you know.

CHRIS: Good God!

ANTHONY: Yes, God is good. But, it would appear, only to them what already have. Now, at one time it was 9 per cent and then . . .

Foreign Department

GORDON: Of course you're growing old. We're all growing old. Especially in this profession. At 32 one's old.

TAMARA: Gordon, can you lend me a couple of pounds, please?

GORDON [*dipping into his pocket*]: I remember when Kruschev died, there was this reporter, one of our top men, tried to phone through to the Kremlin. Didn't stop to think that neither of them would be able to speak the other's language, just automatically reached for the phone. The spark goes. Last night on TV I was watching an awful tragedy and I was thinking – yes, now how can we handle that? This way? Yes, maybe. That way? Yes, well – I'll sleep on it. Years ago I'd have immediately rung up people and started generating ideas.

TAMARA [*referring to newspaper*]: And the slaughter goes on. 'Tanks fire on university students asleep in their dormitories.' We're not reporting foreign news, we're reporting madness.

Political and Features

[NORMAN *exercising with chest expanders*.]

CYNTHIA: I find your piece on futurology spine-chilling.

NORMAN: Brilliantly written though.

CYNTHIA: What's so depressing about the futurologists is their way of wrapping up the future. Nothing to look forward to or be spontaneous about.

NORMAN [*puffing*]: You miss the point. They don't define what *will* happen – only what *could* happen. Know the dangers – prevent them.

　　[RONNIE *enters*.]

RONNIE: What the hell good do you think you're doing?

NORMAN: Healthy body, healthy mind.

RONNIE: What great writer do *you* know who ran a couple of miles before picking up a pen? If you're an idiot, mate, not even an Olympic medal can change that. A lovely bit of private distress, that'll sharpen your wits, not a handful of jerks.

NORMAN [*stopping*]: I'm not suggesting a healthy body *makes* a healthy mind, but given a lively mind to begin with –

CYNTHIA: – such as you've got –

NORMAN: – such as I've got, then it's enhanced by a fit body. Oh my God! I've strained a shoulder muscle.

In Depth

JULIAN: What are the layabouts in our business section up to?

CHRIS: Oh, trying to find a new Arnold Weinstock to write up.

JULIAN: In order to knock down –

CHRIS: – to make room for another Arnold Weinstock to build up –

JULIAN: – in order to knock down –

CHRIS: – to make room for another –

Business News

MORTY: Have you seen the poster of Chairman Mao hanging up in the In Depth offices?

ANTHONY: It's rather like the photographs of nudes which boys hang in their rooms at public school to assert their independence while temporarily trapped by the enemy.

In Depth

CHRIS: I *do* want a cigarette. I *don't* want a cigarette. [*Reaching for phone and cigarettes.*] I *do* want a cigarette. [*Reaching for a bottle of beer.*] And a drink. Bloody bridges!

Arts Pages/Women's Pages

ANGELA: Yes, I do! I do think writing novels is more difficult than writing plays. A play is just dialogue confined to a physical space. Its canvas *can't* be large. A novel demands more attention to detail, greater psychological exploration, a richer grasp of plot. Its space and movement is unlimited and you've only yourself to rely on. No actors to fill out thinly-drawn characters, no director to give rhythms which the material doesn't contain, and no lighting man playing tricks in order to create moods which the plot can't substantiate.

SEBASTIAN: Are you suggesting D. H. Lawrence is greater than Shakespeare?

ANGELA: No, but I *am* suggesting Shakespeare's not as great as Tolstoy.

JANE: Check!

In Depth

CHRIS [*on phone*]: Professor Cobblestone? Good morning. Chris Mackintosh of *The Sunday Paper* here – yes, you've guessed it, those fallen bridges. No – all right, not now. But in fact I didn't want to go into it *now*, only check you're the right man. You are? Splendid. To be frank I don't know how to start thinking on this subject at all and – good! I'll ring you again when I've read through all this material and got a basic shape to the piece and ask you if it makes engineering sense. O.K.? Thanks. Bye. [*Replaces receiver. Closes his eyes.*] Do I want a cigarette? No! I don't want a cigarette. [*Picks up phone to dial again.*]

Sports Pages

[*Phone ringing.*]

RONNIE: Ron Shapiro here.

[*It's from the Editor's office.* HARVEY *has with him* MAC SMITH, *the trade union official.*]

HARVEY: Ron? Look I've got Mac with me. They're querying the agreement we all thought we came to last week and if it's not ironed out now we'll all be in the shit again. Can you come down?

RONNIE: Coming. [*Replaces receiver.*] Who'd be bloody father of a newspaper chapel!

MARVIN: That stoppage again?

RONNIE: They may freeze the messengers. Ring round, get copy telephoned straight through to here and by-pass copy takers. I shouldn't as a union official, but fuck it! I want the paper to come out and I don't care. You agree?

MARVIN: Agreed.

[RONNIE *makes his way to Editor's office.*]

In Depth

JULIAN [*on phone*]: Look, I'm a layman and so if I could explain in layman's language why those bridges fell, rather than in your expertise – yes? Good. As I understand it it goes something like this: I build shelves for 15lb jam jars, test the shelves by putting 20lb jam jars on, use 15lb jam jars for 20 years and *then* return to 20lb jam jars . . . what? Oh, I see. Jam jars are hardly applicable. Of course. Well, let's start again . . .

Political and Features

CYNTHIA [*on phone*]: Yes, well I think it's a very interesting story, workers *should* get a day off on their birthday, but it's hardly for us. Try the News Room.

In Depth

CHRIS: As far as I can make out it's a perfectly decent feat of engineering but no one seems to have taken account of the fact that the things are built by incompetent, lumpen Irish labourers who don't care a damn . . .

Arts Pages/Women's Pages

ANGELA: And shall I tell you why I *don't* go to the theatre? It's pampered. There's more paraphernalia attached to a first night than the appearance of a novel.

SEBASTIAN: Ah ha! Now we have it.

ANGELA: Isn't it true? And there's *no* fuss at all about the appearance of a play on television and *that's* a medium enjoyed by millions!

SEBASTIAN: Demagogue!

Editor's Office

MAC: You see, Harvey, it says there that we've asked for withdrawal of the decision to close down the garage. Now you know that's not true. *We've* never ever said that. Management shouldn't go around sending notes like this to the staff misrepresenting our case. We've only asked that the *date* of closure be withdrawn to give us a chance to negotiate the men's future. That's not unreasonable, is it?

RONNIE: Hasn't that happened already, Mac?

MAC: Now, Ronnie, you *know* it hasn't. They've *changed* the date. But not actually withdrawn it.

HARVEY: Why do you want it withdrawn?

MAC: Now, Harvey, *you* shouldn't be asking questions like that. Supposing we agree to a date for closing down the garages and when that date comes we're not in agreement on redundancy compensation, eh? Come now, Harvey. *You're* an old enough hand.

HARVEY: But for Christ's sake, Mac –

MAC: Now then, Harvey, Harvey. Let's not raise our voices.

HARVEY [*softer*]: For Christ's sake, Mac, we're grown up, intelligent human beings. We've had problems like this before. Why *shouldn't* we come to an agreement on redundancy claims in good time?

MAC: Grown up, intelligent human beings – true. But 'the best laid schemes of mice and men' – you know what I mean? Besides, Ronnie, I'll tell *you* the truth. Because this document has falsified our position it's become a matter of principle for us. And for them? For management? Well, they've decided on a date and they've made it a matter of pride not to shift from it. So there's your problem. Principle versus pride. I'm taking it to my head office now and if nothing happens by the end of the week I'm asking them to make the stoppage official and I hope your men'll give us your support. Good day, lads. [*Leaves.*]

RONNIE: Doesn't look like we're going to have a paper this weekend.

HARVEY: I'll bring the fucking thing out, even if it means working the machines on my own and delivering the sheets myself. But I may need a little help from you, Ronnie.

RONNIE: When not?

In Depth

CHRIS: What I can't understand is how they *test* bridges?

JULIAN: They used to get battalions of guards to walk over them, then if the foundations trembled –

CHRIS: Our army isn't big enough, is it?

Editor's Office

[MARY *visiting.*]

MARY: And what was your lunch like with comrade King?

HARVEY: I can see why you're interested in him. He's a bit too good to be true, isn't he?

MARY: So you agree with me? He should be watched?

HARVEY: Oh, come on, Mary. He's not a spy for God's sake.

MARY: But he's sinister.

HARVEY: He's complex.

MARY: And sinister.

HARVEY: You underestimate him. He's got a good mind and a generous one. He sees the scale of problems in the perspective of history – which always impresses me. Only one very odd thing he said – not odd in its meaning but the words he used. He said: 'One thing I disagree with emphatically is the left's concept of the new man. Misleading,' he said. 'It's not the "new man" we must *create*,' he said, 'but the original man we must *reveal*.'

MARY: Sophistry.

HARVEY: 'Clear away the ignorance and the fear that's gathered around him over the centuries,' he said, 'and when the dust from that job settles then,' and these are his odd words, 'when the dust from that job settles then you'll see all the patterns men can make for the pleasure of their living.'

MARY: 'The patterns men can make for the pleasure of their living.' Jesus! Harvey! Come on! They say that certain poets are bullied by a bad conscience – well this is a conscience bullied by bad poetry.

Foreign Department

GORDON: Why don't you take a year off? Write a book? Everyone's doing it.

TAMARA: Write a book? Ha! I can hardly assemble words for these little bits of so-called foreign commentary. Conveyor-belt work, harsh, destructive, written in a hurry. I'm sick of first-class travel and first-class hotels and the quick friendships with people about whom one has finally to write something unsympathetic. Sometimes I think I'm in journalism because I'm unfit for anything else. A book! I'd like to resign.

News Room

SECRETARY [*on the phone*]: A union official who's *what*? Got a clause in about birthdays? No, it's hardly for the news room. Try our industrial correspondent. You'll find him in Business News.

[MARTIN *rushes in.*]

MARTIN: Paul? That hold-up of the supermarket in Bolton?

PAUL: Yes?

MARTIN: There's been a new development.

PAUL: What are you doing with a crime story?

MARTIN: It may not be a crime story.

PAUL: Not?

MARTIN: Not! Three days later 97 old people living in a new development for old-age pensioners woke up and found boxes of groceries on their front door step.

PAUL: And there's a connection?

MARTIN: The police aren't certain. But I've got another hunch I want to follow. Remember that factory manager kidnapped two months ago, the one that had a strike on his hands for being a bully?

PAUL: So?

MARTIN: When he was released the strike was over and the men reinstated but none of us, no paper, was able to get a statement from him.

PAUL: Go on.

MARTIN: Well, there's another strike in South Wales, place called Llantrisant, and this time it's unofficial and not the manager but the boss himself has been kidnapped.

PAUL: Are you suggesting the unions have become militant urban guerrillas?

MARTIN: Not the unions, but someone! Now there's something else and here's the real break. Since the kidnapping there's been a large bank robbery and though there's no strike pay the men have been given money.

PAUL: A local strike fund.

MARTIN: No! Their *full* wages.

PAUL: How?

MARTIN: Cash, in the post.

PAUL: Well that's The Anarchists Brigade.

MARTIN: No again! The Anarchists Brigade are bomb-throwers not soup kitchens. Besides, they'd announce themselves.

PAUL: Sounds to me as though you'd better consult the brilliant Miss Mortimer. She's got Peter's job for the month.

Arts Pages/Women's Pages

ANGELA: Why do you think the devastating Mary Mortimer has it in for the King of New Lanark?

JANE: Because she can't bear idealism anywhere but in her

own column, where she calls it 'responsibility', while in anyone else it's called 'charlatanism'.

SEBASTIAN: No, no, no! You mustn't talk to her so glibly. We – and she – are much more complex than that. She suffers from the schizophrenia we all suffer from. She can't bear people who make judgements and since, in attacking them, *she* has to judge, therefore she's torn all ends up.

JANE: But we all make judgements, surely.

ANGELA: Only we fear to be seen doing so.

SEBASTIAN: Precisely! It's like a dirty act, to be done in secrecy. If you make a judgement you seem, by your choice, to be indicating those who've not chosen as you've done. And to make it worse Morgan King makes outrageous demands such as that old-age pensioners should get what the national minimum wage is. Capital fellow! But frightfully difficult to tolerate. Doomed of course. I don't personally have much sympathy for the giant-killing Miss Mortimers of this world nor that 'witty, cool and deathly column' of hers.

Political and Features

[MARTIN *visiting*.]

MARY: You've done no investigating yourself?

MARTIN: No, just assembled cuttings and kept an eye on it.

MARY: And the sequence is: a supermarket hold-up, distribution of food to old age pensioners, strike in Wales and a bank robbery?

MARTIN: And then *full* strike pay.

MARY: And *then* full strike pay. Um. And we know it's not The Anarchists Brigade?

MARTIN: Certain.

MARY: What's your hunch?

MARTIN: It's only a hunch.

MARY: Let's hear it.

MARTIN: And it's way out.

MARY: Stop covering your retreats, out with it.

MARTIN: An opposition secret society.

MARY: That's not way out. There must be people in this green and pleasant land simply livid that they're not South American guerrillas.

MARTIN: Exactly! They must be intellectuals.

NORMAN: Easy! Some of my best friends are intellectuals.

MARTIN: They're highly organized, sophisticated, a sense of humour and, probably, opposed to violence.

MARY: And what do you propose?

MARTIN: This: I've made contact with The Anarchists Brigade. They're amateurs, clumsy and highly emotional. Now, if such a secret society does exist they're bound sooner or later, to want to make contact with the Anarchists to tell them to lay off the bombings.

MARY: Not sure I accept the logic of that. Still –

MARTIN: I just want one week free from other assignments.

MARY: I think we can spare him.

[MARTIN *leaves*.]

Arts Pages/Women's Pages

JANE: What do you think of a series on people's obsessions?

ANGELA: Do *you* have obsessions?

JANE: Me? I don't know.

ANGELA: And would you confess them?

JANE: Depends what I discovered I was obsessed with.

ANGELA: Why don't you do a series on 'my best friend'. Find out what human qualities the famed and renowned look for in their closest.

[*Pause*.]

JANE: People sitting around in offices, that's all a newspaper is, sitting around waiting for ideas to come, wondering what the hell to do next.

The Centre Space

[MARY MORTIMER's *lounge. Her three children –* AGNES, JONATHAN
and DESMOND *– have come for a monthly 'family dinner'.*
MARY *is in the kitchen preparing the meal.*
JONATHAN *is reading from a sheet of copy.*
It's a proof of MARY's *current column.*]

JONATHAN: She's attacking him again.

DESMOND: Read it.

AGNES: But please, let's not quarrel this time?

JONATHAN [*reading*]: 'Mr Morgan-fiery-socialist-MP-King is
with us once more. Oh what a dear, human, compassionate
philosopher we have in our midst. And how thankful we must
be, as he constantly reminds us, to have such a learned member
of parliament guiding us through the confusions of such awful
times.'

DESMOND: *Does* he 'constantly remind us'?

AGNES: It's mother's poetic licence to lie.

JONATHAN: 'We quote: "I believe," says the self-styled sage,
"that the first great myth of all time was the story of the creation
of order out of chaos, and all men's greatest endeavours since
then have been the re-enactment of that one first myth. And
because the chaos is endless so man's task will be endless. And if
there is a purpose in life *that* is it." Unquote.'

AGNES: I can remember when he first said that.

JONATHAN: 'We may not know what he means,' says our oh
so witty mother, 'but it's certainly reassuring to have such
serious sounding pontifications as this to pin by our bedside
and read each night before pulling sleep over our troubled
eyes in this troubled world.'

[JONATHAN *has beside him a portable tape-recorder the button
of which he now presses to produce the sound of an audience
whistling and applauding loudly. He throws his arms open as
though presenting this extract to 'an audience' for their acclaim.
The recorder is his latest 'toy' and he'll do this every so often
throughout the scene.*]

DESMOND: They all write so badly, that's what's so depressing.

JONATHAN: Their biggest mistake is to quote the people they want to demolish. Always boomerangs. Much better than their own little fifth-form farts. How about that? 'You've had the *Barretts of Wimpole Street* and now we bring to your screens – da-dum – *The Little Farts of Fleet Street*.'

[*Presses tape for 'applause'.*]

AGNES [*unwrapping a package*]: But no quarrels. Jonathan.

JONATHAN: Yes, elder sister.

AGNES: We only have dinner with her once a month so no more dreary taunts about her being bourgeois. Des?

DESMOND [*deep in newspaper*]: Yes, elder sister.

AGNES: We don't think much of her column but we love her. Understood?

TOGETHER: Yes, elder sister.

AGNES [*revealing a Hogarth print in frame*]: Think she'll like it?

[JONATHAN *presses tape to applaud print.*]

DESMOND: Is that genuine?

AGNES: Not your first edition of course. From a late edition, possibly the fourth, 1838.

[MARY *enters in apron with a tray containing pot of 'stew', plates and cutlery. She plonks it on the table, lifts lid triumphantly, and waits for response.* JONATHAN *switches on tape of applause.*]

MARY: My God! It's going to be one of those evenings.

[*They all begin to help themselves. Then –*]

Well, talk to me, my children. I know we always end up quarrelling over politics but that's no reason to be terrified of telling me your professional gossip. [*All three start at once.*] Whoa! Jonathan, 'the youngest'. You start.

JONATHAN: Directed my first concert.

MARY: Great mistake to televise concerts.

JONATHAN: Agree.

MARY: Good God! We've started with agreements.

JONATHAN: Have you noticed how, at concerts, there are always one or two who leap to applaud almost before the last note has been struck? And you never know whether they do it from enthusiasm or from a wish to get it in that they know the piece so well.

[*Silence. There seems nothing to add or go on to from there.* JONATHAN *presses recorder for his own applause.*]

MARY: We'll try the scientist then.

DESMOND: Three Soviet scientists – G. I. Beridze, G. R. Macharashvili and L. M. Mosulishvili have discovered gold in wine.

MARY: I beg your pardon?

DESMOND: Flowers and plants, you see, contain in their tissues residues of the metals contained in the soil where they grow. Hence bio-chemistry can trace deposits of nickel, silver, copper, cobalt, uranium, lead and other metals by pursuing, picking and analysing flowers and fruit.

AGNES: And?

DESMOND: And so three Soviet scientists called G. I. Beridze, G. R. Macharashvili and L. M. Mosulishvili have discovered gold in wine. [*Pause.*] Which comes from grapes. [*Pause.*] Which grows in soils. [*Silence.*]

Well don't I get a round of applause for that?

[JONATHAN *belatedly switches on tape.*]

MARY: Do you children rehearse your pieces before coming to dine with me?

AGNES: This is a very fine stew, mother.

MARY: There speaks the diplomat of the family. How's the foreign office?

JONATHAN: Mother, don't be so damned bourgeois. We don't *have* to make conversation.

AGNES [*forestalling friction*]: I might be posted to the embassy in Lagos.

MARY: If he calls me bourgeois again I'll –

AGNES: I'll know in a month's time.

[*Silence.*]

MARY: Bloody hell! You're not the most comfortable family to sit down to eat a meal with. Why must you always make me feel I've done something to feel guilty for?

JONATHAN: It's a change from you making others feel guilty in your columns.

MARY: That's my job. Investigation! Democratic scrutiny!

[JONATHAN *presses tape for applause.*]

And turn that bloody machine off! [*Pause.*] Oh, go home. I

swear, I always swear I'll never make these dinners again and each time I relent, each time I think – no! They won't get at me this time, it'll be a happy family event. And each time it happens again. What do I need it for?

AGNES: We're sorry.

MARY: Don't I have enough bloody headaches in that bloody newspaper office and those stupid, vain, self-opinionated people I have to interview?

JONATHAN: You can't exactly deride those you interview as 'self-opinionated' when those interviews appear in a column called 'opinions'.

MARY: Oh can't I just?

DESMOND: Mary, why have you got your teeth into Morgan King?

MARY: Morgan King? What the hell do you care about Morgan King?

AGNES: Desmond, you promised.

MARY: Why Morgan King and none of the others?

DESMOND: It's just that a special kind of savagery comes out with him and it shows.

MARY: I'm a savage columnist, didn't you know?

DESMOND: We're embarrassed that's all.

MARY: Oh no you're not. There's a reason. Why Morgan King?

AGNES: He conducted a series of seminars on local authorities at Jonathan's college in Oxford and we all got to know him rather well, that's all.

MARY: Well, why didn't I get to hear about him? I knew all your other friends from university.

DESMOND: Other students, yes; but we kept the visiting lecturers to ourselves.

MARY: I don't believe you.

AGNES: This is silly. Of course it's not only Morgan King, it's your column in general. We feel it's getting –

DESMOND: – bitchy –

AGNES: – no –

JONATHAN: – strident. That's the word. [Presses tape for applause.]

MARY: Please, please, PLEASE don't push that fucking button again.

JONATHAN: Now don't cry, mother. Tough journalists don't cry.

MARY: You're rather cruel children, aren't you?

DESMOND [*shamefaced*]: Yes, we are, you're right. I'm sorry.

AGNES: We're all sorry. Look, the stew's getting cold.

MARY: Well fuck the stew! You don't get off as easily as that.

JONATHAN: Always dangerous to apologize. The sting is always in the 'tail of a bourgeoise's tears'. Mao?

MARY: I AM NOT BOURGEOIS! Bourgeois is a state of mind, not of wealth.

JONATHAN: Not in the classic sense it's not.

MARY: To hell with the classic sense. Words acquire new meanings. Think! you have to *think* about them. Your lot are so bloody mindless. [*With forced calm and mounting distress.*] I loved and cared for my children, was that bourgeois? That was natural, an old, old cycle tested long before men began exploiting men. I gave you a home to grow strong in, not to seclude you but to help you face an insecure world, was that bourgeois? Did I force you into professions you were miserable with? Look at yourselves. Are you enfeebled, pathetic creatures? Should I be ashamed of you? What's my crime? I'm not bourgeois if I respect the past – people have been fighting and dying for rights since Adam. I'm not bourgeois if I enjoy comfort – only if comfort defuses my angers against injustice. I'm not bourgeois if I fear the evil in men – that's human. If I enjoyed being helpless about evil, you might call that bourgeois. If I indulged in *welt-shmertz*, you might call that bourgeois. If I pretended order existed when it didn't, you might call that bourgeois. But if I try to create order out of chaos, that's human. If I have loves and hates and failures and regrets and nostalgias, if I'm weak and frail and confused and I try to make order out of the chaos of my miserable life, then that's human, bloody human, bloody bloody human!

[AGNES *picks up the proofs of* MARY's *column and gently offers it to her.*]

AGNES: You see, mother, he also talks about order out of

chaos. That's just what we mean. It's as though you're fighting yourself and it shows. In your column it shows. [*Pause.*] Mary, we're our mother's children. [*Small laugh.*] No escaping.

[MARY *is stung but it only serves to deepen her distress.*]
Look. A Hogarth print. We've bought you a present.

ACT TWO

PART THREE

The Centre Space

[*An arbour in the grounds of the home of the Chancellor of the Exchequer,* SIR REGINALD MACINTYRE. *He is strolling up and down with* MARY.]

MARY: And the final question, Sir Reginald.

MACINTYRE: You won't be offended if I say, thank God!

MARY: Three days is a long time, I know. You've been very patient. It's a very personal one. I've asked each minister this and told them they can answer or tell me to go to hell.

MACINTYRE: I'm not very good at saying such things to ladies but I hope your question doesn't tempt me too much.

MARY: It's this. How do you reconcile the needs of your own private standards of living with the needs of those working people whose standards of living you, as Chancellor, are in office to regulate? [*Long pause.*] Please, if you think it too impertinent.

MACINTYRE: Impertinent? Yes, I suppose I do find it that. [*Pause.*] Do you mind if I answer in an oblique way, without, I trust, being evasive? [*Pause.*] It's a terrible problem, democracy. You see, if we could turn round and say all the men who are dustmen are dustmen because of their inequality of opportunity then it would be easy. No problem. We would simply create the right opportunity. But it's not so, is it? Make *opportunity* equal and the inequality of their qualities soon becomes apparent. It's a cruel statement to make but, men are dustmen or lavatory attendants or machine minders or policemen because of intellectual limitations. There! Does that offend you? It used to offend me. Most unpalatable view of human beings. But all my encounters with them point to that fact. Even if we automate all sewage, everything, we're still confronted with the awful fact that some men *are* born with intellectual limitations. Now, what do we do? We can't talk of these things, it's taboo. We can't say in public 'some men are less intelligent than others' – though it's part of any discussion on democracy. So what *should* we do? Compensate their inadequacies with large pay packets? But what of the dustman? Because when he strikes for more pay he may not be asking to be paid for his ability or responsibilities but he *is* asking to be paid for doing what other men *don't want to do*. For what I think should be named 'the undesirability factor'. Isn't *that* a distinction? And a very intimidating distinction I may add. In democracies those who do our dirty work have us these days by, as they say, the short and curlies. Now, government must, you'll agree, remain in civilized hands. So, whose 'short and curlies' should civilized man hold on to?

MARY: Perhaps it's the mark of the civilized man that he disdains from holding on to anyone's 'short and curlies'.

MACINTYRE: No. Only that he *appears* not to be doing so. Does that also shock you? But you make a man feel simple by confronting him with problems beyond his intellect. Wouldn't it be civil, human *not* to discuss with a simple man what was beyond his intellect, or ask him to perform duties beyond his power? Surely you'd want me to *appear* to be his equal which I could only do by not frustrating or humiliating him in that way.

MARY: But supposing your judgements are wrong? Supposing the man is capable of more than you give him credit for?

MACINTYRE: Supposing all our judgements are wrong? Yours of me, mine of you – so? Do we cease making them? We are appointed because our judgements are more often right than wrong. That too is one of the risks of democracy, unless you can find me a man who can create a system – or a system which can create a man – whose judgement is right, all the time, about everything. Do you find an answer shaping in all that? Am I making myself clear?

MARY: Perfectly.

MACINTYRE: You will, of course, let me see the typescript before going into print?

Business News

DOMINIC: Well, people who fuck up the system appeal to me. [*Phone rings. He picks it up. It's* PAUL *from the News Room.*]

PAUL: Dom? I've just had an earbending fink on the phone who says he's got damaging documents implicating Leonard Crafton.

DOMINIC: Head of Onyx Foods? Oh, a charming man, a con but charming. Everyone wants to rubbish him.

PAUL: Will you see him?

DOMINIC: If we must.

PAUL: He sounds interesting if erroneous.

DOMINIC: Interesting if erroneous. I'll remember that.

Editor's Office

[*An editorial conference.*]

GORDON: Well, do we have a newspaper this week or not?

ANTHONY: The problem, old friend, lies in the difference between the production side and the creative side. We're prepared to work at all hours in order to get a newspaper out and production doesn't care a damn about the kind of journalism we think we produce. And why should they? They don't read it.

GORDON: *There's* your technology versus politics problem, Harvey. Right in your own back yard.

ANTHONY: And a back yard it is – *that's* the problem. We've got Victorian machinery. Thousands to man it. Millions to buy it. Six years to install it. And all you really need is half a million for a Web off-set machine and a handful of typists to run it instead of expensive, obsolete printing men. Of *course* you'll always have stoppages.

HARVEY: Anyway gentlemen, it's in the hands of their head office and our management boys – let them fight it out and may the best man win. Now our little Middle East war. What about *that* bloody mess?

In Depth

PAT: Well someone on your sodding paper ought to be interested.

CHRIS: I've tried, love, honest I have.

PAT: I mean it's more than just another abortion story, it's a story about your knotty medical problems and your callous authority.

CHRIS: That's what I said: 'Knotty medical problems and callous authority,' I said. Try it on Mary. She's got Pete's job for this month.

Editor's Office

[*Editorial continuing.*]

HARVEY: And as far as I can see we're going to be the only ones to give the cholera epidemic a big spread. The dailies have hardly touched it. Map with arrows showing its route, three nine-inch columns – front page.

ANTHONY: Don't believe in epidemic scares personally.

GORDON: *You* don't believe in the pollution scare either, so you're no judge.

ANTHONY: Pollution's different.

HARVEY: Which nicely brings me to my next point. I want to cover the Mersey, long diagram, showing who's pouring what into its waters and from where. Every firm named, questioned, challenged.

Sports Pages

[DOMINIC *visiting*.]

DOMINIC: If you want me to cover your tennis championships it'll cost you high in expenses. I'll spice it with the obligatory champagne-and-strawberries atmosphere, you pay for it.

RONNIE: You'll get what my budget will allow.

MARVIN: You're not the *most* brilliant tennis reporter we have.

DOMINIC: Oh I am, I am. And you know that I am.

MARVIN: Besides, your expenses come from Business News.

DOMINIC: It's true. I can't lie. My expenses are the highest on *The Sunday Paper* on account of the terrible terrible amount of bribing I have to do among the trade union officials.

RONNIE: You're a cynical man, Dominic.

DOMINIC: Cynical I am not. Spoilt, perhaps. But then we can't all have interesting backgrounds like you, Ronnie. Russian Jewish immigrants from the East End of London? Were you really born in the East End? God! How I resent my father for being so rich. All the best people were born in a ghetto. If only my father had bought *us* a ghetto, one we could go to for weekends. Now that would have been something.

Arts Pages/Women's Pages

JANE [*reading a women's magazine*]: Ooooh! Look! Moira Hartnel's entered the battle for women's liberation.

ANGELA: A top model gone politicking?

JANE: Think she's worth pursuing?

ANGELA: Any staying power?

JANE: I only have to do her once. She's not *star* quality.

ANGELA: Thank God for the woman's magazine. Jane can always rely on them to fill a hole in her column.

JANE: How about 'from women's waists to wasted women'?

ANGELA: Or 'model mauls men'?

JANE: Or 'from liberated fashions to fashionable liberations'?

SEBASTIAN: Meeow!

Sports Pages

MARVIN: So there I was, in Northern Ireland, soldiers shot at, civilians murdered, bombs going off everywhere, reporting on a game of golf. Jesus! I thought, what the hell am I doing covering a game of golf?

Business News

[THE FINK *is introducing himself to* MORTY.]

MORTY [*shaking hands*]: And you're the gentleman with information on Onyx Foods?

FINK [*patting his briefcase*]: Minute research. It's all here. I take it I can speak openly? Good. The basis of my information is this: that Leonard Crafton – Crafty Crafton I call him – has stated a share price since 1967 based on a false market, and that he's been able to achieve this through a complicated system of interlocking holdings which work roughly in this way: the English company takes over a French company which then buys shares in a subsidiary of the French company and so on. Clever? Ah, very clever is our crafty Crafton. Now look at these graphs of share price rises and rising profits . . .

Arts Pages/Women's Pages

SEBASTIAN: Oh my God! Another poem. We always get them after disasters or Prince Philip's birthday. Says a great deal for the soul of the British public I suppose but doesn't contribute much to British poetry.

Business News

[THE FINK's *story, continuing.*]

FINK: Now, I'd been following him so closely that I understood the pattern of crafty Crafton's behaviour, his psychology as it were, and of course, when his shares were at 71 I bought them because I knew, from watching his dealings, that they'd soon go up to 93 or thereabouts, which they did, and at which point I sold. And who's the Mafia, as it were, in all this? Snuff! Oh don't laugh. [*Dips into his briefcase for large foreign magazines.*] Snuff is the new narcotic. You can put your LSD into it. Kids in Germany and Sweden are doing it all the time. And so Mr Crafty Crafton and his Jewish backers are putting their money into snuff. Large profits, you see. Now, that's not all . . .

Arts Pages/Women's Pages

ANGELA: Oh yes, I agree, the elegant sneer is always admired. And if it's like Pope it's very good indeed.
JANE: Problem is, it's rarely like Pope.

Business News

[THE FINK's *story, continuing.*]

FINK: So, you're asking, where is all this leading? His saga seems endless and many-vaulted, you're thinking to yourself. Nearly there. I've told you about Crafton's dealings on the continent and at home. I've told you his motives and about the habit of his Jewish brethren in helping poorer members of their community. So, we know, they stick together, now why?

Editor's Office

[*Editorial continuing.*]

HARVEY: What's your centre-piece this week?

GORDON: A finely argued piece of demolition on the myth of the silent majority which makes the very simple but devastating point that the convenience of such a concept as silence is – the silence.

HARVEY: Quite right! If you say nothing anybody can claim to speak for you.

Business News

[THE FINK, *who has gradually become excited by his own story, allows his enthusiasm to take over his judgement.*]

FINK: I'll be honest, lay my cards on the table. I'm obsessed by the European Jewish Mafia. Been reading about them as far back as the time Napoleon freed the Jews. And here's my point, think about it. There's the tightly-knit Jewish families of Rothschilds, Mannheimers, and Herzens on the continent, and Messrs Morgenstein, Rosenthal and Crafton in this country. And now [*clasps his fingers together*] with the European Common Market – click! The opportunity they've been waiting for – a highly closed plot in the traditional Jewish manner trying to dominate the important areas of food and leisure. [*Pause.*] You must not, however, think I'm anti-semitic.

Political and Features

MARY: Shall I tell you what's wrong with your article on futurology?

NORMAN: I'd prefer you not to.

MARY: You believe the futurologists!

NORMAN: That's not true.

MARY: You ask a very reasonable question: Has technology rearranged the genes of political issues? and then you give *their* answer: yes it has!

NORMAN: I happen to agree with them.

MARY: Have you ever asked yourself why their books are so thick?

NORMAN: Scholarship.

MARY: Balls! It's because men aren't robots, they're human, unpredictable, millions of individual wills, all different – hence, a large book of hedged bets.

[MARTIN enters.]

Any luck?

MARTIN: To be honest I changed tactics.

MARY: Meaning?

MARTIN: I went to Llantrisant, where the strike was. Thought I'd get more of a lead there.

MARY: So, if your secret society did plan to contact the anarchists you've missed them. And we don't even know if they exist.

MARTIN [handing her a sheet]: I think I've got evidence to prove that. I picked up this stencilled document which was in the latest strike pay packet. A sort of manifesto. Very flowery stuff. Not like the anarchists at all. Correct grammar and statements with some degree of lucidity, except the end, which–

MARY [who's been reading it]: Eureka! Martin, keep on to that anarchists cell. It may lead to something fantastic. Fan-tastic! 'Scuse me. [She rushes out.]

Arts Pages/Women's Pages

JANE: It's a terrible confession – but my colleagues depress me. They play this great game at work and then they shuffle home on the commuter-train to suburbia.

ANGELA: Got to have something to compensate for lilliputian lives.

JANE: That's what we are. Lilliputians! Always wanting to bring down giants.

ANGELA: I seem to spend my time building them up.

JANE: They are paper giants. But the real ones – we never celebrate the real ones.

SEBASTIAN: Oh, I don't know. Business News celebrate Arnold Weinstock. Women's Pages celebrate Hughie Green.

JANE: Fashions! Novelty! We celebrate fashions and novelties.

ANGELA: Well, do something about it.

Editor's Office

[MARY *visiting*.]

HARVEY [*who's been reading* MARTIN's *document*]: It's slim, Mary.

MARY: The *exact* words, though. 'The patterns men can make for the pleasure of their living.' The same awful words: Morgan King! The man himself. Behind all those boyish Robin Hood antics.

HARVEY: Maybe they're not his words. Maybe I made a mistake and he was quoting from a poem or a Hazlitt essay or something, and he and this group – whoever they are – were using the same source, coincidentally. Have a look, Gordon.

MARY: Coincidentally? Bloody strange coincidence. Harvey, Morgan King has formed a secret society of political Robin Hoods. I *know* it. It all fits in with his shifty passions. One of my sons attended a series of seminars he gave at Oxford and from the way he describes him he sounds quite capable of seducing a small band of over-heated romantic imaginations into playing urban guerillas.

GORDON: Not good enough, Mary. I'd say you needed more evidence.

MARY: I think you're all frightened.

HARVEY: No, cautious.

MARY: So am I. I'm not asking us to print anything, but it's worth following up for God's sake.

HARVEY: You're relentless.

MARY: So you keep saying. Hell! I can see I won't get much joy here. [*She leaves.*]

Foreign Department

[MORTY *visiting*.]

MORTY: And suddenly I realize. This Fink's spinning me the old yarn about the Jewish conspiracy to take over the world. Poor bloody Jews. Can't do anything right, can we? Jesus, Marx, Freud, Trotsky, you, me – all part of some conspiracy or other.

Editor's Office

[JANE *visiting*.]

JANE: Well, we're staking pretty big claims as the most serious paper in the country.
HARVEY: And it's true.
JANE: Then let me bring the Women's Pages into the science versus politics issue.
HARVEY: What are you thinking of?
JANE: Oh, I don't know. Are women more attracted to science than politics and is there a reason? That sort of thing.
GORDON: You think women aspire to the practical rather than the empirical?
JANE: Could be. I just want the go ahead in principle.
HARVEY: You've got it, you've got it.
JANE: Hallelujah!

Political and Features

[TAMARA *visiting*. NORMAN *has been reading the proofs of her latest piece*.]

NORMAN [*handing it back*]: It's reasonable, Tamara, reasonable.
TAMARA: That's a good word, Norman. Succinct and diminishing. Thank you.

NORMAN: Now don't sulk.

TAMARA: Oh, how I'd just like to slide around, with no purpose, having little conversations.

NORMAN: Only you can't quite give up the glamour of catching a plane and having access to important people.

TAMARA: Can't I?

CYNTHIA: None of us can.

TAMARA: *Important* people? My contempt for the Western European politicians I've had to meet is gradually extending to the whole spectrum of human beings – important or not.

News Room

[MARY *visiting, with* PAT *at her heels.*]

MARY [*to* PAUL]: Paul, who the hell turned this away?

PAUL: It's only another abortion story.

MARY: Another abortion story? Another *abortion* story?

PAUL: I can turn you up a dozen stories about girls of thirteen, twelve, eleven, even ten having abortions.

MARY: That's why I have to go through everything myself.

PAUL: Look, Mary, as news editor *I* judge the kind of news story we should be printing.

MARY [*storming off*]: I want this woman hung, drawn and quartered. She's a National Health Service gynaecologist and she's not paid with my money to offer moral judgement to twelve-year-old girls in need of help . . .

PAT: Thanks!

Political and Features

NORMAN: Well, I'm sorry – it *is* just a reasonable article because it *is* rather difficult to generate excitement about obscure Indian tribes in Latin America. I mean it may look good in print when you read a D. H. Lawrence novel, but Quetzalcoatl *does* sound funny when you actually have to *say* it.

TAMARA: Oh your bloody English upper-class wit! You still

go on making pale jokes about the funny names of aliens. Haven't you heard that no one finds you funny any longer except your pudding-faced working class? They can always be relied upon to find the sound of Vladivostok good for a giggle.

In Depth

[MARY *rushes in followed by a bemused* PAT.]

MARY: Right! Drop your bridges.

CHRIS: Did she say 'drop your breeches'?

MARY: I want this gynaecologist investigated.

JULIAN: Hell, Mary, it's a news story not an In Depth exposé.

PAT: It's more important than a news story. The mother herself has asked us to investigate.

MARY: Problem is the doctor's clammed up. Refuses to speak to the press.

JULIAN: I don't blame her.

MARY: What we want is the story of a guilty gynaecologist. Was she married? Did she have an unhappy love affair, broken marriage? Are there any children?

CHRIS: That's Harold Robbins, not journalism.

MARY: And get a photograph, even if it's of her peering reluctantly round a door.

JULIAN: A classic news room story.

MARY: Pat, get this photostated.

PAT: How many?

MARY: About ten. Julian, you can get up there in two and a half hours on the M1.

JULIAN: Three.

CHRIS: Four.

JULIAN: And basically what you want is all the dirt I can get on her?

MARY: Yes. And get photographs of the girl and her mother. Doorstep them if necessary.

JULIAN: How can you take a moral position about the gynaecologist if you start invading people's privacy?

MARY: I'll worry about that. [*She leaves.*]

Arts Pages/Women's Pages

JANE [*entering*]: I'm in business.

ANGELA: He's agreed?

JANE: Of course he agrees. I don't know why I didn't push earlier. Do you think the story of Lysistrata comes under the heading of science versus politics?

ANGELA: That's sex versus politics.

JANE: But the Greek girls didn't have contraception – and that's science.

ANGELA: So?

JANE: Well, the general's ladies could last out longer today by safely taking their favours elsewhere.

SEBASTIAN: Bit of a strain on the imagination, that.

Editor's Office

[*Editorial continuing.*]

ANTHONY: Has the Chancellor read the typescript of his interview with Mary?

HARVEY: Not yet. Why?

ANTHONY: I hardly think he's going to approve of all her witty little interjections. '"It is a cruel statement to make," the Chancellor continued, "but men are dustmen or lavatory attendants or machine minders or policemen because of intellectual limitations." I resisted the temptation to ask if he had statistics on how many intellectually limited sons of the upper classes became dustmen.'

HARVEY: Heavy-handed but he does need knocking.

ANTHONY: Well why didn't she simply make the point to him and get his reply?

HARVEY: Nor is the Commissioner of Police going to be happy to have his force labelled 'intellectually limited'.

Political and Features

MARY: I think I'm tired.

CYNTHIA: You *think* so? You're not sure?

MARY: And I've got my mother for dinner tonight. She's never tired.

CYNTHIA: Don't you ever think of peppering evenings with mum?

MARY: Oh, Jason'll be there.

CYNTHIA: Your ex-husband seems to be the only man you ever see these days.

MARY: Only really intelligent man I know. God knows why I agreed to divorce him.

CYNTHIA: Why did you?

MARY: Used each other up. Why else? Some couples accept it, others don't. Simple.

CYNTHIA: Oh, very.

Foreign Department

GORDON: Now, this is what I mean about religious dogma leading to massacres. [*Reading from* The Times.]: '"My dear countrymen, peace be with you," he said in his speech announcing war. "Our enemy has again challenged us. His dislike and enmity of us is well-known the world over. We have shown great forbearance but the time has now come when we must give the enemy a most effective answer. One hundred and twenty million crusaders, you have the support and blessings of Allah".'

TAMARA: Uch! Vain! Pompous! Demagogues! How I despise them.

Business News

MORTY [*to someone off-stage*]: Yes, well I believe in the Capitalist system so I have no conflicts. Conflicts? Hah! I've been looking for them for years. Always wanted to be able to resign on a matter of principle.

Foreign Department

GORDON [*still reading from* The Times.]: '"Your land is filled with the love of the Holy Prophet."'

TAMARA: I just don't believe it.

GORDON: '"Rise as one for your honour and stand like an impregnable wall of steel in the face of your enemy."'

TAMARA: And on and on and on . . .

Business News

MORTY [*to someone off-stage*]: And what's more, Arnold Weinstock is one of the most intelligent men we've met who's more intelligent than us, and we don't meet many of them!

Foreign Department

GORDON [*still reading from* The Times]: '"You have right and justice on your side"'.

TAMARA: Always!

GORDON: '"Pounce on the enemy in a spirit of confidence."'

TAMARA: No one ever learns.

GORDON: '"Let the enemy know that every one of us is determined to stand up for the defence of the dear motherland."'

TAMARA: As though history never happens for them.

Arts Pages/Women's Pages

SEBASTIAN: . . . It was Beethoven's violin concerto and Carl Orff's 'Carmina Burana' and our music critic overheard one of the musicians saying, in a very loud voice: 'now that we've buggered up Beethoven we'd better fuck Orff . . .'

Foreign Department

GORDON [*still reading from* The Times]: ' "The enemy knows that victory in war does not go to those who have numerical strength and large quantities of military hardware. It goes to those who have faith in their mission and in the ideals of Islam and who believe God helps the righteous." '

TAMARA: And who will help us? Dear God, who will help the rest of us?

PART FOUR

The Centre Space

[*A table in a restaurant.* MARY *is dining with* OLIVER MASINGHAM, *Under Secretary of State for Foreign Affairs. They are friends. She is slightly drunk.*]

MASSINGHAM: I hope you're not disappointed, Mary. Lumbered with a mere under secretary rather than the Foreign Minister himself?

MARY: You think I'm drunk for that reason, Oliver?

MASSINGHAM: He hates interviews. All that personality cultifying.

MARY: Who does he think – no! I mustn't.

MASSINGHAM: Mustn't what?

MARY: I've been told by my children that my only contribution to British journalism is to have elevated the gutter question 'who does he think he is?' to a respected art form.

MASSINGHAM: And that hurt of course.

MARY: It *should* have hurt. Everything should hurt. But nothing does. Oliver – this is off the record, but here's a question I've been dying to ask one of you only I didn't dare. It goes like this: you're a minister. I've watched the House in action: fights, battles of wit, of personality, intellect – but, that's not all is it? There's personality conflicts also – in the cabinet, in ministerial departments with cantankerous old civil servants.

And then – tact! Diplomacy! Different kinds, in different ways, to different people. The public face on the one hand and the private reassurance to industry, the unions, the foreign ambassadors on the other. A great juggling act, wits alert all the time. And on top of all this, on *top* – of all *this*, there's the problems of being a husband, a lover, a father, a friend, uncle, brother – God wot! [*Pause.*] How-do-you-do-it-for-God's-sake? How? How don't you become overwhelmed by it all? Do certain arteries harden? Is part of you callous? Like the doctor, or the writer? Tell me.

MASSINGHAM: Mary, I think you're very drunk.

MARY: But still functioning, eh? My lovely brain still ticking – tick-tick-tick-tick.

MASSINGHAM: Perhaps I should take advantage of your lovely, drunk brain and get you to talk about yourself for a change.

MARY: Me? Oh, I had a famous father, didn't you know? Famous for what they called in his day 'thought-provoking' novels. Only his thoughts provoked very few, very shallowly, and his day didn't last long. I used to taunt him in front of my university friends about having nothing to say to my generation and he used to take notice and rush to read my required reading. I had to grow up in his growing darkness and watch his lively pleasure, at being recognized in the streets, change into a grey anonymity. He was a gentle man, made for the comforts fame brings and which the Gods gave him only a taste of. And I, with innocent devastation, went into competition with him. I won, of course. Because good fathers never let their children lose. He stepped back, graciously, for the sake of a healthy family, following the false principle, which many indifferent artists follow, that, if he couldn't create a healthy, happy family he couldn't create a worthy work of literature. He created nothing from that moment on. Defeated! And I understood none of that.

News Room

[*It's a Saturday.*
The still slide of the printing presses now becomes a film of men

preparing the machines ready for use.
The paper is being laid out. Mainly the front page. Movement is reaching towards a height.
(This area can now be filled with actors who've played other parts.)
HARVEY *is standing beside a man who's sitting drawing possible layouts on a blank sheet.]*

HARVEY: Right, we'll have our Middle East war on the left, conductor and his baby centre space, cholera here and map over the top, here, and that leaves this area for the gynae-cologist story, if there is one. Mary? Where's Mary?

ANTHONY [*Taking* NORMAN *aside*]: Will someone tell me why we're featuring a photograph on the front page of a fifty-one-year-old opera conductor with his eighteen-month-old baby in his arms?

NORMAN: Well, we've got a story about an outbreak of another little bloody war, one about the spread of cholera, a morbid piece about a mother urging her daughter to death, and so, with a gruesome front page like that, don't you think we need a drop of human warmth? To make our millions of readers like the world just a little better on their Sunday off work?

ANTHONY: May I remind you, Harvey, that our messengers are still on strike and copy's not moving?

HARVEY: Ronnie's with Mac now.

Sports Pages

MAC: Pensions are rotten in this place, Ronnie, and you know it.

RONNIE: I know it, but –

MAC: And I'm not advising my men back until management agree to postpone the date for cancelling closure of the garage so we have time to discuss them.

RONNIE: Mac! Sometimes you boys cut your nose to spite your face.

MAC: That's not friendly, Ronnie.

RONNIE: Friendly? Do you know that your boys stopped the

Securicor van from bringing in the cash the other day? Now who do you think that affects? Not us, or management. We all get paid monthly by cheque, straight into our banks. No! The office girls. The poor, bloody office girls. We had to whip round in this office and pay the secretary.

MAC: All wars have their innocent casualties.

RONNIE: Cant! Don't give me cant, Mac. Look, time's pressing. Release your messengers, get copy flowing again so's we can get the paper out and I promise you I'll persuade our chapel to give two weeks notice of strike if no agreement is reached on redundancies. Agreed?

MAC: Can you guarantee it?

RONNIE: Come on, Mac. You know I can't *guarantee* a thing like that. Agreed?

MAC: If it doesn't work, Ronnie, I promise you, we'll get the whole of Fleet Street out and no one, anywhere, will have a paper.

[MAC *leaves.* RONNIE *has been dialling meanwhile.*]

RONNIE [*Into phone*]: We've got a newspaper!

News Room

SECRETARY [*yelling to* HARVEY]: We've got a newspaper!

HARVEY: Great! Mary, where's Mary?

[MARY *appears with copy.*]

MARY: All right I agree, it *is* a news story. As long as she goes on the front page I don't mind.

HARVEY: And the bridges story'll go into In Depth where it belongs. Good. Got a photograph?

MARY: Messengers should've brought one from the dark room.

HARVEY: The first interviews read splendidly, by the way.

MARY: Thanks, but don't patronize me, Harvey.

HARVEY: Cheer up, Mary. We nearly didn't have a paper this week.

[MESSENGER *arrives with photo.*]

My God! She looks so hounded.

MARY: It'll be a lesson to other moralizing gynaecologists. *She* hounded that poor child.

[*She leaves.*]

Sports Pages

RONNIE: I mean all strikes are like a marriage conflict, aren't they? Just one minor incident is needed and out comes all the bitterness of past abuse, magnified by the years. Do you think that when a union leader sits facing an employer he's merely confronting a man who wants to pay him less than he's asking? Never! Have you ever seen the conference rooms in trade union offices? Replicas of city board rooms. And when he wins his five pound a week extra he's not only getting more money for his men he's also telling the other class what they can do with their elegant culture. I understand it, I can even defend it historically, but frankly, between thou and I, I loathe its spirit, its mean, I'll knock-you-down-spirit.

News Room

[*The following snatches of conversation fly back and forth among the miscellaneous characters who flood this area.*]

PAUL'S SECRETARY [*clutching phone*]: Our copy taker is in chaos and Ian is sitting in his hotel waiting to dictate – can anyone do something about it?

HARVEY'S SECRETARY: Right! We're going to that wedding after all. It's royalty and the chief feels a little responsible *to* them or *for* them or *something* . . .

HARVEY [*to* HARVEY'S SECRETARY]: Ring him up, tell him copy is O.K., but ask him what he means by the top of page 7 where it says 'the secret transcripts have been released'! *What* transcripts have been released by whom, to whom and about what . . .

HARVEY'S SECRETARY: It *was* a good story until the subs got at it – inky-fingered bloody maniacs . . .

PAUL [*to* HARVEY]: Harvey, first edition of the *People* look. They've got an exclusive on the Prime Minister's private earnings.

HARVEY: Damn! We got anybody on to it?

PAUL: No one free.

HARVEY: I'll do it myself.

LAYOUT: Where you thinking of putting it, Harvey?

HARVEY: That's the problem.

ANTHONY: Do you really think it's that important?

HARVEY: What, after we published his diary extracts? We'd be laughed at to miss this. Right! We'll take the cholera map out and cut the last quarter column.

LAYOUT: And put the money story where?

HARVEY: Bit at the top here, across five columns, over the Middle East headline.

ANTHONY: Then we won't be the 'only one going to town on the cholera epidemic'.

HARVEY: Not the moment to be facetious, Anthony.

Political and Features

MESSENGER: Letter for Miss Mortimer.

Sports Pages

MARVIN [*on phone*]: But, Ned, we haven't got the space. We've already had to cut down on the swimming championships – it's a small paper this week. Wait, that's not a decision I can make, I'll ask Ronnie. Ronnie, Ned reporting the Arsenal West Ham match, he says the Hammers' new player is the greatest genius in the history of football.

RONNIE: That's because Ned's a university graduate who wants to write about football as poetry. How much does he want?

MARVIN: Another three hundred words.

RONNIE: Tell him 150!

MARVIN [*into phone*]: 150!

Political and Features

MARY: Jesus Christ! [*She moves quickly to the door to call the* MESSENGER *back.*] What did he look like?

MESSENGER: Who, miss?

MARY: The man who gave you this letter, describe him, quick.

MESSENGER: Well, I don't know, do I? Reception give it to me and I just give it to you, didn't I?

[*He leaves.* MARY *whips up phone, dials. It's picked up in the* NEWS ROOM.]

MARY: Harvey, please.

SECRETARY: For you, Harvey.

MARY: Harvey. Can I see you? Alone?

HARVEY: I'm just about to start on the P.M.'s earnings. What is it?

MARY: Something on Morgan King. I've *got* to see you.

HARVEY: Well, briefly then, in my office.

[MARY *is about to rush out.*]

CYNTHIA: What's all that, then?

MARY: Morgan King and kidnappings.

[*She leaves.*]

Business News

DOMINIC [*he's slightly drunk*]: Women! Ah, women! I love them! Their touch, their look, their smells. I *love* a woman who smells of action. When she works in a garage there's a smell of oil lingering around her. If she's a doctor – it's medicinal. A painter – the smell of paints. I love the smell of alcohol on her breath when she drinks; of her body after she runs. Anything that tells me she moves, is alive with decisions, agitated. Fuck your art! Fuck your politics! Fuck your conversation! Even your wine. Women! I can't bear to be without them.

News Room

[JULIAN *visiting.*]

SECRETARY [*on phone*]: Time Life? Paul Mannering's secretary here. Yes, the same one. We can't afford two. It's about that article he promised you. I forgot it! Will tomorrow do? Thanks. 'Bye. Holy Mother of God forgive me for my sins.

JULIAN: How much are they paying you for all that, Kathy?

SECRETARY: Well they get a separate bill for every lie I tell – if that's what you mean.

Arts Pages/Women's Pages

ANGELA: I can't review this book.

JANE: You write novels. I don't think you should review them.

ANGELA: I find his writing so awful and I gave his last one such a knocking that I'm beginning to feel it's unfair. Gives me guilts. No reviewer should have to feel guilts.

JANE: Especially if she's also a novelist!

SEBASTIAN: Meeeow!

Editor's Office

[HARVEY *has just finished reading the letter* MARY's *handed him.*]

MARY: What do you think?

HARVEY: It's suspect.

MARY: Not to me it isn't.

HARVEY: And we'll end up with the biggest libel suit in the history of Fleet Street.

MARY: Here's what I suggest. We've got three hours till the last edition. Can the bridges hold over till next week?

HARVEY: Till eternity I should think.

MARY: This man's waiting for me across the road in the pub. I'll take Chris and see what he's got to say. If the documents look authentic then we'll reproduce them and just ask questions. No comment.

HARVEY: They'll have to be bloody authentic.

MARY: We'll spend an hour with the fink, an hour to write it and it can be on the stone in good time for the last press as an In Depth story.

HARVEY: You're rushing, Mary.

MARY: I *know*, I just know in my bones – these documents will be conclusive. I've pursued this man for a year now, Harvey, and I've warned – he's a phoney of the most offensive sort and it's our responsibility to –

HARVEY: Mary, have you thought, that if he's linked with the robbing of supermarkets for old-age pensioners, bank robberies to pay strikers, kidnapping managers to give them lessons in civility, then you'll do just what you don't want, you'll make him a martyr.

MARY: Nonsense! The English temperament can't stand martyrs.

HARVEY: And there's another thing. I've got a sneaking admiration for the enterprise. It appeals to me.

MARY: Well, it doesn't to me. It's the wrong tone of voice. Half-baked revolutionaries who've borrowed other people's tongues. Its sentimental nonsense which belongs neither to our nature, our history nor our situation and I despise it.

HARVEY: Mary, some advice.

MARY: Not now, Harvey.

HARVEY: Yes, *just* now. We're only engaged in handing on fragments of information. You can spice it with comment, but don't fall into the trap of exaggerated pronouncements.

MARY: Harvey, I don't think –

HARVEY: Well I *do* think. You can't reveal, you can only inform. Don't simplify what's complex and then imagine you've clarified the truth. And it *is* complex. New states being born, new classes, races finding their voice, feeling their strengths. A time ripe for opportunists, ripe for platitudes about suffering, ripe for revenge. Anything can happen: a release of all that's noble in men or a murderous unleashing of spites and envies. And we have the power to tip it one way or the other; not simply by what we say but *the way we say it*. The habit of knocking down gods is very seductive and contagious. I'm not all that proud of the history of journalism, Mary, but I don't want to see *The Sunday Paper* perpetuating it.

MARY: But why *this* – *now* – and *to me*.

HARVEY: Because each 'god' you topple chips away at your own self-respect. The damage you do to others can boomerang and destroy you. That's why.

MARY: The duty of this paper, since we're handing out advice, is to investigate secret and well protected misbehaviour – of any kind.

HARVEY: And there's no institution more 'well protected' than a newspaper.

MARY: But that doesn't mean we can afford to limit democratic scrutiny of our society and its politicians, for Christ's sake!

HARVEY: I'm simply warning you. You might want to deflate the egos of self-styled 'gods' but be careful you don't crack the confidence of good men. We haven't got that many. Think of it.

MARY: I don't really think I needed all that.

[*She leaves.*]

Political and Features

NORMAN: She's lucky, Mary. She can insult fools. Not me. I was born to suffer the fool for ever. And why? Because when the stupid man is being stupid he *knows* he's being stupid, and I know that he knows, but I can't offend him by letting him know that I know! I'm a gentle soul. People must be allowed to be stupid like dogs going off into corners to lick their wounds.

In Depth

[MARY *visiting*]

MARY: Chris, take a break and come and have a drink with a fink.

CHRIS: A gentle fink or an evil fink?

MARY: A Morgan King fink.

JULIAN: Ah! A king-sized fink.

CHRIS: Gossip or documents?

MARY: You know I never listen to gossip. Hurry, if it looks good I want to catch the last edition.

CHRIS: St George moves in for the kill.

MARY: All right, all right! He's misunderstood. *I'm* the dragon. Shall we move?

CHRIS: I fly, I fly. Watch me how I fly.

[*They leave.*]

Political and Features

CYNTHIA: I once knew a beautiful young boy who was like that. Everyone wanted to embrace him, me for example. And he was so sensitive to the embarrassment of refusal that he let me. Men, women – they all wanted to touch him. The more brazen seduced him outright – some people have a nose for those things, they can smell out victims. That's what he was, a victim. And so gradually he began avoiding people, shunned all contacts, withdrew. At the age of thirty he was consigned to a home, morose, confused. Born for abuse.

Foreign Department

[*The urgent sound of 'tick-tack'.* GORDON *and* TAMARA *standing by the telex.*]

GORDON [*reading*]: 'At least 250 doctors, professors, writers and teachers, the cream of the intellectuals who could have helped create the state were found murdered in a field outside the capital.'

[TAMARA *turns away.*]

'All had their hands tied behind their backs and had been bayoneted, garrotted or shot.' Tamara, get this down to Harvey. It's Reuters, everyone'll have it. Tamara!

TAMARA: I –

GORDON: For Christ's sake, you're a journalist. Is this any worse than your reports on the Eichmann trial?

TAMARA: Darkness, there's such darkness in that act.

GORDON: It's war.

TAMARA: War? It's Mary's 'who-does-he-think-he-is?' gone insane. The poisonous side of the sweet apple of democracy. It's what your lovely ordinary Everyman would like to do in order to feel equal – massacre the thinkers.

GORDON: Don't be a bloody fool. Men have been slaughtering their thinkers for centuries.

TAMARA: How blithely you say it.

Business News

[JANE *approaching* DOMINIC *with a bottle of whisky.*]

JANE: With the compliments of Women's Pages.

MORTY: And what's he done that we haven't?

DOMINIC: Gave the girls a little anecdote about the man who was refused sterilization on the National Health.

MORTY: You selling your life story again?

DOMINIC: Oh very funny. But I tell you the population explosion is serious. I can hardly park my car for people in the way.

Foreign Department

TAMARA: I don't think I can really cope much more, Gordon.

GORDON: Go home. I'll finish your story.

TAMARA: Between the oppressors and the fanatics there's the rest of us.

GORDON: Go to a cinema, or the opera.

TAMARA: Helpless. We're always so helpless.

GORDON: Spoil yourself. Buy yourself a present – what about those antique markets you love so much?

TAMARA: Uch! Depressing! Cracked plates, torn lace, threadbare shawls. Old ladies' homes bought for a few pence and sold at such a terrible profit. All fraudulent, cheating – and insulting. Above all insulting, and offensive, and greedy, and insulting and greedy, greedy, greedy!

Sports Pages

MARVIN [*slamming down phone*]: Thank you very much! Another bloody adviser. Why do they always come through on a Saturday, the day when we're the only office working our balls off.

RONNIE: Occupational hazard, mate. Unlike the other departments in this autocratic establishment we have democracy forced on us. Everyone's an expert on sport and every Sunday morning spiteful little eyes race down our columns in the 'let's-catch-'em-out-game'.

Business News

MORTY: Tell me, Jane. That feature on dressing fat ladies, your model, where did you find her?

DOMINIC: Thinking of modelling fat men's wear, are you?

JANE: The less we talk of that little fraud the better, I think.

MORTY: But she was beautiful. Fat, beautiful, happy and well-dressed. Tremendous morale booster for stout ladies.

JANE: She got hundreds of offers of marriage, but what those photographs didn't show, and we only discovered it afterwards, was that the clothes she was given to wear didn't meet at the back and had to be kept together with safety pins.

News Room

HARVEY: Right! My copy's gone down. [*To* LAYOUT.] Sam, you laid out the new shape yet?

LAYOUT: It'll look like this. What's your headline?

HARVEY: Any ideas?

ANTHONY: How about 'Earnings I ain't got'?

HARVEY: He had earnings all right.

LAYOUT: How about 'Earnings: P.M. tells all'.

HARVEY: No. We'll keep it straight. 'P.M. I've still got an overdraft'. That's what he said. Will it go in?

LAYOUT: I think we can fit *that* in.

[MESSENGER *arrives with proof sheets.*]

HARVEY: Anthony, do me a favour and sub that for me, please.

Arts Pages/Women's Pages

SEBASTIAN [*on phone*]: No, no dear fellow, you know it's much better to cut an entire paragraph rather than re-arrange it. The printers invariably make a balls of it.

In Depth

[ANGELA *visiting.*]

JULIAN: And so our ex-prime minister, Hotspur Hoskins as he was fondly known to us all, said of her, in one of his more jovial and confiding moods: 'Political commentator? Huh! That bitch'd get a scoop wrong if you gave it to her at dictation speed.'

ANGELA: Did he actually use the word 'scoop'? Jesus!

News Room

[MORTY *arrives on the scene.*]

HARVEY: Morty, your fink's story. Anything in it?

MORTY: The problem is, if a company like Onyx declares an overseas profit of £1 million they don't have to say where it comes from.

HARVEY: On the other hand don't you always do business with your friends?

MORTY: Right. That's what business is about, and Crafty Crafton was only going about his business.

HARVEY: Good. So we forget it.

MORTY: And a plague on all their houses.

HARVEY: Tony, that piece Chris did on Atlantis Insurance.

ANTHONY: All true, Harvey. Every word of it. But no documents.

HARVEY: We'll print it but it weakens the story without names.

ANTHONY: The old problem, loyalty to sources of information.

HARVEY: My piece O.K.?

ANTHONY: O.K.

HARVEY: Good. We'll push out the first edition.

PAUL [*into phone*]: Let's go! Roll 'em!

[*Now the film on the backscreen becomes a film of the machines beginning to roll out the first edition. And with it comes the full blast of their noise which, though subsequently reduced for the remaining dialogue, continues till the end of the play.*]

In Depth

JULIAN [*on phone*]: Yes, the Atlantis story is going in, it's a big story – very eye-catching – pretty diagrams and all that – most impressive. No! Of course no names are mentioned.

Arts Pages/Women's Pages

ANGELA [*on phone*]: Yes, yes. Your air tickets are in the post, now concentrate on the paragraph you're going to cut for me. How about the one comparing his playing to a 'flight of homeward flying fleas'? Yes, it may be accurate and funny but we do try to discourage our distinguished critics from being gratuitously offensive.

News Room

[MARTIN *rushes in.*]

MARTIN [*calling* HARVEY *aside from main table*]: Harvey?

HARVEY: What is it, Martin?

MARTIN: I was right. There does exist a secret society.

HARVEY: Let's have it.

MARTIN: It's hot.

HARVEY: Well let's have it for God's sake.

MARTIN: I'm sitting on top of an Anarchists cell when in burst three youngsters, nylon stockings over their faces, one carrying a gun, and they tell the Anarchists to lay off the violence.

HARVEY: With one of them carrying a gun?

MARTIN: It turns out to be a water pistol.

HARVEY: Go on.

MARTIN: So I trail the three rivals –

HARVEY: Make it short.

MARTIN: And one of them turns out to be Mary's youngest son.

HARVEY: Oh no! Bloody hell! No.

ANTHONY: You're looking harassed, Harvey.

HARVEY [*to* MARTIN]: Tell him.

Business News

JANE [*reading a letter*]: 'And what's more,' she writes, 'I think you should not only be urging people not to have babies but you should encourage them to save our resources. Water for instance. I mean, soon the world will run out of water. Forgive the personal touch but *I've* stopped pulling the chain on my urination.'

DOMINIC: I see. Save our water and start a dysentery epidemic.

News Room

ANTHONY: You can't tell her, Harvey.

HARVEY: Not in front of this lot, I can't. And it can't be *her* story either.

MARTIN: You bet it can't. I've stood in the cold for days on this one.

ANTHONY: Don't be a fool, Martin. Yours is only half the ditty.

MARTIN: Half?

ANTHONY: At this moment Saint Maria Mortimer is out gathering dirt which she believes will topple the dragon of Lanark.

MARTIN: I don't connect.

ANTHONY: You should, my boy, you should. 'Only connect,' says Forster.

MARTIN: I didn't go to university.

ANTHONY: I thought everyone went to university. She's in a pub across the road, talking to an evil fink, who's offered her documents proving a link between Morgan King and your so-called secret society.

MARTIN: Jesus!

ANTHONY: Well, Harvey?

HARVEY: I'm still thinking.

In Depth

JULIAN [*on phone*]: And so I walked into El Vino's for the first time in my life, 'cos everyone assured me I had to do my drinking there or I wouldn't know what was going on in the world, and I was thinking to myself: that perhaps I'd come into the wrong profession after all, when a bloke comes up to me, pissed out of his mind, and says, as though he'd read my thoughts, he says: 'Psst. A journalist is a man who possesses himself of a fantasy and lures the truth towards it – remember that and you'll go to the top.'

News Room

HARVEY: Right! The bridges story comes back. [*Picks up the phone.*] Frank? Don't hold that last edition. Yes, *don't* hold it I said. The bridges story stays in. Yes, in! In, in, IN!

ANTHONY: Martin my boy, what you now do with your story is your own decision. Can you believe it?

Foreign Department

[*Urgent sound of 'tick-tack'.* TAMARA *is in the middle of reading a long telex.*]

TAMARA: 'The most horrific episode carried out by the guerrillas was in the midst of celebratory prayers which turned into cries of revenge for the 250 murdered intellectuals. The rally ended with Islamic prayers in which five prisoners, whose crime was alleged to have been an attempt to abduct two women, joined their captors in offering praise to Allah. The crowd began to beat the trussed up men until a group of the guerrillas, wearing black uniforms, pushed them back, fixed bayonets and began to stab the prisoners through the neck, the chest, and stomach. The crowd watched with interest and the photographers snapped away. A small boy of ten, the son of one of the prisoners, cradled the head of his dying father, which act infuriated the crowd who proceeded to trample on the child.' [*Breaks down.*]

GORDON: Go home!

News Room

[MARY *and* CHRIS *rush in.*]

MARY: They're authentic. I knew it. Look.

CHRIS: True, Harvey. Front page material.

HARVEY: It's too late.

MARY: Too late? You've held the last edition, haven't you?

HARVEY: It was too late I tell you.

MARY: Too late? Too late? Whose nonsense is this? We agreed.

HARVEY: It came from the top. The bridges story had to stay.

MARY: Bloody hell! Didn't you tell them we had an important story coming up?

HARVEY: They wanted to see the evidence first. Too risky.

MARY: What cock and bull story is that, Harvey? *You're* the editor aren't you?

HARVEY: And that's *my* decision.

MARY: But I promised I'd bring him down.

Business News

JANE: Do you know, I never ever see any of you working. You're always standing around reading magazines with incomprehensible graphs and tables.

DOMINIC: Not work? My dear lady. First of all it's Saturday and our work's all done. Secondly I'm reading the opposition, and that's work.

News Room

MARY: I demand a better explanation, Harvey. That man's a politician and in the running to be on the party's executive. That makes him dangerous, a national risk.

Business News

DOMINIC: Ah! Now, what we *should* do is one thing, what we're *able* to do is another. I tell you, the cigarette packets carry a notice saying: 'Warning! Smoking can damage your health!' But what about all newspapers carrying a notice on the front page, just below their names, saying: 'Warning! The selective attention to data herein contained may warp your view of the world!' What about *that*, eh?

News Room

MARY: But I could have brought him down. I promised you I'd bring that man DOWN!

HARVEY [*to* SOMEONE]: The bloody idiots have cut the wrong story.

MARY: He doesn't even listen to me now.

Sports Pages

RONNIE [*on phone*]: I can't help it. It'll have to wait over till next week. It's a small paper this week and fishing's a small sport – NO! I don't care if it does feed multitudes . . .

Business News

JANE: I like it. 'Warp your view of the world.'

DOMINIC: Just below the name. Imagine it. '*The Sunday Paper* – Warning! The selective attention to data herein contained may warp your view of the world.' Po-pom!

News Room

MARY: Harvey, answer me!

Business News

JANE: *Daily Mirror* – warning –
DOMINIC: *The Times* – warning –
JANE: *Private Eye* – warning –
TOGETHER: 'May warp your view of the world!'

News Room

MARY: HARVEY!

ANTHONY: Mary, my dear, look, I've got a problem . . .

[*He takes her, consolingly, from the scene.*]

MARY: But why isn't he listening? He's not even listening.

[*Now, as they move off, everyone in all departments talks at once, a babble, a crescendo of voices melting into the full blast of the machines. The sound continues but – the stage darkens – except for the bright image on the screen of the presses turning – turning.*]

THE WEDDING FEAST

A play in two acts and a prologue freely adapted from a short story called *An Unpleasant Predicament* by Fyodor Dostoevsky

FOR NIKKI AND BOB GAVRON

WITH LOVE AND GRATITUDE

The Wedding Feast received its world premiere at the Stadtsteater, Stockholm, on 8 May 1974, directed by Gun Arvidsson.

It received its British première, greatly revised, at the Leeds Playhouse on 20 January 1977, with the following cast.

LOUIS LITVANOV	David Swift
KATE WHITE	Fiona Walker
DAVID LOWERY	Noel Collins
STEPHEN BULLOCK	Brett Usher
MR HAMMOND	Michael Egan
BONKY HARRIS	Andrew Jarvis
KNOCKER WHITE	David Troughton
TOSH WHITE	Dickie Arnold
EMILY WHITE	Barbara Atkinson
TINKER WHITE	Nigel Gregory
DAPHNE DAWSON	Stephanie Fayerman
MR DAWSON	Ted Morris
MRS DAWSON	Mary Ann Turner
MAUREEN DAWSON	Carol Leader
MARTIN DAWSON	Michael Troughton
RINGO RAY	Sebastian Abineri

Directed by John Harrison and Michael Attenborough
Designed by John Halle
Lighting by Mo Hemmings

This version results from further cuts and revisions from the Birmingham Rep. production of 5th June 1980 directed by Peter Farago, and differs from the earlier Penguin edition.

CHARACTERS

LOUIS LITVANOV, *a shoe manufacturer*
KATE WHITE, *his secretary*
DAVID LOWERY, *his manager*
MR HAMMOND, *managing director of chain of shoe shops*
KNOCKER WHITE, *Kate's brother, a shoe operative*
TOSH WHITE, *their uncle, a shoe operative*
EMILY WHITE, *Tosh's wife*
TINKER WHITE, *their son, regular in the army*
DAPHNE DAWSON, *Knocker's bride, a shoe operative*
MR DAWSON, *her father, a shoe operative*
MRS DAWSON, *her mother*
MAUREEN DAWSON, *her sister, a shoe operative*
MARTIN DAWSON, *her brother, a building worker*
RINGO RAY, *Martin's friend, a shoe operative*
STEPHEN BULLOCK, *Kate's friend, a journalist*
BONKY HARRIS, *a shoe operative*

(MR HAMMOND and MR DAWSON can be played by the same actor)

PROLOGUE

There are four small sets for the Prologue to suggest: LOUIS's *lounge,* LOUIS's *bathroom,* LOUIS's *office, streets of Norwich. All could involve the use of a screen with projected slides and/or film, though this is not essential. There is one main set for Acts One and Two: interior of the* WHITES' *house for the wedding.*

SCENE ONE

[*Lounge of a large country mansion in the outskirts of Norwich in Norfolk. Four people, three men and a woman.*
A drinks trolley, four chairs around a small table. Late evening. Behind, a huge screen.
The host, LOUIS LITVANOV, *is serving and chatting with his guests:* MR HAMMOND, KATE WHITE, DAVID LOWERY.]

LOUIS: And *why* do you think I make my office of glass? To be *seen* working! And why do you think that office is on the shop floor? To discuss business where work is done! Noise! Activity! I'm a worker. I work hard.
  [STEPHEN BULLOCK *steps forward. In the* PROLOGUE *he has the fuction of a narrator.*]
STEPHEN: This – uncomfortable story occurred about the time our elected representatives decided bravely that we should take our fortunes into the European Common Market.
LOUIS: My operatives see me work hard. They respect me!
STEPHEN: A courageous time when our cool captains of industry streamlined their factories, sacked superfluous labour – albeit with a touching impetuosity – and, fortified by high hopes of new destinies, struggled firmly to calm the anticipated though unreasonable industrial unrest which followed. A time

111

of optimism and regeneration owing much to men of high commercial idealism. We think, ourselves, that such men have been a little unjustly castigated for the harsh measures they were forced to take: prosperity, after all, has its price and in the beginning must always take a sad toll of victims. Or must it?

LOUIS: When the men get there at eight in the morning who do they see? The night-watchman? No! Me! The first to arrive, the last to go. And they respect me.

STEPHEN: And so you see, not every businessman was ruthless when faced with the challenge of streamlining for entry-into-Europe-day. This tale adjusts the balance, a little at least. And if for the moment capital has failed to find a modus vivendi with labour, well – it will not have been, as we'll show, for the want of trying. However, before the main story – the preamble, a filling-in, a few – vivid brushstrokes.

DAVID: Mr Litvanov –

STEPHEN: – is our central character.

DAVID: – I don't think you're being very honest.

STEPHEN: Honest, in the formal sense of the word, that is.

LOUIS: Not honest? Have you ever known me do a crooked deal, break a contract, abuse my workers?

STEPHEN: But we're talking about –

DAVID: – the private sense, Mr Litvanov –

LOUIS: Louis, please, it's out of office.

DAVID: – the private sense. You won't face the lessons of experience.

LOUIS: Experience! Experience! What, what, what experience?

STEPHEN: What experience? We'll soon hear. To begin, then [*flicks switch of control which projects interior on to screen*], a country mansion in the outskirts of Norwich in the county of Norfolk. Four people. One Sunday evening. No! To begin with: me! Name: Stephen Bullock. Education: Norwich Grammar and the London School of Economics. Profession: Journalist. For whom? The local daily press. Temperament? Unreliable. Achievements? Mediocre. Vices? Self-pity when drunk. Virtues? Honest – when drunk. But now, the story in which, later on, I play a not too worthy part, though I wouldn't have missed it for worlds! So, a country mansion in the outskirts of our lovely city of Norwich in the county of Norfolk. The country – rich in agriculture; the city – a centre for shoe manufacturing industry; the epoch – one of softening class barriers with the Alps two hours away and the moon a mere thirty-six hours away. Next, background –

LOUIS: One thing I was brought up to be and to be absolutely: honest! I can remember my father telling me that when he was a boy in Russian he saw a pogrom – houses burning, peasants looting – you know what I'm talking about? And he got angry, my father, and wanted to go in there and fight – a boy of fourteen with drunken peasants! But his father, my grandfather, grabbed him and shouted 'Take no notice! TAKE NO NOTICE!' So my father told me the same, 'Take no notice! Don't learn the wrong lessons! That's the way *they* want to behave? Let them! But not you. Honest! Always be honest and peaceful. Don't learn the wrong lessons.'

STEPHEN: And so Louis Litvanov, son of an impoverished Jewish cobbler and grandson of an impoverished Jewish cobbler, came with his poor, bewildered parents to our hospitable land and became one of its grateful, prosperous sons. But not a –

LOUIS: – millionaire! I could have been a millionaire, but no! I love my workers and they love me and because they love me they trust me and because they trust me I can run a factory. A simple philosophy.

STEPHEN: Louis's guests–

KATE: A simple guilt!

STEPHEN: – are not in agreement with him.

KATE: You're like a man who couldn't ever be a doctor – you'd associate too much with the patient's pain. You look at your operatives, you watch them do the same monotonous job every day and it hurts you. Guilt! You should have grown out of it by now.

LOUIS: You see how they talk to me?

KATE: But he enjoys it.

LOUIS: What other employer would let his secretary talk to him like that?

KATE: See how he enjoys it?

LOUIS: No! I say. It's her right. Every human being's got the right to talk to his, or her, employer as an equal.

KATE: How he enjoys himself in the act of tolerating his – to use an indelicate word – employees.

DAVID: He'll never understand the nature of British democracy.

HAMMOND: And what's that?

DAVID: You can only tolerate those who know their place.

STEPHEN: That's David Lowery –

LOUIS: – My tough, matter-of-fact Scottish manager. Listen to him. You're not interested in people, that's your trouble. You're not even interested in shoes, are you?

DAVID: Frankly, no! I'm interested in making money. That's what you pay me for and that's what I'm good at. Shoes bore me.

LOUIS: Pretending he's tough. Playing at big business. And you'll fail. People aren't stupid, you've got to *earn* their trust. The public *and* your workers. Respect them and earn their trust. It pays dividends. Both ways! In profits and human dignity. Believe me!

KATE: You're shouting.

STEPHEN: That's Kate White –

LOUIS: I'm Jewish. I shout!

STEPHEN: – his attractive secretary, my dear school-friend, my school girl-friend, and the teacher's dearest, brightest pupil.

KATE: Louis can never resist the sensation of standing alone in defence of a principle.

STEPHEN: I nearly married her.

KATE: Especially one so seasoned with a touch of evangelic fervour.

STEPHEN: But she is cursed with divine discontent: she is right for most men but not one is right for her. Kate, a tired Marxist, who learned her Marxism from me but her tiredness from the world. Louis accepted her affectionate bullying because he once contemplated running off with her, and she bullies because she would have liked to have gone but didn't, couldn't, as none of us can do what it's not in our nature to do. He was older and she was younger. He was married and, though he was married to an ageing coquette with a small brain supporting too much energy, and Kate knew it and Louis knew Kate knew, yet Kate was no home-breaker! Not that Louis's *politics* weren't a substantial appeal. He'd also once been a Marxist. As we all had once been. In our brave youth. In 1936, during the fascist riots in the East End of London Louis was a young communist messenger taking instructions from headquarters to strategic field positions. On roller skates! But – it *was* in his brave youth.

HAMMOND: And what, tell me, is the experience that Mr Litvanov won't face?

STEPHEN: That's Duncan Hammond –

LOUIS: Louis, please. I'm at home now.

STEPHEN: Managing director of a chain of shoe shops. An honourable man whose presence – as a weekend guest, no less – is especially gratifying to Louis Litvanov, because it's a sign that Louis has mastered those rough sides of his peasant origin which he prefers to keep apart from those rough sides of his peasant origin which he finds it wise to boast of on occasions.

HAMMOND: Mr Litvanov –

LOUIS: Louis –

HAMMOND: Louis has always struck me as a pretty practical man. Can't really see him not learning from experience.

STEPHEN: But listen –

DAVID: We'll tell you then.

STEPHEN: Just listen to this.

DAVID: Where shall we begin?

STEPHEN: A real roll-call of honour, this.

KATE: At the beginning.

STEPHEN: Oh, I'd better add –

DAVID: In the beginning?

STEPHEN: This little gathering is to celebrate Louis's very youthful fifty-second birthday –

DAVID: You start then.

STEPHEN: – and they're all a little drunk.

KATE: When he first bought over this ailing factory and I was a little girl and a bit –

DAVID: – Mr Litvanov said, right! Huge bonuses for everyone in the first year of profit.

KATE: And Louis, being an honest man, kept his word. We reorganized, the workers responded, and in two years we were making profits.

DAVID: Handsome bonuses all round.

KATE: In the third year bigger profits still.

DAVID: Even handsomer bonuses all round.

KATE: In the forth year still bigger profits.

DAVID: And up again went bonuses.

KATE: But, Mr Hammond, as you and every good Marxist knows, nothing stands still in capitalist society. You don't expand, bor, you stagnate. So, he added a wing, bought more plant, employed more men.

DAVID: Good for the business, good for employment, good for the country but – profits were down.

KATE: Inevitably –

DAVID: – and quite properly, as any good businessman –

KATE: – or Marxist –

DAVID: – will understand –

KATE: But the workers being neither good businessmen nor Marxists instantly sent deputations.

STEPHEN: [*but to us*]: Excuse us, Mr Litvanov, but why are our bonuses down?

DAVID: [*still to* HAMMOND, *of course*]: We've expanded, we explained. Profits are down.

STEPHEN: Excuse us, Mr Litvanov, but *you've* expanded, *your* profits are down, that's not our fault. Us've worked hard as any we worked 'afore an' we've come to rely on it.

LOUIS: I understood their arguments.

KATE: And Mr Litvanov –

LOUIS: Louis –

KATE: – understood their arguments.

DAVID: So, we had a discussion and agreed to a *fixed* bonus *not* geared to profits.

LOUIS: I'm sure Mr Hammond is familiar with all this . . .

HAMMOND: Oh, I'm not so sure.

KATE: Story number two. One day one of the wives visited Louis.

STEPHEN: Excuse me, Mr Litvanov, but could I borrow some money? My husband's bin ill five weeks, look.

DAVID: 'What?' cried Louis. 'Doesn't this firm pay sick pay?'

KATE: And up he jumped, called in David here, and the accountant – everyone! and asked with child-like amazement: no sick pay?

DAVID: We pointed out that no one in the industry pays sick pay.

LOUIS: I spoke to the federation of shoe manufacturers – no! It would be abused, they said. Spoke to the union – no! Other demands more important, they said.

KATE: So, Louis went ahead alone and instituted sick pay –

DAVID: – and a very, very interesting situation arose. As you know, a long time ago we had machines requiring three men to run them and so, because workers have a fine sense of history, they insisted that even though technology had produced a machine operable by one man yet, for historical reasons, of course, they should continue using three.

STEPHEN: And good luck to them I say.

DAVID: Now, what happened when one of those three was ill? Not only was he paid sick pay but the remaining two insisted that the third man's wage be divided between them, *and* that they should be paid the overtime needed to catch up on the backlog which the third man's absence created.

KATE: And what backlog was there?

DAVID: None! Because the machine only needed one man anyway.

KATE: And where was the sick man?

DAVID: Temporary work! In another firm!

LOUIS: But reasons! There were reasons! Behaviour like that has historical reasons.

DAVID: We appealed to the unions who said don't pay sick pay then. But Mr L, being a humanitarian, paid the price of over-manning *and* sick pay, and illness rose from fifteen days a year to thirty.

LOUIS: But profits rose. You've got to keep pointing out that profits rose also.

KATE: And so Louis felt he had to humanize relationships

even more. He had an idea.

DAVID: The football saga?

KATE: Ah! The football saga!

DAVID: One day, I remember the very day, a Friday, we were together in the packing room, looking outside where the men were playing football in their lunch hour.

LOUIS: How about a match between the men and the management I suggested.

STEPHEN: Smashing! One Saturday afternoon. Crates of beer. Sandwiches. Beat them seven-one, of course.

DAVID: Then it grew.

STEPHEN: What about a regular team, Mr Litvanov?

LOUIS: Splendid, I said. Great idea. I'll hire the grounds, pay for refreshment –

KATE: – until one day one of them came and said –

STEPHEN: – excuse me, Mr Litvanov, but we play a team the other day, and they had a special kit paid for by their management.

LOUIS: Don't worry, I said, we'll have a team kit, best money can buy –

STEPHEN: – and boots, Mr Litvanov, we get through helluva lot o' boots in a season.

LOUIS: Nothing easier, I said.

STEPHEN: And can we hev Wednesday off for the league matches?

LOUIS: Now wait a minute, I said.

STEPHEN: Can't stay in the league otherwise, y'see, Mr Litvanov.

KATE: So Louis agreed, didn't you, Louis?

DAVID: And then we found they weren't coming in on Thursdays because of bruises to their ankles –

KATE: – and that they had to have time off on Tuesday for training sessions –

DAVID: And that they needed supporters which meant time off for other workers –

KATE: – and always these veiled threats about leaving if each new demand wasn't met.

LOUIS: Which I didn't like. No! *That* I didn't like. *I'd* encouraged the idea in the first place and that wasn't nice. But I tell you what –

KATE: – he understood.

LOUIS: If you have a deprived upbringing, a job that's monotonous, you grab at all the recreation you can get. I know. I did it myself.

KATE: And therefore Louis Litvanov understood their motives.

HAMMOND: Tell me, Mr Litvanov –

LOUIS: Louis, please.

HAMMOND: Louis. Tell me, are all Jewish businessmen as paternalistic as you?

LOUIS: That's what you call it? Give everything a name and dismiss it. All right! So I'm paternalistic. You think my workers care if it means good wages and a pleasant atmosphere?

HAMMOND: Pleasant atmosphere? That's interesting now. And it doesn't occur to you that because you insist on putting your office on the shop floor it might disturb your operatives?

LOUIS: Disturb them?

HAMMOND: Disturb them, for example, to watch you giving us drinks, as you so kindly do before we visit your collection? And it's in the middle of the morning, don't forget.

LOUIS: Disturb them? Why should that disturb them? They know why it's happening. Buyers come to look at a collection you've got to give them a drink. The operatives understand this. More, they want it! The more I sell the more they earn. What *should* they say?

HAMMOND: What *could* they say? They're on your territory. You confuse their diplomacy for honesty. Am I correct, Miss White?

LOUIS: Don't ask her. She's an old-fashioned Marxist. It confuses her that I get on so well with my workers. Right, Kate?

KATE: You *imagine* you get on with them.

HAMMOND: Yes, what about when they're *not* on your territory?

KATE: And he's planning to expand into Europe.

LOUIS: I'm a European, of course I'll expand. The European

business community needs men like me. The worker must be loved, cared for, respected as a human being. How else can you make an Industrial Relations Act work, or a Treaty of Rome or any other of those agreements which, we all agree I hope, are only aimed at the benefit of all?

HAMMOND: Oh we agree, we agree. But your theories, Mr Litvanov, the men of Europe are tough and hard and won't so easily respond, I fear.

LOUIS: Then we must teach them, mustn't we, Kate?

KATE: Yes, Louis. You, me and David here. We'll do a lecture tour of company board meetings. 'Mammon and manual worker: how to love both and survive!'

LOUIS: She's beautiful when she's witty.

HAMMOND: But what about the worker *outside* his work situation? They like to keep their distances, you know. I mean, supposing you went to their homes. There. Where they live. What then? Would your sense of equality stand up there do you think? Between four dreary working-class walls? Stand up? Would it?

DAVID: Ah ha! Now there's a question.

KATE: I bet that'll give Louis something to think about.

DAVID: To keep him awake at nights.

KATE: Poor Louis.

[*The guests leave.*]

STEPHEN: Poor Louis! The party came to an end. [*Switches off slide.*] It had been a good way to celebrate a fifty-second year. Civilized. They'd been frank, witty, flattered each other's intelligence. Louis Litvanov had cause to feel pleased with himself.

SCENE TWO

[*A bath, many tall mirrors, a handsome dressing gown, bathroom boxes.*]

STEPHEN: And so, man of habit that he was, Louis undressed, meticulously folded his clothes in neat piles and laid them on one of his tapestry-covered chairs [*switches on suitable new slides of tapestried chair*] in one of his oak panelled bedrooms [*switches on slide*] alongside one of his mirrored bathrooms [*switches on slide*] in this, one of his two country homes, and prepared to soak in that hot bath all hard-working bodies need in preparation for sleep and tomorrow's enterprise.

Yet, something irritated him. The little party, for all the expansive attention he'd given to it, had left some vague uneasiness in his soul. What?

[*Sound of telephone.*]

His wife, telephoning from their London flat.

[*It is a machine necessitating a mere button so that he can talk to and hear it from any part of the room. This enables him, now, to undress and look at himself in the mirror while talking.*]

WIFE'S VOICE: Louis?

LOUIS: I'm here.

WIFE'S VOICE: Where are you?

LOUIS: In the bathroom.

WIFE'S VOICE: You alone?

LOUIS: No!

WIFE'S VOICE: Who's with you?

LOUIS: Everybody. You finished with the Inquisition?

WIFE'S VOICE: What you so irritable for?

LOUIS: I always think maybe this time you'll ask me first how I am, how's the factory.

WIFE'S VOICE: I hate the factory.

LOUIS: Or happy birthday.

WIFE'S VOICE: Oh, Louis, I forgot.

LOUIS: So why you ringing?

WIFE'S VOICE: You asked me to ring – I'm ringing.

[*He grimaces at his wife – the telephone machine.*]

LOUIS: How are the boys?

WIFE'S VOICE: They also hate the factory.

LOUIS: I know. And you teach them to hate me too. I'm a very lucky man. Blessed.

WIFE'S VOICE: For goodness sake, what are you doing there?

LOUIS: Undressing. What else should I be doing in a bathroom?

[*She is silent.*]

[*To himself*] Not only am *I* a peasant but I'm married to one.

STEPHEN: Ah ha! The words slipped out. Was this the reason for his vague uneasiness? Louis was an honest man. Strange tensions tugged at his hard-won equanimity.

WIFE'S VOICE: I can't hear you. Stop undressing and come nearer to the phone.

LOUIS: Tell me something. Tell me something interesting. Tell me a beautiful story, something beautiful you've done.

WIFE'S VOICE: Hurry up, Louis, please. I'm late for an appointment.

LOUIS: An appointment? This hour?

WIFE'S VOICE: I'm in London, remember? The big city? We don't die with the sun here you know.

LOUIS: Go, go.

WIFE'S VOICE: I'll buy your present tomorrow.

LOUIS: I'm much obliged.

WIFE'S VOICE: 'Bye!

LOUIS: [*mocking her tone*] 'Bye, 'bye!

[*Switches off contraption. Looks at himself in the mirror.*]

You're growing old.

[*Confronts another mirror.*]

You're growing fat.

[*Falls to floor and attempts press-ups. Collapses and gives up after four.*]

And you're a peasant.

[*Slowly rises. Takes up a magnificent dressing gown over his shoulders. Again sees himself in a mirror. Draws himself up to his full height.*]

No! You're a tycoon.

[*Defiantly throws open his arms. Dressing gown falls off.*]

No! You're a peasant. [*Pause*] Who the hell needs so many mirrors? And so many doors? And so many rooms? And so many houses and so many cars? [*Mimicking, shouting*] Louis, you're shouting.

[*Takes off pants, finds himself confronting another mirror — naked and vulnerable.*]

[*Softly, sadly*] I'm human, I shout!
[*He enters bath, slowly crumbles, sinks, dejected.*]

SCENE THREE

[*The factory. To begin with, the sounds of machines from the shoe factory. Then — Film or articulated slides of morning on the shop-floors of* LOUIS's *factory. Visuals match sounds:*
first — the hum of the electric current revving up;
then — the first large sound of the enormous 'clicking' (cutting) machine called 'the revolutionary press';
then — the 'in-sole moulder' moving up and down;
then — the machine for bevelling the sole's edges, spinning round;
then — the long rows of girls at the machines which stitch the uppers together and the linings to the uppers.
A symphony! a visual poem! Ah!]

STEPHEN: Poor Louis Litvanov, husband, father, confused idealist, factory owner on the threshold of big, European industry, his age at odds with the stubborn enthusiasms of a reluctantly fading youth. Who would dare pass judgement on a man's actions when such awful conflicts are at work in his soul?
  [*Glass office is set up.* LOUIS *inside.*]
  But 'stubborn' is an admirable word to apply to our hero.
LOUIS: Harris!
STEPHEN: The next morning brought fresh energies, and all doubts were drowned in dreams where, they say, most unsolved problems settle themselves.
LOUIS: Harris!
STEPHEN: He found time, on his way to work, to pause and climb a tree, which action — though it irritated his sceptical chauffeur — boosted his own morale. His chauffeur, besides, was a slothful unimaginative man who, for example, failed to appreciate the need to drive to work in a modest Ford rather than the ostentatious Rolls which was only reserved for week-end visiting. And so, fortified with new resolves, Louis began a new day with special bounce.

LOUIS: Harris! Harris!

[BONKY HARRIS, *an operative, appears.*]

LOUIS: Bonky? I've got something special to discuss with you. But first, this. You've made a good job of it. [*He's referring to a wooden model of a new style shoe and drawing from which it was made.*] Excellent! But this line, from the sole to the heel. Look [*pointing to drawing*], a little steeper.

BONKY: Do you really think it can rise so sharp?

LOUIS: I know it can rise so sharp. Apart from that you've copied it beautifully. An artist! You're a real artist! Which brings me to my special thing: your secret hobby.

BONKY: Who told you about that?

LOUIS: No matter who. It's true, isn't it?

BONKY: My hobby is my hobby, Mr Litvanov.

LOUIS: You paint, don't you?

BONKY: My hobby is my –

LOUIS: And I want to see them.

BONKY: I don't show –

LOUIS: I mean, *may* I see them? Please?

BONKY: I don't show no one what I do.

LOUIS: I want to buy some.

BONKY: I don't sell –

LOUIS: I mean I'd *like* to buy some. Please.

BONKY: But I don't do them for selling, Mr Litvanov.

LOUIS: [*impatiently*]: Oh, come on, Bonky. Let me see them.

BONKY: Yes, Mr Litvanov.

[BONKY *moves off. Employers must be indulged.* KATE *enters.*]

LOUIS: Good morning, Katherine.

KATE: You're shouting.

LOUIS: I'm in good spirits, I shout. [*But softer*] Good morning.

KATE: Good morning.

LOUIS: You think I made a fool of myself last night?

KATE: I have a favour to ask you.

LOUIS: You did, didn't you?

KATE: It was your birthday.

LOUIS: Drank too much.

KATE: Your hearty concern –

LOUIS: Talked too much.

KATE: – it irritates me.

LOUIS: Made a fool of myself.

KATE: You were at your worst.

LOUIS: What favour?

KATE: My brother is getting married. There's some wedding shoes –

LOUIS: Take. Now, ask me a real favour.

[BONKY HARRIS *enters with some paintings on hardboards.*]

BONKY: Oh, sorry, Miss White. I'll come back later.

LOUIS: Come in, come in. Look, Bonky's paintings. Did *you* know one of our operatives painted in his lunch hour? You didn't did you? No! You're so busy criticizing my black sins that you miss the jewels around you. [*Pause.*] I like them. [*Pause.*] Bonky, tell me, help me solve a little argument we've been having. When the buyers come, to look at our collection, and I bring them into this office for drinks, and you can all see us – does it upset you? To watch us? You know, in the middle of the morning and all that? You mind? You? Any of you?

BONKY: No, sir. Don't worry me none, Mr Litvanov, no sir. Drink yourselves to death for all I care, if you'll pardon the joke.

LOUIS: And the others?

BONKY: Can't talk for the others, master; no one can't talk for no one else can they?

LOUIS: But what do you think?

BONKY: Well, reckon they might some on 'em want a pint watching you, but they don't think on it much. They know it's not their time o'day, see. They think you people gotta drink then. They think it's your way, don't they? Not the same way as them, is it?

LOUIS: [*he's scored*]: You're a wise man, Bonky. [*Holding up paintings for* KATE] Look! Good, yes? I'll buy them. How much?

KATE: For God's sake, you're embarrassing him.

LOUIS: You embarrassed, Bonky? Miss White's ashamed to talk about money matters; are *you*? [*Pause.*] See, wrong again. So. Five pounds each? Ten? Twenty? Tell you what, fifty pounds for the three of them. [*He proceeds to count out notes to an oppressed-looking* BONKY HARRIS].

[*The film of the operatives working is now full stride into its rhythm.*]

STEPHEN: When a good man's determined to do good there ent no stopping him, there ent. Fired by principles he'll defy all scorn. It is said by men of spirit and short sight that it is only greed which drives the working man to harder work. But such a view ignores the subtle paradox that, in order to satisfy this so-called greed, men must cooperate! They must! One man don't produce a car do 'ee? No! Takes a whole lot on 'em, cooperating together. And is not cooperation a worthy human aspiration?

[*To prove which the rhythmic sound of the machines intensifies and the visuals showing men and women 'cooperating' are even lovelier and, somehow, holier.*]

SCENE FOUR

[*The streets and landmarks of Norwich projected on the screen as and when* STEPHEN'S *continuing story indicates.*]

STEPHEN: How happily that next week passed; and when the next Saturday came his good humour persisted and Louis took his chauffeur and the chauffeur's wife, who was his house-keeper, and their children into the colourful market of Norwich, bought them presents, fed them lunch, took them to admire the city's castle and cathedral and walk the old delightful cobbled Elm Hill Street. And when teatime came fed them cream and jam squashed between soft scones, after which he whipped them into a late afternoon film showing of *Nicholas and Alexandra*. Whew! What a purring troupe it was that spilt out from the celluloid world of regal living into the cold, brisk, starry night of a Norfolk sky and, laden with parcels and giggling when their Ford was discovered to be hooked bumper to bumper to a Rolls-Royce, finally drove out of the city centre through the suburbs towards fields and a sort of home.

[*Pause.*] Until –

CHAUFFEUR'S VOICE: Don't worry, Mr Litvanov. Be fixed in five minutes.

    [LOUIS *walks into a background of a projection of a starry night.*]

STEPHEN: Not even a puncture can disturb the good humour of our munificent manufacturer. The night air is fresh and good. The sky is razor keen with sharp stars, and from round about come the domestic sounds of families, alive with their week-end pleasures and pastimes. A baby cries, momentarily frightened out of sleep; a dog barks at an owner's return; children play hide and seek in the shadows and, why – there's even the sounds of music; a party, a wedding, a birthday feast? Can there be so much misery in this world if settings of such charm are possible? But wait! Who's this? Those voices are familiar.

    [A FATHER *and* SON, *arguing, walk past.*]

SON: And I tell you Knocker said *one* more crate.

FATHER: What in hell do 'ee know. 'Is sister say two crates an' two crates is what I'm buyin'.

SON: But he'll be riled. He say to get only one.

FATHER: Never mind what 'ee say. 'Ee say many things what no one wanna take notice of. She say two, and two it'll be.

    [*They pass by.*]

STEPHEN: Crates of beer? Knocker? Can it be? Kate's brother's name is Knocker. Surely not. Everyone's got a nickname like that in these parts. Still, it is a coincidence. But no! The wedding wasn't today. Or was it? Perhaps it was. Perhaps he'd forgotten.

    [FATHER *and* SON *return. A crate to each.*]

SON: Well, I'm telling you, that's all, just warnin'. He'll be riled.

FATHER: Oh give over. You ben't afeared of Knocker White, surely?

SON: Me afeared of Knocker White? Him? That accident-prone lump of merchandise?

FATHER: He is that. Narthin' what stand is safe when he's talkin'. Ole Knocker White.

    [*They pass by.*]

LOUIS: Knocker White. It is. The wedding.

STEPHEN: It is well known that whole trains of thought sometimes pass through our brains instantaneously. However, we'll
try to unscramble our hero's thoughts, at least to give you a
kernel of them, as they say, the most essential and nearest to
reality. 'Why,' flashed through his mind, 'Hammond's right. I
talk and talk and only test my notions in the factory, but not
in their houses. Here, for example, is one of my workers,
Knocker White . . .

LOUIS [taking over]: . . . just returned from a moving ceremony, full of hope, excitement, looking forward to his wedding
feast. One of the most blissful days of his life – sharing it with
his nearest and dearest, thanking them, with a banquet. Modest
naturally, poor but gay. Full of genuine gladness.

What, what if he knew that outside, at this very moment, I,
his boss, someone *he* felt was his superior, was toying with
thoughts of coming in? What would he say? What would he
feel if suddenly I *did* walk in? [Thinks.] Ha! Dumb! He'd be
dumb with embarrassment. Stands to reason! I'd be in his way,
upset everything. [Thinks.] Or would I? With anybody else,
perhaps. But with me? A man who's known poverty half his
life? How I'd transform that embarrassment into a sweet
pleasure, a real human moment. [Pause.] What would happen?
I'd go in. Silence. They're amazed. Anxious. Dancing stops.
They back away. Understandable. But, I go straight to the
groom. A smile. Simple words. Tell him about the puncture,
the voices going for crates of beer, the sounds of music I heard,
the coincidence. 'I don't suppose you'll turn me out,' I say.
Turn me out! Ha! He'll be ecstatic! He'll take my coat – rush to
get me an armchair –trrrremble with delight. And one by one
I'll make the acquaintance of the guests, the bride, compliment
her, tell jokes – about coming again in nine months time to be
godfather. I'll beg them not to stand on ceremony . . .

But not for self-honour. I won't be looking for special
attention, laurels, flattery, servile humbleness. No! My actions
will evoke nobler feelings. Our conversation will be modest,
natural, men facing men in a human situation. For only a half-
hour, just to offer respects, or perhaps an hour, and one or

128

two or maybe three drinks. But no more! Before the food comes I'll leave. 'Business,' I'll say. And they'll understand that.

Then I'll leave, with a joke about the wedding bed which'll make them roar with laughter, and then I'll kiss the bride, gently, on the forehead, and I know how they'll all look at me, because it's a beautiful gesture, in the right proportion, at the correct moment, everything correct, most important. For to every action is a time and place and they see that I know that. And then, in the factory, next week, the efficient industrialist, kindly but firm. Not the place to remember weddings and kisses. Work! The world must turn on. Men must be fed, houses built, shoes cut out and sewn up. Two sides! They'll see two sides of me. And when they're old they'll tell their children and I'll be spoken of with affection, honoured, remembered.

STEPHEN: These, or thoughts something like these, flashed through Louis's mind. Though, it must be remembered, that the most virtuous and honourable intentions felt in the heart take on a shade of vulgarity when actually put into words. So that it was more the *sensation* of his intentions rather than their crude articulation, such as we have had to record for you, that spurred him on to his final decision which, with his star carrying him, was to walk confidently in through the gate, along the pathway, push open the front door – which the happiness of the occasion left ever open – and . . .

[*Dance music! Screen lifts to reveal interior of the* WHITES' *house, guests dancing. On his way through the passage,* LOUIS *trips over a heap of coats, steadies himself by placing his hand into a large blancmange, draws back in horror and covers his coat with the white mess –*

– in which state he finds himself drawn inexorably into the room where –

– guests see him and freeze.

And our hero seems to have recognized, with a chill of certainty, that he's about to embark upon one of the most mortifying episodes in his life.]

 END OF PROLOGUE

INTERVAL

ACT ONE

[*As at the end of the Prologue.*

There is no longer need for STEPHEN *to help keep the story going – it has its own inexorable momentum! Background has been established and now no 'plot' need hold up the rhythm of the disastrous wedding scene about to be enacted.*

Inside the WHITES' *house.*

We see the passage, the stairs up, the area under the stairs, possibly the kitchen, or part of it.

The dividing doors between front room and dining room have been parted for the dancing. In the dining room area are set up trestle tables and the beginnings of 'the spread'.

The wedding scene. Frozen. Then –]

KNOCKER: Well go t'hell! The master!

[*A buzz of mumbling 'Liftoff, Liftoff, Liftoff'.* LOUIS *smiles, weakly. Raises his arms.*]

LOUIS: Knocker White, don't you recognize me?

[*Silence.*

LOUIS *reaches for a paper serviette to brush away his accident. The mess is multiplied.*]

Blancmange! [*Another dead smile.*] You won't turn me out, will you? I mean even if you're not pleased to see me. [*An even deader smile.*] We-have-to-welcome-our-guests, don't we? [*Not even an attempt to smile.*] If I've stopped anything, interrupted, disturbed – please, I'll go away.

[KNOCKER *makes a dash to grab a chair which he plonks in the middle of the room.*]

KNOCKER: I'm sorry, Mr Liftoff – er – Litvanoff. Sit you on a chair, look.

[*Gratefully, though it's in the middle of the room, attached to nothing, to no one, he sits.*

And he sits.
And he sits. Then –]
Your coat.
[LOUIS *stands to be relieved of his coat, and again sits.*
And sits.

KATE *and* DAVID *enter from the kitchen – and freeze!*]

LOUIS: Just fancy, on my way home, a puncture, here, near here, on the way back from town. Shopping. With the chauffeur and the housekeeper and their family. I took them out for the day. Do it frequently. Lunch, tea, pictures, the lot. [*Pause.*] Beautiful city, Norwich. [*Pause.*] The market. Those coloured stalls. Back streets. The Castle. [*Pause.*] The Cathedral. [*Pause.*] Bought a pair of wellingtons. For country walks.

KATE [*at last*]: Well, well, well! Mr Litvanov, how unexpected.

[DAVID *steps forward to end* LOUIS's *lonely stand in limbo, and take him to another less conspicuous seat.*]

DAVID: And welcome. Bring yourself over here and be a bit more comfortable.

[*A grateful* LOUIS *allows himself to be led and now talks torrentially to relieve his tensions.*]

LOUIS: And then this puncture came and my chauffeur – Hoppy Johnson, you know, who helps me drive this old Ford I've got – he says 'I'll mend the puncture.' Because you know I'm useless with mechanical things. And while I wait I hear this music and I see these two men carrying big boxes of beer – these two, over there [*pointing*], am I right? And they talk and I hear the name 'Knocker White' and so I know, I guess at once, the wedding of one of my workers – there can't be two Knocker Whites. What could be nicer? Share his joy, drink his health, that's what friends are for, am I right? You can't *not* look in to drink a toast I say to myself. What sort of man would that be? He won't turn me out, pleased or not pleased, Knocker White won't do that. We have to welcome our guests. Excuse me, if I'm in the way I'll GO! [*He's suddenly aware that everyone is listening.*] I'm shouting, aren't I?

KATE: Knocker! The first thing you do is introduce your wife and then you offer Mr Litvanov a drink.

[KNOCKER, *who's stood holding* LOUIS's *coat, thrusts it un-ceremoniously away, grabs* DAPHNE *and storms on his guest.*]

KNOCKER: This-is-my-wife-Daphne-what'll-you-have?

LOUIS: Of course we know each other, Miss –

DAPHNE: Mrs White.

LOUIS: Mrs White. Congratulations. I'll have a whisky, Knocker, and your wife must come and sit with me and point out who all the other guests are, and everyone must carry on as though I wasn't here.

[RINGO *seems to oblige. Very seriously he begins to catch flies, but creeping around the room, calling to them gingerly more as if they were cats.*]

RINGO: Here, bluebottle, bluebottle, bluebottle! Here, bluebottle!

[MRS DAWSON *pulls him aside for a silent reprimand. It was not what* LOUIS *had intended.*]

LOUIS: Please. The music. Dance. Carry on dancing.

[An *attempt to regain balance is made. Pop music had been coming from a tape recorder which is again switched on.*]

DAPHNE: Well, you could've blowed me down with a feather. When I see you, you could've blowed me down with a feather.

DAVID: I'm sure everyone is delighted you've come, Mr Litvanov.

MR DAWSON [*to* MRS DAWSON]: Who *is* that?

MRS DAWSON: Thaas Liftemoff, what own the factory.

MR DAWSON: Who?

MRS DAWSON: Liftemoff!

LOUIS: Er – excuse me, it's Litvanov, Litvanov.

EMILY [*to* TOSH]: Did we invite the owner?

LOUIS: I'll stay for half an hour or so –

EMILY: Why didn't you tell me we invited the owner?

LOUIS: – then you can relax.

EMILY: I didn't know we invited the owner.

KATE: I'll get you some appetizers.

[KATE *moves to get a tray of 'canapés' from the other side of the room. On the way* KNOCKER *bumps into her and spills the whisky on her frock.*]

KATE: What fly – you bring down! What stand – you knock down! What's knocked down – you tread on!

[*In the confusion* KNOCKER *hands* LOUIS *the empty glass.*]

DAPHNE [*to* LOUIS]: Knocker hev this tendency to bump into things.

[KATE *leaves him for the 'canapés'.*]

EMILY [*raising a glass*]: Would you do us the honour, Mr Liftoff, now you've come?

[LOUIS *raises empty glass,* KNOCKER *dives to fill new one.*]

Can't 'spect no big feasts like what you're used to, but a little ole drink, to the health o' bride and groom.

DAPHNE: Thaas already done a hundred times, look.

EMILY: No matters. Not by 'im it ent, and you be a little more respectful.

LOUIS: Now let's see, you're whose mother?

EMILY [*pointing to* TINKER]: His, sir. He's mine, and [*pointing to* TOSH] Knocker an' Kate are nephew an' nieces to him who be brother to their mother what's bin dead these last few years. She die of a broken heart she did, when their father die –

MRS DAWSON: She's off!

EMILY: – an' he die of cancer which were just the same as what his father afore him die of an' thaas no good saying it ent heredity 'cos I knowed it were an' you're not going to convince me otherwise 'cos look here, look, I had a friend what live up alongside me an' she died –

TOSH: 'Course she didn't wanna live a'ter he'd gone, their mother, she didn't, that she didn't. 'Tosh,' she say to me –

MRS DAWSON: Now he's off!

TOSH: – 'Tosh, I don't think I want t'go on anymore,' she say. 'I hed 'nough!' She'd made up her mind, see. Made it up, she hed. So she took to her bed, refused to eat an' just died. Like that. Two hours later the doctor he come an' he put a stethame-thing on her an' I ask him: 'Doctor, what you looking for? The woman's bin dead two hours, look.' But he didn't listen to me, no, he had to make sure hisself.

[*During all this* KNOCKER *has tried to hand over a new drink to* LOUIS. *The chattering defeats him, he drinks it himself!*]

KATE *has returned and moves in with 'canapés' to save a bamboozled* LOUIS.]

KATE: Now that you've honoured us this far, Mr Litvanov, you'll share our humble table, won't you?

RINGO [*piss-taking and mumbling his question here and there*]: Is ours a humble table?

LOUIS: U-uh-uh! No bullying, Kate.

RINGO: A humble table?

LOUIS: You know very well yours won't be a humble table.

RINGO: Ours, is it, a humble table . . .?

DAVID: No office quarrels, they'll not be understood, Mr Litvanov.

RINGO: . . . humble, humble, humble?

LOUIS: Well tell your girl-friend this is no time for silly sarcasms.

DAVID: She's not, alas, my girl-friend.

LOUIS: She's not, alas?

DAVID: Alas, not, proposition her though I have.

LOUIS: Then if you can be here, I can be here. What are you doing here anyway if you're not her boy-friend?

DAVID: I've been asked for moral support and by popular request.

LOUIS: And I'm neither moral support nor popular request I suppose?

KATE: Right!

LOUIS: Now that's rude, Kate. You know you'd've been very upset if I'd told you I walked right past your brother's wedding, wouldn't you?

[TINKER *has been making faces at* DAPHNE *of the 'Oh-so-you're-mixing-with-the-hoi-polloi-now-are-you' sort. She's giggling.*]

LOUIS [*irritably*]: What are you laughing at, young woman?

DAPHNE: It's him, Mr Litvanov, look at 'im, the ole fool.

KATE: Daphne, stop it!

DAPHNE: Oh you don't wanna mind me, Mr Litvanov. Anything make me giggle, and that Tinker White, he's their cousin you know, he tell me this funny story –

TINKER: Go on, tell 'im!

DAVID: Here we go.

KATE: Shut you up, Daphne. Mr Litvanov don't wanna hear no Tinker stories.

LOUIS: Of course I do. Where else would you want to tell stories if not at weddings? I'm listening. [*But with trepidation.*]

DAPHNE: Well, there was this field mouse, see, an' she've a date wi' her bor what live the other side o' the field, and she doll herself up for him, you know [*she titters*], lipstick an' powder an' special dress an' ribbon – an' then [*titters again*], an' then she go 'cross the field to her bor friend. But on the way [*tittering becomes less easy to control*], on the way she stumble right into a threshin' machine what was gathering the harvest an' she go in at one end [*long titters*], an' she get mauled an' scratched [*now* TINKER *joins in the laughter*] an' battered an' beaten, but she still go to her bor friend an' he open the door an' see her all bleedin' an' torn an' a right ole mess, an' he say [*she has great difficulty in getting the last part out*], he say – 'Blimey, gal [*great laughter*], blimey, gal,' he say, 'what happened to you?' An' she say [*now everyone except* KATE, LOUIS *and* DAVID *are laughing*], an' she say 'I – I – I bin REAPED!'

[*Everyone is convulsed*]

LOUIS [*to* KATE]: I been what? [*She refuses to answer, then to* DAVID] What did she say, I been what?

DAVID: Reaped.

LOUIS: Reaped?

DAVID: When you gather in the harvest you call it reaping.

LOUIS: I know. So?

KATE: Leave it alone, for God's sake.

DAVID: The word 'reap' sounds like the word 'rape'. [*Blank.*] I wouldn't pursue it too hotly, Mr Litvanov. Just laugh.

LOUIS: Oh! Reaped! I see.

[*He laughs, loudly. But everyone else has finished. Silence. Embarrassment.*

Suddenly –]

MR DAWSON: You'll look after our children, 'ont you?

DAPHNE: My father.

MRS DAWSON [*loudly in his ear*]: Well, 'course he will, father.

DAPHNE: My mother.

MR DAWSON: I mean you're master and they be young and thaas not an h'easy life. Not afore and not now, no time. No matters what any on 'em say. Not an h'easy life.

MRS DAWSON: Don't you fret, father. 'Course he'll look after them.

MR DAWSON: Well thaas all right then, 'cos thaas none on it an h'easy life, an' –

MRS DAWSON: An' don't start goin' on an' on an' –

RINGO [still piss-taking, as though working it out for himself]: The word 'reap' sounds like the word 'rape'. Reap, like rape, Rape, rape. Reap reap.

MRS DAWSON [taking over. To LOUIS]: 'Course, they hed to hev their bachelor's night out. [Shouting over to KNOCKER] I said you hed to hev your bachelor's booze-up, didn't you? [Back to LOUIS] I said to Daphne I said, 'Do you take a hold on him or you'll find him a sketch in the mornin'.' An' he were. Didn't I tell you, Daphne?

DAPHNE: They were so plastered, look, that even though they were round the corner in Flowerpot Lane they took the map out to find their way home.

TINKER: Plastered? Us plastered?

MRS DAWSON: Jimmy Leist went, Arthur Shanks went, John Jolly went, Ernie Holland, Harry Nunn, Eddie Bush, Herbie Kay, Dickie Pemberton, Arthur Calton, John Bally.

MR DAWSON: She know a lot o'people don't she?

DAPHNE: I reckon if they'd bin given the breathalyser the bugger'd've disintergrated.

[Silence.]

LOUIS: What about this toast? I'm here to drink their health so why not now? And I'll do it Jewish style.

MRS DAWSON [distantly]: I met a Jew once.

LOUIS: Three whiskies, please.

MRS DAWSON: I didn't see narthin' wrong wi' him.

TOSH: Comin' up. [Gives three glasses to LOUIS.]

LOUIS: Good. So. First. I – er – I'm particularly, no – specially, yes, specially glad of this opportunity that I can express, that I may with this express thought – er – wish, as your employer, as your fellow worker, extend to you, the bride – the very pretty bride of this lucky man who will, no, who must – er – let's see now – who – er – [*gives up*] in short, your very many good healths for the future.

[LOUIS *quickly swallows first whisky to cover failure.*
Silence.]

DAVID [*rescuing*]: The bride!

EVERYONE: The bride!

[KATE *joins in but very half-heartedly, hating this circus.*]

LOUIS: And next I'm particularly – [*thinks twice*] – the groom!

[*Swallows second whisky.*]

DAVID: The groom!

EVERYONE: The groom!

LOUIS: And lastly [*desperately searches for another excuse to toast. Sees* EMILY.] – the mothers. No! in this case it's aunts, yes? And, of course, the bride's mother, I forgot the bride's got a mother – and so – mothers and aunts – that old generation of ladies we'll see no more, tough like we could never be. God bless them, I love them.

[*Downs third to mixed and bewildered murmurs of* 'aunts', 'mothers', 'mothers and aunts', 'aunts and mothers'.]

TOSH: You missed out the real mother, if you'll pardon the correction, Mr Litvanov.

[TOSH *reaches for a full glass of beer each, for the two of them.*]
She [*pointing to* KATE] be mother of this family. Keepin' us together, rememberin' birthdays, sortin' out tax claims, explainin' me to her, and her to him. She be the tough'n. Tough as any what we were, if not tougher. And we'll drink it Norfolk style. [*Hands* LOUIS *full pint of beer.*] Kathy, to her!

LOUIS: Of course. Miss White. How could we forget? Katherine!

EVERYONE: Katherine!

[TOSH *drinks his glass in one and urges* LOUIS *to do the same.*
While they drink – EMILY, *a compulsive talker who doesn't really care if anyone's listening to her or not, will simply chatter on. Every so often we hear the beginning of her utterly inconsequential chattering which after the first seconds settles to become an inaudible background drone. One such begins now,* EMILY *addressing herself to whoever is nearest, they – ignoring her.*]

EMILY: Now you were talking about freezers, I'll tell you this: there's lots they say can be bagged up for freezers but you gotta know how t'do them. You have! My neighbour she've got one but she don't know how to bag up apples, she don't. She ask me! She ask me how to bag up apples an' I tell her . . . [*Drones on.*]

> [LOUIS *finishes his long draught to round of cheers from youngsters.*]

LOUIS: Oh good God!

> [*He's away! Eyes glowing. A pint in one. On top of three whiskies! Anything can happen.*]

Please. I beg you. Music. Dancing. You mustn't stop for me. It's a wedding. Dance. Sing.

> [*The tape which had come to an end is now turned over.*]

DAPHNE: Oh excuse me, won't you? When I hear music I just gotta go.

> [*She kisses a surprised* LOUIS *with a too wet and too familiar kiss on the lips. He takes out handkerchief to wipe away lipstick.* KATE *takes over.*]

KATE: And are her kisses sweeter than wine?

LOUIS: Why haven't you been helping me, Kate?

KATE: Did you need it, then?

LOUIS: She can be really cruel when she wants.

DAVID: Were those toasts really Jewish style?

LOUIS: No, but I needed three whiskies quickly.

KATE: Well now you've had them.

LOUIS: Look at her. Angry all the time. Just because I'm getting on with her family and friends.

KATE: Louis, I'm warning you. You're a dear man, but don't depend on my affection to see you safely through social experiments with my family.

> [*He kisses her, a defiant peck.*]

I'm issuing no safe-conduct passes.

LOUIS: She's beautiful when she's determined.

KATE: None!

LOUIS: Isn't she beautiful?

KATE: None!

LOUIS: Beautiful!

KATE: I'll go and lay the table for food. Mrs Dawson, we'll lay up, shall we?

MRS DAWSON [to MR DAWSON]: I'm goin' to lay up.

MR DAWSON: Lay who?

KATE: Aunt Emily, you and Uncle Tosh work on those serviettes.

[MRS DAWSON *follows* KATE, *who moves towards the kitchen just in time to be swept up into a dance by the swiftly entering* STEPHEN.]

STEPHEN: Sorry I'm late, shall we dance?

KATE [*dancing*]: How many times must I tell you not to use the side door?

STEPHEN: I want to feel one of the family.

KATE: And this is not a waltz.

MRS DAWSON: Who's he? I ent never seen him before.

STEPHEN: Kate and I went to school together to learn how to change the world. If she'd have married me we would have done! And who are you?

MRS DAWSON: Only the bride's mother, me.

STEPHEN: The bride's mother! Shall we dance?

[STEPHEN *dances away from* KATE *to sweep up* MRS DAWSON *in a dance. She protestingly whirls with him till he sees* LOUIS, *at which he stops dead.*]

I don't believe it.

[KATE *leaves him to figure that one out and takes off* MRS DAWSON *to lay up the food. Meanwhile,* KNOCKER, *who's retreated, glares at his wife, who's dancing closely with his cousin,* TINKER.]

KNOCKER [*to* TOSH]: See 'im.

TOSH: See who?

KNOCKER: 'Im. See 'im?

TOSH: I see 'im.

KNOCKER: Well look at 'im.

TOSH: He's your cousin, you look at 'im.

KNOCKER: Oh yes, I'm lookin' at 'im.

TOSH: Thaas all right then.

KNOCKER: Yes, I'm looking at him all right. I see him.

[STEPHEN *introduces himself to* LOUIS.]

STEPHEN: Excuse me, Mr Litvanov. I'm Stephen Bullock, friend of Kate's, reporter on the local press. Mind if I mention that you came to Knocker's wedding?

LOUIS [*relieved*]: Mind? Of course I don't mind. I'd like you to. Tell them – Louis Litvanov came to drink the health of one of his workers, uninvited, unprompted, came and sat among the guests, like one of them. Go ahead. My pleasure.

STEPHEN: I won't be using quite those words, but thank you.

LOUIS: Any words. Use any words. You know better than I how the reader thinks.

STEPHEN: None of us knows how the reader thinks. One of the reasons newspapers are always running opinion polls is that they don't know how the reader thinks.

DAVID: I thought journalists claimed to know –

STEPHEN: – nothing! We claim nothing except the moral right to expose those whose moral righteousness we suspect.

DAVID: And who, sir, will be left to expose your moral righteousness?

STEPHEN [*bouncing away*]: Ho, ho! Hum, hum! There's always the readers' letter column, isn't there?

[LOUIS, *who'd anticipated a longer interview, is abandoned in mid-flight.*]

LOUIS [*calling vainly after him*]: I say! What about –?

[*Every moment is undermined, seems menacing, unnerving.* DAVID *tries to help.*]

DAVID: Have you noticed Bonky Harris's painting on the wall?

LOUIS [*relieved once more*]: Ah! Bonky Harris!

[*They begin a tour of inspection.* RINGO, *showing a disquieting interest, follows respectfully behind as if to see what knowledge he can pick up.*]

Lovely colours. Good sense of colours. I bought some you know. Brighten up the home.

DAVID: Colours? You think he's colourful? Funny, I'd have thought colour wasn't his strong point.

LOUIS [*undermined*]: Wasn't?

DAVID: Atmosphere. Good atmosphere.

LOUIS: Atmosphere? [*Looking*] Ah! Yes.

DAVID: This lake with the trees. Very tranquil, don't you think?

LOUIS: Tranquil. Yes.

DAVID: Only look at the way he does reflections on water. It's more like a polished surface than a wet surface. Wet surfaces quiver more.

LOUIS: I see. [*Amazed his manager can talk about painting.*]

DAVID: Still, that's the charm of the primitive. As in this one here. Or that. Nice sense of shapes but no sense of textures.

RINGO [*to* LOUIS]: Nice sense of shapes but no sense of textures.

[DAVID *takes* LOUIS *out of range, back to his seat.*]

DAVID: Now sit there, Mr Litvanov. Relax. I promised to help Kate. I'll try not to leave you too long. [*Leaves.*]

[*Meanwhile,* RINGO *has beckoned* MARTIN *to look at the paintings. They go back over the tour.* LOUIS *anxious, overhearing, as they intend. As always in Norfolk the irony is dry, not raucous or savage.*]

RINGO [*to* MARTIN]: Nice sense of shapes, no sense of textures.

MARTIN ['*learning*']: Nice sense of shapes, no sense of textures.

RINGO [*moving on*]: Charm of the primitive.

MARTIN: Charm of the primitive.

RINGO [*moving on*]: Lovely atmosphere. Very tranquil.

MARTIN: Very.

[*But over their chat comes* EMILY'*s louder chat.*]
Poor Louis. Nothing has happened quite as he'd fantasized. Every encounter stretches him on the rack of his foolish impulse.
EMILY *at her serviettes, or whatever.*]

EMILY: Now you talk about transport. I can remember when it was all bicycles and buses. These days you need cars! You haven't got a car you can't get nowhere. You can stand waiting all you like an' no bus'll come an' pick you up. I know! I stood! You talk about transport . . .

[MARTIN *and* KING *decide to approach* LOUIS.]

MARTIN [*to* LOUIS]: Good on you to come. [*Pally faces.*] I'm Martin Dawson. Daphne's brother. Soon get warmed up, won't we, Ringo?

RINGO: Yerp!

MARTIN: You got something wrong with your motor-bike, he'll take it to pieces and put it together again before you can say Louis Liftoff – er – vanov. [*Pause.*] Even though that *do* take a long time to say. Right, Ringo?

RINGO: Yerp.

MARTIN: He work in your factory, don't you, Ringo?

RINGO [*going after it*]: Here bluebottle, bluebottle, bluebottle.

MARTIN: Everyone work in shoes 'cept me. No shoe factory for me I ses. More money on building sites. An' money count. Money count, don't it, Mr Liftoff?

[MAUREEN *has approached and is now sitting in* RINGO'S *place.*]

MAUREEN: You boastin' o' your wage packet again, an' your ole buildin' sites again, an' your being cleverer than us again?

MARTIN: An' this be our Maureen, Ringo's girl-friend an' my sister.

MAUREEN: Hev 'ee bin showin' you photos o' his big manly body heavin' bricks an' pushin' cement yet?

MARTIN: She also work in your factory an' I tell her too, no money in shoes –'cept for you that is.

MAUREEN: Come on, Ringo. Leave them ole bluebottles alone. I wanna dance.

RINGO [*moving away with* MAUREEN, *to* LOUIS]: Nice sense of shapes, no sense of textures!

MARTIN: Now, Mr Liftoff. How would you like to see an art exhibition? [*Takes* LOUIS *by the arm on a second 'tour'.*] Did you know this here mansion was an art gallery? Yes! Very high-class house our Knocker lives in.

LOUIS: Oh I know, I know. You see, young man –

MARTIN: Martin.

LOUIS: Martin. You see, the painter is one of my – er – he works in my factory.

MARTIN: In shit grow roses, they say.

LOUIS [*totally at a loss how to respond*]: They say that? Yes, well, of course – er – I was saying, Bonky's paintings, I even bought some. Lovely atmosphere they've got.

MARTIN: Atmosphere? Don't know about that, but he can paint bricks.

LOUIS [*again undermined*]: Bricks?

MARTIN: Bricks. Look on 'em. You can tell he've had to build a wall some time or other. May only hev bin the wall in his garden but he've had a brick in his hand. You can tell it. [*Leaves* LOUIS. *Suddenly*] Soon warm up. [*More pally faces.*]

    [LOUIS, *again left alone, wanders back to his chair, until –* DAPHNE *and* TINKER, *exhausted, giggling, settle on either side of him, and sit, and sit.*

    Meanwhile, STEPHEN *grabs* MARTIN.]

STEPHEN: What's he done since he's been here?

MARTIN: Done?

STEPHEN: Done. Said. Happened. Since he's arrived?

MARTIN [*feeling* LOUIS *is threatened, defends him*]: He've drunk three toasts.

STEPHEN: Who to?

MARTIN [*raising his glass to* LOUIS *across the room*]: Bride, groom, and the mothers and aunts. Very good on him.

STEPHEN: What was he saying to you just now?

MARTIN: He tell me he've bought some paintings from Bonky Harris.

STEPHEN [*getting what he's been looking for*]: Boasted about that, did he?

    [KNOCKER, *his eye on what* DAPHNE *and* TINKER *are up to, takes a drink over to poor, abandoned* MR DAWSON.]

MR DAWSON [*taking a drink*]: We got a thrashin' last week.

KNOCKER [*but looking at his wife*]: So I heard.

MR DAWSON: Couldn't double out.

KNOCKER: Yerp.

MR DAWSON: Played two of their worst darts players and we got a thrashin'.

KNOCKER: Yerp.

MR DAWSON: Couldn't double out, see!

    [*Meanwhile, the awkward silence between* DAPHNE, TINKER *and* LOUIS *is breaking.*]

TINKER: Shoes – them difficult things to sell, Mr Liftoff?

LOUIS: Excuse me, I don't really care what people call me but in fact the name is Litvanov. Russian. Not Liftoff but LIT-VAN-OV. Not difficult really.

TINKER: Liftemoff, yes. Well, you mustn't mind me. In Norfolk we soon find a handle for people. Me, I'm Tinker. Not much like Derek, is it? Derek's me real name, only they call me Tinker on account I always had lots o' gals an' I keep ringing them up, see? Ringling, tingling, Tinker?

[LOUIS *catches sight of* KNOCKER *glaring at them.* KNOCKER *backs away, falls into an armchair near* MR DAWSON *and in which lies* LOUIS's *coat still, and drops tray. The clatter disturbs* MR DAWSON.]

MR DAWSON: Blast bor! There you go again. There ent never no tellin' where you'll end up. [*Directly at* KNOCKER] I say there ent never no telling where you'll end up.

DAPHNE: Well hang it up, Knocker. [*Pause.*] Go on. [*Pause.*] SHOO! [KNOCKER *flees.*]

TINKER: Daphne! Whisky! Get your employer some whisky as befits his station in life.

LOUIS: I didn't come here to drink you know. It wasn't my intention to –

TINKER: Thaas all right, thaas all right, my mannie.

[*At the other end of the room, where* KATE *and* MRS DAWSON *are laying out food, have collected a knot of* STEPHEN, DAVID *and* KNOCKER.]

KNOCKER [*who's just turned off the tape*]: Well he've done it, ent'ee, eh? He've really put the last touch to my matrimonial festivications, that 'ee 'ave.

MRS DAWSON: You should be proud, Knocker. That ent everyone has 'is boss come to 'is wedding.

STEPHEN: There's not everyone has a boss so presumptuous.

KNOCKER: Proud? They're gettin' 'im drunk in there! Anythin' can happen. But she don't care. [*Indicating* KATE.] She's his pet an' she's laughin'.

KATE: She's not his pet and she's not laughin' and you listen to me. You're on your own now, bor. I made you this weddin', I'm leavin' you this house, but you're host. That ent my fault he've come but he have come, so you be civilized and look after him and learn to take your own decisions. There ent no more I can do for you.

KNOCKER: I'll lose my job, you see.

KATE: I sometimes wonder we're in the same family.

KNOCKER: There's men out of work an' women ten a penny. Who'll pay the mortgage then?

DAVID: You won't lose your job, Knocker, don't be an ass. But he's right, Louis is getting drunk. He shouldn't be left.

STEPHEN: He's a pompous ole fool. What in hell does he imagine he's doin' any road?

DAVID: Kathy, use your wits.

KATE: What wits do I have left? Wouldn't have happened ten years ago. But we fought to change the times and the times they've changed! We kept saying we're equal to any man! Right? Some've been listening and now they've come to eat at our table to prove it and we're going to be gracious about it. [Pause.] For as long as we can. [Pause.] We'll keep our creepy, crawly spites and envies to ourselves, shall we? Please?

STEPHEN: What you looking at me for?

KATE: We went to school together to change the world, remember? So I know you, Stephen.

STEPHEN: Poor Kate, straddling two worlds. In love with both, and none of you in either, is there, my love?

MRS DAWSON: Well I don't know what all you clever people is on about but I do know I'm the bride's mother an' there ent no one takin' a blind bit o' notice o' me. There ent no one bin bothered to introduce me to him nor nathin'.

KATE: We've all been a bit put out, Mrs Dawson. Once we're sittin' eatin' it'll be better, look.

MRS DAWSON: So you say, my gal, so you say. But I reckon I bin made a fool on, that I do. You took over all the arrangements for the weddin' an' I weren't asked about narthin' an' I bin quiet all this time but I hevn't bin any too happy about what's bin happenin' no! that I hevn't. All the cookin' *you* done. All the invitations *you* sent out –

KATE: There weren't anyone to invite. All our family is dead, you don't speak to yours – who's left?

MRS DAWSON: No matters. I should've bin asked. An' now he've come an' I'm left lookin' like a bloody skivvy.

[DAVID, STEPHEN *and* KNOCKER *try, discreetly, to disappear.*]

Yes, that's right you go my mannies – bloody little mice.

[LOUIS *is high in conversation with* TINKER. *Others have gathered round.*]

LOUIS: What's an employer's responsibility? To provide work and not care about his employees? That's all? I say no! I say an employer's got to show an interest in his workers. The days of fighting between management and labour are past.

TINKER: Well, I'm impressed to hear it, 'cos thaas what I say too. Workers is men like others an' no one should push them around. There's unions an' there's rights an' no one's gonna tell me to do things I don't want.

MARTIN: You ent got much choice bein' in the army hev you, bor?

RINGO: Here bluebottle, bluebottle. Here bluebottle.

LOUIS: What *are* you chasing?

MARTIN: Flies. He catches them, trains them an' sells them, you know?

[*But* LOUIS *doesn't know. Is blank.* RINGO *sees* KNOCKER *gloomily alone.*]

Knocker! Come on, lad, join us.

[*He refuses to budge.*]

LOUIS: What's wrong with you? It's your wedding isn't it?

KNOCKER: Beginnin' to wonder, I am. I'm really beginnin' to wonder.

LOUIS: So join us.

[KNOCKER *sulkily moves forward.*]

Knocker, Knocker, Knocker. Look at you. You feel uneasy I'm here, eh? Feel you need a special behaviour because he must be a special kind of boss who can find the time to come to an employee's wedding and sit and drink and talk naturally, eh?

[*Affectionately*] Knocker, Knocker, Knocker. You all got funny names. Tosh –

[EMILY '*descends*'.]

EMILY: You talk about Tosh and his eating?

LOUIS: Tinker –

EMILY: 'You hev sandwiches all day,' I tell 'im –

LOUIS: Knocker –

EMILY: 'Get you that inside you,' I say, 'you want something hot when you come home!'

LOUIS: Knocker, Tinker, Tosh!

EMILY: He complain but I tell 'im, 'Tosh, you get that inside you . . .'

LOUIS: Funny names!

MAUREEN: You know what I'm called?

LOUIS: No, what're you called?

MAUREEN: Skirts.

LOUIS: Skirts?

MAUREEN: Skirts Dawson, on account I like showin' my legs.

[*To a slow 'woooah' she draws up her skirt to show a leg.* LOUIS *is embarrassed.*]

DAPHNE [*during the 'woooah'*]: Maureen Dawson, stop that, blame fool! Drawin' attention to yourself. Blame fool!

MAUREEN [*with Slavic passion*]: I WANT MUSIC!

KNOCKER [*to* MAUREEN]: You do that too often I'll be sacked and he'll hev a hert attack!

[*She ignores him and switches on tape. The crowd disperses leaving* LOUIS *alone again.*

The deaf old man, DAWSON, *passes by.*]

MR DAWSON: 'Course, them used to be rough ole times, the ole days. My father, he used to flog me when he were riled, used to flog me an' then used to cry a'ter he'd done it, used t' cry. [*Pause.*] Never flogged *my* chil'un, though. But them's still rough ole times. *I* can't see no improvement, no, I can't. They keep tellin' me there is an' maybe there is, but I can't see it. There's none on it gotten a great deal better.

[*He wanders off, leaving* LOUIS *again in mid-air.*

Then, for no reason, except presumably taking advantage of LOUIS's *philosophy that all men are equal,* MARTIN *makes another of his faces and screams a loud 'cock-a-doodle-doo' into* LOUIS's *face.*

LOUIS *jumps, uncertain whether to be angry or not.*]

LOUIS: Now that's not nice. That's taking liberties. I didn't like that at all.

[*But* MARTIN *does it again and others take it up in merriment.* LOUIS *offers a weak smile and a weak 'cock-a-doodle-doo' of his own. But* MAUREEN *saves him.*]

MAUREEN: Wanna dance? Come on, Mr Litvanov. I'll show you how.

LOUIS: I'm not very good at this you know.

MAUREEN: Ent narthin' to it. Make it up for yourself. Just hop, jump, sway, twist – anythin' anyhow.

[*Slowly at first, self-consciously, but gaining confidence, he tries.*]

Smile, then, thaas not a funeral.

LOUIS: I'm concentrating.

MAUREEN: Relax, loosen up, flop.

[*He tries to do just that. Then, to his horror, he realizes that* MAUREEN *is swaying seductively and slowly sliding her skirt up to reveal a suggestively rotating pelvis.*]

MAUREEN: Thaas right. Very good. Good boy. Yes. Mmmm!

LOUIS [*stopping*]: Stop that. No. Really. That's not nice. Stop it. Stop doing that.

KATE: THE FOOD IS READY!

[*He's saved and everyone moves to help arrange the half-laid-up tables.*]

EMILY: Tinker! Get these tables away from the walls. You and Martin get hold on this one. You and Stephen or someone get hold of this other one.

[*Now follows a set of 'table-setting' lines. Other lines in other productions may be needed instead of, or additional to, these. They should be discovered in an ad-libbing situation but once found should be firmly planted and uttered as bold text.*]

KATE: Mr Dawson, can you get me a couple of chairs from the kitchen?

MRS DAWSON [*to* STEPHEN *and* DAVID]: Will you put that little table down here.

KATE [*anxiously*]: *Not* you, Knocker. Don't you touch the tables.

KNOCKER: OK, I'll get the chairs from upstairs.

STEPHEN: Which way does it go?

DAVID: Bottom of a 'T' – this way, I think.

TINKER: Where does the big table go?

KATE: That's the top of the 'T' – with the four best chairs.

KNOCKER: I got three chairs here.

DAPHNE: You would have to carry three! Why can't you carry two at a time?

KNOCKER: I can manage. [Drops one.]

DAPHNE: So I see!

KNOCKER: Who needs these chairs?

TINKER: Give me one before you break them.

KNOCKER: I got two chairs here.

MARTIN: I'll take one.

KNOCKER: I got one chair here.

[No one calls for it so he places it himself. In the midst of this reshuffling, BONKY HARRIS appears with a painting.]

MARTIN [standing on a chair]: The artist himself to honour us.

KATE: Why, Bonky! You said you couldn't come.

BONKY: No more couldn't I. The wife's still queasy but her mother's there to sit awhile so I brought over this wedding present.

[DAPHNE goes up to take it from him.]

DAPHNE: Oh, Bonky! Thank you. [Kisses his cheek.] Look everyone! Bootiful, ent it? [Holds it up to them. Everyone applauds.]

RINGO [to DAVID]: Nice sense of shapes, no sense of textures!

LOUIS: What a touching wedding present. Very original. Look at that house. You can tell you've handled bricks at some time in your life, eh?

BONKY [incredulous to see him there]: Never! Never touched a brick in my life, Mr Litvanov.

[LOUIS, again undermined, is also ignored while BONKY is fussed over as LOUIS wasn't.]

KATE: Stay and eat with us, Bonky.

BONKY: I can't, Miss White, honestly.

KATE: I'm Kate in this house and I insist.

MARTIN: We all insist. Here's a chair, Maureen! Another plate and things.

MRS DAWSON: There's plenty of food, look, plenty of it.

KATE: That's settled.

EMILY: You can eat and then you can go, so long as you eat first.

KATE: Come on now, settle everyone. Mr Litvanov, will you sit in the centre here? Be the guest of honour?

[*All turn to* LOUIS. *But in the general melée it hasn't been noticed that he's put on his coat.*]

LOUIS: Now really, it wasn't my intention to impose on you – not eat as well as to –

EMILY: Thaas not what you might call a banquet but it's wholesome an' plentiful an' you're welcome.

MRS DAWSON: Now then, Mr Liftoff, I'm the gal Daphne's mother an' I say you're very welcome to share with us our daughter's celebration. Had us knowed you was comin' we'd've laid on something special, I'm sure, but howsomever we've not done badly for ourselves so do you take you your seat in the middle an' we'll begin. [*Pulls out chair for him.*] If you please, sir.

[KATE, *feeling she's perhaps overdone her stern reproach, extends a friendly, reassuring arm of 'peace', and takes his coat.*]

LOUIS [*relieved somewhat*]: In that case it'll be a privilege to join you.

[*General approval.* TOSH *appears.*]

TINKER: Where *you* bin?

TOSH: I reckoned with an important guest like the one we got it's only right to have a little champers.

TINKER: How far you reckon thaas gonna go, Poppy?

TOSH: That ent for you for a start. This here's so's we can do the right thing by the bride an' groom an' the guest of honour. Watch out! [*Pops bottle.*]

TINKER: You don't pour champagne into beer glasses, dad.

KNOCKER: Well we ent got no champagne glasses so shut you up.

DAPHNE: Oh, real champagne!

KNOCKER: Don't say it like that – haven't I ever bought you the stuff?

DAPHNE: You! You did your courting on a single gin or half o' bitter.

KNOCKER: Now thaas not fair, Daphne Dawson.

DAPHNE: White – remember?

TINKER: I can't stand this. What sort of toast is that with only three on you able to drink the stuff? No one's gonna say I was ever mean. I'm gonna buy a coupla more o' these.

LOUIS: Good idea, Tinker. Here, buy two for me. No, four – make it six!

[*He peels off four £5 notes from a big bundle.* KATE *glares,* DAVID *winces.* STEPHEN *smiles.*]

Now, no more formalities or I'll feel guilty for coming. Let's eat.

[*Everyone tucks in.*]

Mmm! Who made this beef?

DAPHNE [*nodding towards* KATE]: Her!

MARTIN [*to whoever is near him*]: Glad thaas not lamb.

DAPHNE: She do everything.

MARTIN: 'Cos I'd've bin sick.

DAPHNE: She go away to all them foreign places an' she come back wi' strange, newfangled ideas for food.

MARTIN: I pass by lambs every day an' they smell.

MRS DAWSON: 'Course, anyone can make a thing if they hev the mind an' time.

MARTIN: I can see pigs up to *here* in shit an' I can still eat them, but lambs smell so.

MRS DAWSON: No one don't ever complain about *my* Sunday joint.

MARTIN: I *should* really *like* eating sheep 'cos they're so stupid, but–

DAPHNE: But Knocker 'ont get no fancy stuff from me though, not that I can see 'im eatin' half-done beef anyways.

KNOCKER: No, it'll be fish an' chips or Kentucky Fried Chicken from little boxes for us.

DAPHNE: Knocker White, I don't ever eat fish an' chips from boxes. I make it. 'Sides, even if we did it'd be 'cos I'm out workin' an' such.

[KNOCKER *in his agitation is eating quickly and reaching out wildly for this and that and exchanging anxious, resentful or apologetic looks with* LOUIS.]

KATE [*loudly*]: Mr Dawson. You're not eating.

[MR DAWSON, *at the other end of the table, sits before an empty plate.*]

MR DAWSON: What she say?

MRS DAWSON: She say eat up, look.

MR DAWSON: Tell her there ent narthin' I recognize.

[MRS DAWSON *ignores her husband and fills up his plate.* LOUIS *points to the new painting that's been leant against the wall.*]

LOUIS: Now *that* painting, Bonky, you may never have laid bricks, but that new painting has atmosphere. You've got real talent, believe me.

BONKY: Atmosphere, Mr Litvanov?

LOUIS: Yes. Er. Atmosphere. You paint good shapes. [*But he's not really confident any longer.*]

BONKY: Don't know about shapes, Mr Litvanov, I just paint the earth.

LOUIS: Earth?

BONKY: Earth! In everything, ent it? Everything you touch –

MARTIN: Earth!

RINGO [*musically, as though joining in a search for the right* note. High]: Earth! [*Low*] Earth!

MAUREEN [*middle*]: Earth!

[*All the young ones take it up. A game but – a raucous noise.*]

LOUIS [*silencing them*]: Now seriously, everybody, seriously. You do like your jokes about everything, don't you? Let's hear what Bonky has to say. Bonky?

BONKY [*slowly, shyly*]: Well. I love earth. That's all. I mean – everything you use in this world comes from the earth. Your own self comes from the earth, don't it? The water you drink comes from the earth. The food you eat in some shape or form, the bricks you use, the tools you use, the wood you use, the match you use, the chairs you sit on, they all come from the earth. [*Pause.*] And when you die – you go back there. Don't you? [*Silence.*] I mean – don't you?

[*Then, at last, the youngsters seem to have found the right note, and a sweet chord rises, as if the table is singing; comes, dies away, to the old ones' 'mms' and 'aahs'. Till – KNOCKER, whose agitation never really subsides, rises to reach for a sauce bottle and knocks a glass of champagne over LOUIS, who jumps up. KATE, MRS DAWSON and EMILY all jump up with him.*]

MRS DAWSON: Knocker, you clumsy oaf, Mr Liftoff's expensive suit ruined. I'm sorry, Mr Liftoff.

LOUIS: LITVANOV!

MRS DAWSON: Liftemoff, yes. Now don't you fret, we'll have it cleaned, the firm's expense. That ent too bad. Knocker, you're a real burden.

KATE: Don't get excited, Mrs Dawson. I'll get a cloth.

LOUIS: Please, sit down. It's all right. It's only a suit.

STEPHEN: I'm sure Mr Litvanov has many suits.

[TINKER *returns.*]

TINKER: Here she is, my lovelies. A crate of the best. Martin, you open up one. Knocker, you struggle with another. Ringo, one for you. And Mr Litvanov, you must be used to this – one for you. I'll pop this beauty.

KATE: Please, now let's eat and get it over with or it'll be time to go before we start.

TINKER [*to* MR DAWSON]: Champagne, look.

MR DAWSON: What?

TINKER: Champagne.

MR DAWSON: What?

TINKER: CHAMPAGNE!

[*The bottles go 'pop, pop', the glasses clink, the voices rise in sounds of real pleasure, and –*]

THE FIRST ACT ENDS

ACT TWO

[*Post-banquet torpor.*

The dishes are washed. The left-over food placed on the trestle table now lying along the wall to make more room.

The tape is low. DAPHNE *dances with* TINKER. KATE *with* DAVID. MAUREEN, RINGO *and* MARTIN *sitting it out, listening, sprawled. All are in various stages of drunkenness and watched by a sober and miserable* KNOCKER.

In a corner sits MR DAWSON, *deaf to everyone, if not asleep. Sitting beside him, eyes closed, is his wife singing an old song, totally at odds with the taped music.* KNOCKER *moves to them.*]

KNOCKER [*to* MRS DAWSON]: Ent that time you took him home?

MRS DAWSON [*singing*]: And though I grow too old to dream,
   Your song will live in my heart.
   Kiss me and then, until we meet again . . .

   [KNOCKER *moves to where his aunt,* EMILY, *is ecstatically and with glazed eyes watching the dancing and clapping her hands out of rhythm with the music.*

   From the kitchen comes the sound of an argument between STEPHEN *and* LOUIS.]

STEPHEN: You don't know how the other half lives.

LOUIS: I *was* the other half!

KNOCKER: No one don't think o' me, do they?

EMILY: Oh, Knocker, thaas a lovely wedding.

KNOCKER: What about me, though?

   [*She is beyond caring.*

   STEPHEN *and* LOUIS *stumble through from the kitchen. To* KNOCKER'S *consternation they're quarrelling violently. Both are very drunk.*

   TOSH *is struggling with a last bottle of champagne.* BONKY *is sitting, melancholic and drunk, near by.*]

LOUIS: And how do you imagine I started? You think *my* parents had money?

TOSH: Here she comes.

LOUIS: Fill me up. So don't tell me I don't know about workers and hardship and how the other half lives.

STEPHEN: That's not my point.

BONKY: I mean, everything come from the earth, don't it?

LOUIS: I know what your point is.

STEPHEN: Workers' control that's what my point is.

BONKY: Your own self come from the earth.

LOUIS [*to* STEPHEN]: I know, I know! Think I'm a fool? I can't follow a dialectical argument?

STEPHEN: Workers' control, not to be confused with silly ole participation.

LOUIS: Well, I'm not a fool. I was debating things like that when you were a twinkle in your mother's eye.

STEPHEN: My father's. I studied business management.

LOUIS: While I actually managed business.

STEPHEN: And I've studied reports on participation experiments.

LOUIS: While I actually carried out those experiments.

STEPHEN: And I've studied –

BONKY: I've studied rocks. Earth! It's all earth.

STEPHEN: I've studied –

LOUIS: And did you study how two thousand workers can *each* have a say in how to manage a large factory? Did you do that?

STEPHEN: I know –

LOUIS: You know nothing.

STEPHEN: Oh yes I do.

LOUIS: Oh no you don't.

STEPHEN: I do!

LOUIS: You don't!

STEPHEN: I do! And if you'd stop going on so much and didn't commandeer the bloody discussion I might be allowed to make my point.

KNOCKER [*trying to pull* STEPHEN *away*]: Why must you always go an' start quarrels?

STEPHEN: Now you keep your hands off me, Knocker White, 'cos you know nothing.

KNOCKER: If you write about any o' this in your newspaper I'll –

STEPHEN: You'll what?

KNOCKER: Never mind what I'll do, you just don't, thaas all.

BONKY: Everything at your wedding, Knocker, all on it, come from the earth . . .

LOUIS: And another thing, young man, another thing.

STEPHEN: What other thing?

LOUIS: I don't like the way you talk to me.

STEPHEN: Ah ha! There we have it. That's it.

LOUIS: No respect.

STEPHEN: I knew you'd give yourself away if I just let you carry on, Mr Liftoff.

LOUIS: And you call me by my right name. You know it, don't you? It's Litvanov, L-I-T-V-A-N-O-V. Litvanov.

STEPHEN: Yes, Mr Liftoff, that's what you'd really like, wouldn't you? No answering back.

LOUIS: That's distortion. I didn't say that –

STEPHEN: Know thy place.

LOUIS: Always win by distortions.

STEPHEN: *That's* what *you* call respect.

LOUIS: What am I doing sitting here talking to a little fool like this for? [*Tries to stand but finds his legs unsteady.*] Oh my God, no. No! How did *this* happen?

[*Tries to stand once more and fails.*

STEPHEN, *to press his point even more, shows he can not only stand but can mount a chair from which he continues.*]

STEPHEN: Yes, Mr Liftoff. We can see you'd like us just to love you –

[KNOCKER *shifts uselessly between them, threatening* STEPHEN *and pacifying* LITVANOV.]

KNOCKER: I'm sorry, Jesus, I'm sorry, Mr Litvanov. [*To* STEPHEN] An' you shut up, get down an' get out.

STEPHEN: You came here to court popularity, didn't you? Good ole Liftoff. Just one of the boys.

LOUIS: I said remember who you're talking to, young man.

STEPHEN: I'm talking to you and I'm not a young man. You spoilt everyone's enjoyment. Do you know that? You came, they *had* to buy champagne, and then you humiliated them by buying not one but six bottles yourself. Good ole Liftoff, yes. I'll write about you all right. This wedding and you. The event of the year. One of the boys ... [*But the effort is too much and he comes crashing down, throwing his drink over* LOUIS *on the way.*]

KNOCKER [*rushing to dry his employer*]: Oh, my sainted aunts. Take no notice on him, Mr Litvanov, leave him now. [*But his employer pushes him away.*] Well, come you out to my sister an' the others then.

[LOUIS *struggles to take control of himself. The sight of* STEPHEN *stretched out on the floor helps restore some of his dignity. He does up his collar and tries to straighten his tie.* KNOCKER *attempts to help him.*]

LOUIS: Get the hell out of it, you. You've been no help right from the start.

KNOCKER: I know what, Mr Litvanov, Bonky Harris's paintings! You like his paintings, don't you? We got them all over the house. Kathy had 'em framed. I'll show 'em you.

LOUIS: Paintings? [*Savagely*] I hate paintings.

[BONKY *sadly rises at this and moves away, out of the room.* LOUIS *stretches his arms out in apology, but too late. Now angrily he struggles to put on his jacket.* KNOCKER *attempts to help, and with his employer resisting and pushing him away, a minor lunatic battle ensues. Still, poise is regained, of a fashion, and with a smile* LOUIS *staggers into the other company.*

KATE, *tipsy herself, has now grown used to the situation.*]

KATE: Ah, our guest of honour. We bin neglectin' him. Louis, come here.

TINKER: Louis! Ah! Looooois! Welcome back, Louis.

[*Everyone mockingly picks up the name and calls it out at varying levels of the harmonic scale.*]

Come on, Louis, take your jacket off. Tape's finished. Besides, the neighbours, noise you know, so we sorta gotta 'muse ourselves.

[KATE *unbuttons* LOUIS's *jacket. Their faces are close together.*]

157

KATE: Enjoyin' yourself, Louis?

LOUIS: Not 'Louis', Kate, have pity.

KATE: So, you want to get on with my family, do you?

LOUIS: I wish I could be sick.

KATE: It's a family only a member of which could love.

LOUIS: What you unbuttoning me for?

KATE: Not even I ever really got a foothold in it.

LOUIS: Don't unbutton me, I'm going home.

KATE: Look at this house. All my life, my home.

LOUIS: What you loosening my tie for?

KATE: But what of me do you see in it?

LOUIS: Don't loosen my tie, I'm going home.

KATE: What – what of me?

LOUIS: I wish I could be sick.

[TINKER *from behind whips off his jacket.*]

TINKER: Now then, friends, party games! Thaas forbid to dance so we're left to our own natural resources.

LOUIS [*trying to put his jacket on again*]: I must go now. Please. You've been very hospitable, all of you. Not my intention to stay and intrude – and outstay – by intrusion – my welcome – must say – goodnight – [*But he can't make it and staggers collapsing into a chair.*]

TINKER: Ringo, give us a hand.

[*They lift* LOUIS *in his chair and set it to one side.*]

DAVID [*To* KATE]: Stop him.

KATE: Can't! When a good man's determined to do good there's no stopping him!

DAVID: I do not think we should let this go on, Kate.

KATE: Well, I do think we should let this go on, Kate. The lesson will enrich his character.

DAVID: You're too drunk to play God. [*Moves to* LOUIS.] Mr Litvanov, how would you like me to drive you home now?

LOUIS: Hello, David. It's a lovely wedding. You enjoying yourself? We're going to play games now.

DAVID: Mr Litvanov, if you'll take my advice –

LOUIS: Don't keep telling me how to run my business, there's a good fellow. [*To* TINKER] Pretends he's tough, says he's only interested in money. [*Conspiratorially tapping his nose to say* '*we know better*'.] Says he doesn't care about shoes and people. [*Back to* DAVID] Pays dividends! In profits and human dignity!

DAVID [*To* KATE]: And it'll be me has to gather the debris, stifle the jokes, restore the pecking order.

TINKER: Now sit there, me ole son an' we'll show you a game we play in these parts, an' when we've done one round you'll join in, right? [*Pause.*] Yes, well, you'll be all right in a second or two, never fear, my mannie. Now –

BONKY [*returning, presumably from the lavatory*]: Earth! The water you drink comes from the earth –

[STEPHEN, *recovered, staggers around with a soda syphon in his hands. He's douching himself with it.*]

STEPHEN: Look! Lovely! Refreshing! I'm awake all over again.

[*He squirts some at* DAPHNE *who giggles, and then at* TINKER *who's less amused.*]

TINKER: Now cut that out, ole son, we're going to play games.

STEPHEN: I am playing games. [*Turning to* LOUIS] Now here's a man who needs waking up.

[*He's about to squirt soda at* LOUIS *but* KNOCKER, *who's been keeping a wary eye open, rushes in the way and takes the blast.* DAVID *steps forward to take the syphon away.*]

KATE: All right. Enough now. It's time to go home.

KNOCKER: You bin dyin' to do that all evenin' haven't you?

KATE: Mrs Dawson, your husband's asleep, look.

KNOCKER: I see you. I watched you. You done it – now you go home. This party's finished for you.

KATE: Uncle Tosh, look at Aunt Emily.

STEPHEN: The little men rise up at last –

[KNOCKER, *though smaller, rushes to hoist the drunk* STEPHEN *in a fireman's lift. The action is greeted with cheers – except from* KATE.]

KATE: Put him down, Knocker White, this instant, now – put him down.

KNOCKER: This is my house you tell me? Right – I'm making the decisions then, startin' from now, an' this is my first decision. He be your friend? Now you take him to *your* home.

[KNOCKER *wants to carry* STEPHEN *to the front door but has lost his sense of direction and is swinging and staggering about in all directions. This enables* STEPHEN *to retake the soda syphon and fire his weapon in a swinging circle at everyone.*

Pandemonium! Which is increased as KATE *and* DAVID *try to pull him down — which battling quartet lumbers on through the passage.*

But KATE *and* DAVID *have to reach for their coats which leaves* STEPHEN, *still on* KNOCKER'S *shoulder, free to pick up the syphon again and squirt it on* KNOCKER'S *backside.* KNOCKER *staggers so far back into the room that he's even able to squirt it, finally, over* LOUIS, *before he's dumped in the street and wanders off, chanting —*]

STEPHEN: I woke him up, I woke him up, I woke him up.

KATE [*rushing back into room to* LOUIS]: Don't go. I'll be back and take you home. [*To* KNOCKER.] Knocker White, I want this party over by the time I get back.

[*She and* DAVID *go off.*]

KNOCKER [*calling after them*]: Well, were it my fault? Did I invite the master? Did I make him stay?

[*Nevertheless, he's quite pleased with his feat and returns in triumph to the company.*

The women are tidying up, men putting chairs and bottles away. TINKER *is attentive to* LOUIS.]

LOUIS: My jacket, I want my jacket.

TINKER: Your jacket, ole son? You want your jacket? You shall have it. His jacket, where's Mr L's jacket?

[*But* LOUIS *has already succeeded in putting it on.*]

TINKER: Why, you've got it on, my mannie. You got me all confused, look it's on you.

LOUIS: Oh yes, well, that's kind of you, you're a good man, very kind.

TINKER [*helping*]: Thaas right, you button yourself up an' sit there an' it'll be civilized again, you see. We're going to have a nice party an' we're goin' to send you away with good impressions and pleasant memories.

[*Seated,* LOUIS *now sinks into reverie to sort out this mess.*]

LOUIS: That's what I came for, pleasant memories —

RINGO [*draped over a chair, dreamily*]: I think Litvanov's right.

LOUIS: – to wish you all good health, show I'm human, you're human, everyone's human –

RINGO: I think he's right – very praiseworthy, Litvanov.

LOUIS: – good intentions, pleasant memories, human contact –

RINGO: An' very noble 'tis, too, Mr Litvanov.

LOUIS: You're very kind to me, I'm very grateful.

RINGO: Very praiseworthy, Litvanov is, very praiseworthy indeed.

LOUIS [*woken, irritated*]: What the hell's the matter with him? He silly or something? You silly or something?

TINKER: Now you don't wanna take any notice of Ringo there.

LOUIS [*still exploding at* RINGO]: I mean even mockers get tired of their own voice.

TINKER: He's only a boy.

LOUIS [*calming down, returning to reverie*]: Yes, I know, only a boy. I mean – what I want to say was – was –

[*Long pause. Everyone waits.* LOUIS *is very drunk.*]

– not one of you love me, do you? Not one. Whereas me – I – I love you all – and – and –

[*Acute embarrassment.*]

BONKY: The food you eat in some shape or form, the bricks you use, the tools you use, the wood you use, the match you use, the chairs you sit on – they all come from the earth. [*Pause.*] Don't they?

[*Silence.*]

TINKER: Now then, everyone – the shoe game.

KNOCKER [*confidently*]: Oh no, Tinker White. No games. We bin at it a long time and I reckon we're all fit for our beds. I am leastways.

TINKER: Knocker! You were marvellous. Weren't he marvellous? – You picked that snotty nose up like he were a feather.

DAPHNE: Who'd've thought.

TINKER: A feather!

DAPHNE: My Knocker.

TINKER: I ent never seen 'im do anything like that before, have you?

DAPHNE: He deserves a drink.

TINKER: Did you see 'im, Mr Litvanov? That loud-mouthed little journalist what squirted soda on you? Well, our Knocker here soon showed him.

KNOCKER [*disarmed and taking drink*]: Soon ever I see 'im do that I weren't hevin' any on it. I wanted to throw him out afore but you seemed like you was coping wi' 'im nicely. Nicely I thought. All his daft ideas. I don't know anyone what read what he write, that I don't.

DAPHNE: But him being a friend o' your sister's –

KNOCKER: No matters! No one's gonna go insultin' my guests –

TINKER: You married a hero!

KNOCKER: – an' now it's all peaceful an' we can sit, talk an' drink in peace –

TINKER: an' play the shoe game.*

KNOCKER: Oh well, I don't know about that. Mr Litvanov here don't wanna play our silly ole games, Tinker.

TINKER [*plying* KNOCKER *with drinks*]: Mr Litvanov's all right now, aren't you, Mr Litvanov?

[LOUIS, *completely melancholic, offers a confused smile – rather like a reluctant and crippled old king confronting a mob he despises and wishes had his ailment.*]

He's goin' to sit there an' watch us an' then he's gonna join in, ent you, ole son? It's very simple.

[*As he talks the action takes place with everyone except* MR DAWSON *and* BONKY *forming a circle round him. The following positions are taken.*]

Note: *This layout is based on the Leeds production which took place on an apron stage confronted by a high raked auditorium. In a proscenium stage* KNOCKER *and* DAPHNE *would probably need to be to the fore*

---

* Note: as this is the dramatic high point of the play, precise (though not mechanical) orchestration is essential. It's advisable, after the first week of rehearsal, to rehearse these three rounds of the shoe game for half an hour every day before rehearsals begin – a good way to warm up! Or for half an hour at some point in the day. If it's left to be worked out towards the end of rehearsals then the result will be sloppy instead of electrifying.

DAPHNE   KNOCKER

RINGO   MRS DAWSON

TINKER

EMILY   MARTIN

TOSH   MAUREEN

Someone's blindfolded, see? I'll do it first, this handkerchief here, round my eyes, can't see a thing, an' everyone forms a circle around me an' then, someone takes off his shoe.

[TOSH *does so, throws it to* MRS DAWSON.]

I don't know who 'tis. So I've got to follow the sound of the throw. Then they hev to hit me on my backside an' I gotta turn round quickly to see if I can lay hands on them.

[*Someone swipes at him, he turns, but fails to grab them.*]

Like that! see? They can't hit you anywhere but your backside' cos thaas the point of the game. You gotta turn the moment you think someone's comin' up behind you, like this [*he turns*] – then, of course, he can't wallop you so he hev to throw the shoe to someone else or just pass it along. Passing it makes less noise, of course. Sometimes you stick your backside out to tempt them, slowly, and then – spring!

1st Round

[TINKER *springs and catches* MAUREEN *who had just tapped him but couldn't escape in time. She's blindfolded. But while he was talking, the following was happening:* TOSH *threw to* MRS DAWSON.*

The sound made TINKER *turn to* MRS DAWSON.

But then MRS DAWSON *passed to* DAPHNE

who passed to RINGO

who passed to EMILY

TINKER *held his attention to* MRS DAWSON *and had not heard the swift and silent movement of the shoe back to* EMILY. EMILY *swiped successfully,* TINKER *turned but failed to grab her. Then –*

EMILY *threw to* MAUREEN *who*

threw to DAPHNE *who*

    threw to MARTIN *who*
    passed to KNOCKER *who*
    passed to MRS DAWSON *who*
    passed to DAPHNE *who*
    passed to RINGO *who*
    passed to EMILY *who*
    passed to TOSH *who*
    passed to MAUREEN *who swiped and*
    TINKER *caught her.*]
See? Simple. Now, Mr Litvanov, you can play that, can't you.
Up you get.

    [*He hands over a jelly and staggering* LOUIS *to* KNOCKER *and*
    DAPHNE.]
That's it. You'll manage.

2nd Round

      DAPHNE   LOUIS   KNOCKER
RINGO   MRS DAWSON
            MAUREEN
EMILY   MARTIN
        TOSH   TINKER

[MAUREEN *seems to enjoy offering her bottom for a 'whack',*
though no one slaps hard. She moves slowly round, seductively.
TINKER *throws to* DAPHNE *who*
throws to MARTIN *who taps* MAUREEN *and*
throws to EMILY *who*
throws to MRS DAWSON *who*
passes to LOUIS *who*
gaily and too obviously is about to swipe and walk straight into
MAUREEN'S *arms but is held back by* DAPHNE *and* KNOCKER.
DAPHNE *shows* LOUIS *he must wait till* MAUREEN'S *back is turned,*
then she swipes and
passes to RINGO *who*
passes to EMILY *who*

throws to KNOCKER *who taps* MAUREEN *and*
passes to MRS DAWSON *who*
throws to LOUIS *who taps* MAUREEN *with slow relish and is*
caught.
They begin to blindfold LOUIS.]
KNOCKER [*loud whisper*]: No! Not the master!
[*But he's outvoted.* LOUIS *is* blindfolded, placed in centre.
KNOCKER *folds his arms stubbornly.*]
KNOCKER: Well, I ent goin' to hit 'im!
[*The circle is the same as before only* MAUREEN *is between*
MRS DAWSON *and* MARTIN.

3rd Round

This round begins in a friendly spirit. Nothing menacing.

MRS DAWSON *throws to* TOSH *who*
throws to KNOCKER *who obviously is terrified to handle it, it's*
his boss! and passes the shoe on like a hot potato to MRS
DAWSON *who throws to* TINKER *who taps* LOUIS *and*
throws to RINGO *who*
throws to MAUREEN *who taps* LOUIS *and*
throws to TOSH *who*
throws to KNOCKER *who quickly wants to pass it on to* DAPHNE
but realizes how eager she is and instead
passes it to MRS DAWSON *who*
passes to MAUREEN *who*
passes to MARTIN *who*
throws to EMILY *who excitedly taps* LOUIS *and passes to* RINGO
who becomes badgered by an irritated DAPHNE *who has not had*
a go at LOUIS
RINGO *teases her and finally*
throws to MARTIN *who*
throws to RINGO *who taps* LOUIS, *again teases* DAPHNE, *and*
throws to MARTIN

In exasperation DAPHNE *snatches off her own shoe, her wedding slipper.* EMILY *gasps.* MAUREEN *gives a little hysterical giggle. Everyone freezes. Two shoes? Is that fair? She wouldn't dare. Surely. But she does. And what's more it's a slightly harder, more vicious whack. The sound stings through them.* DAPHNE *defiantly holds on to her slipper. They all look at each other, sheepishly at first.*

Then the mood changes. There's still no menace but there is a heightening of tension and excitement.

MAUREEN *with a nervous laugh takes off her shoe and taps* LOUIS. *Then* RINGO *takes off his shoe and taps* LOUIS. *Then* TINKER *takes off his shoe and taps* LOUIS.

What's happening?

TINKER *raises his shoe like a triumphant sword above his head. The other three follow. Defiance, however futile, is contagious in a crowd, and so the remaining ones take off their shoes and all stand with shoes poised high.*

LOUIS *is alert. Something's in the wind. One by one they each step forward to tap him. He's confused. They become intoxicated. The beating grows. It is no longer a game. A mob mentality takes over and each tap becomes more malevolent, the sound of the whack more frequent, until all control is lost and they simply crowd in and beat him about the body. (Not the face.)*

LOUIS *realizes he's being beaten. He wrenches off the blindfold with a profound howl of great rage. Then –]*

LOUIS: WHAT ARE YOU DOING TO ME? I came here –
I wanted to – it was my intention –
   [*He sways, reaches to sit on a chair by a table and lays his head to rest – in the remains of the blancmange!*
   The shock temporarily revives him. He pulls himself up, striving for dignity, and like a huge, tragi-comic clown, staggers about, falls and passes out.
   The aggressiveness of the company turns to sheepishness, shame and a touch of fear.]
BONKY: It all comes from the earth. And when you die – you go back there.
   [*Is he dead?*]

166

KNOCKER: Oh, bloody hell! Oh, creeping, jumping, bloody hell. Well thaas it. Thaas done it. Thaas my lot, ent it?

[*Silence. Then – the sound of snoring.*]

TINKER: I go t'hell! Listen to him, then. [*Pause.*] Knocker, ole son, the night has come – that great special moment. Precious to every man. An' thaas all yours.

[TINKER *and others move for their coats.*]

DAPHNE [*unbelieving*]: Tinker?

MR DAWSON [*passing prone figure, mumbling*]: They keep telling me there's an improvement but I can't see it. There's none on it gotten a great deal better. None on it ... no ... none on it ... none on it ...

KNOCKER: You can't leave him like that. What – us up there an' 'im down here? That'll kill my first night's activities, hell if it won't.

TINKER: Well, what you wantin' of us?

KNOCKER: Call a taxi, take 'im 'ome. That's what I'm wantin' o' you.

TINKER: An' put 'im to bed? Not likely, ole son. He's your boss.

DAPHNE: An' you got 'im like it.

KNOCKER: An' I'm left wi' it. Thaas me. Thaas my luck all right. Born wi' it I was.

TINKER: Good night, Knocker. Daphne, look after 'im.

DAPHNE: Tinker White, if you go now, us like this, I'll not speak to you ever again. Thaas true that is, not ever again.

TINKER: I'll hev to spend my leave in foreign parts then, won't I?

DAPHNE: Mother! Do something.

MRS DAWSON: No one don't ask my advice for narthin' an' I ent givin' it. Ask her. [*Referring to* EMILY.]

EMILY: Don't be daft, Tinker, we can't leave 'im like this.

TINKER: Well what am I supposed to do? What you all looking at me for? Did I lay 'im out? You all wanna pass the buck so quick, don't you? 'Sides, he wouldn't spoil my first night's activities. In the mornin' he'll wake up, give hisself a wash, phone for his chauffeur – that man what 'help me drive my little ole Ford' – an' go 'ome. What's the panic for?

[KATE *has returned and at the sound of the door slamming they all turn to her. She is furious.*]

They think it's all my fault.

KATE: Go on home now. We'll see to him.

[*All move homewards.*]

EMILY: Lovely wedding, Knocker.

MARTIN: This is it then, bor.

TOSH: We'll leave you to it, Knocker.

MAUREEN: Leave you to it, Knocker, Knocker. Thank you, Knocker. Treat her well, my sister, treat her well . . .

RINGO: Better'n what she did.

EMILY: Lovely wedding, Knocker.

MR DAWSON: Good on you, Kate. I enjoyed all that.

KATE: Not you, Tinker. You ent gettin' away without some help.

[*The four remaining stand around the heavily-breathing body.*]

He's ill. He can't be taken home. Take him upstairs to the bed.

KNOCKER: The bed? *Our* bed? An' where do *us* sleep? You took your bed away to your new flat. Where do *us* sleep?

KATE [*pointing to narrow divan*]: There!

DAPHNE: There? Two on us?

KATE: For one night, you'll manage.

KNOCKER: It's got a broken leg.

KATE: It'll last.

KNOCKER: On my wedding night?

KATE: He's gonna feel rough enough when he wakes up after all you've put him through and I aren't lettin' him wake up to find himself in all this mess. Knocker, get me a flannel. Daphne, go make up that divan. Tinker, take off his shoes.

[*Each sets about their task. When the jacket is removed* KATE *gently wipes* LOUIS'S *face.*]

Now Louis, you must take a long holiday, restore your spirits. Perhaps you'll listen to me from now on. Just give them the rate for their work and the sweet, sweet *illusion* that they're equal to any man. Stop pretending it's a reality. [*Pause.*] And don't be kind or ashamed or apologetic for your money. You go around behaving like that, how shall we be able to hit you when the time comes, bor? [*Pause.*] There! You're ready for your bed, I reckon. In the morning I'll bring flowers, make you coffee and nurse your wounds. Huh! Wounds! You won't think you've got any will you? Tinker, Knocker – carry him up – and gently.

[KATE *turns to see* DAPHNE *struggling to make up the divan. She helps.* KATE *is systematic, folding in the corners hospital-style.* DAPHNE *is chaotic, shoving them under. When it's done the two men have returned.*]

KATE [*to* TINKER]: Come on, you. You can walk me home. Goodnight, you two. I'll be here before you're up in the morning.

[*Gently, to a brother she's leaving.*] Sleep well.

KNOCKER: Huh!

KATE [*washing her hands of him*]: Or not well, as you please!

[*They leave.* DAPHNE *throws a hateful look at* KNOCKER *and storms past him.*]

KNOCKER: Where are you goin'?

DAPHNE: And what do you reckon I should sleep in?

KNOCKER: What you wanna sleep in anythin' for?

[*She ignores him, contemptuously. Leaves.* KNOCKER *undresses, not without some last remaining vestige of excitement and anticipation, and gingerly creeps into bed. Soon* DAPHNE *returns in a night-dress and lunges onto bed.*]

KNOCKER: Careful!

[*Though angry, she too gingerly creeps into bed, reaches to switch off remaining bedside light, and slams heavily down. In the darkness there is a crash.*

KNOCKER *puts on light again to reveal them lying in a collapsed divan.* DAPHNE *is hugging the blankets and whimpering.*

KNOCKER, *rigid and wide eyed, returns to a prone, horizontal position, resigned.*]

A sacred night *this* is gonna be. Oh yes! Witch-cursed White, thaas me. Howsomever, this is only the beginnin'. Tomorrow the pipes will freeze and burst. I know it! Pneumonia! And then next week the chimney'll catch fire. Burn to death! Or those stairs. What lunatic built them? Someone who hated my ole Nanny White, sure to fall down them. Or there'll be a war, or I'll get knocked over by a car, or cut me fingers off in the machines, or lose a winnin' pools coupon, or be assassinated by mistake. Every day! Somethin' new! Some lousy, rotten, little accident, some great, black tragedy. For the rest of my life an' ever an' ever amen! Thaas me!

[KNOCKER *turns off light and hugs himself back to sleep.*

The night passes. A slow dawn light filters into the room.

The wreck of LOUIS *shambles downstairs. Stands in centre of room, surveys the mess. Walks to get overcoat, then across the room to pick up his shoes.*

He surveys the mess and memory of the evening before, clenches his teeth, hardens his face.]

LOUIS: Yes, that's the way it has to be.

[*And a great melancholy settles upon his heart.*

He shuffles off. Lights fade, and –]

CURTAIN

SHYLOCK

A play in two acts

This is the ninth version of the play, resulting from the London Workshop production of 1989, and differs from the version world premièred in Stockholm in 1976, the English-speaking version premièred on Broadway in 1977 and the version further revised for the production in Birmingham in 1978.

I do not use despair, for it is not mine,
only entrusted to me for safe-keeping.

Wislawa Szymborska, Polish poetess

ACKNOWLEDGEMENTS

I have always depended upon my friends for comments and criticisms of early drafts of my plays but with *Shylock* (formerly *The Merchant*) my gratitude also extends to many scholars whose works provided the background to a period and setting I only barely knew.

Of those friends and scholars three must be mentioned for my especial debts. Dr D. S. Chambers, lecturer in Renaissance Studies at the Warburg Institute, who read the third draft and made many helpful observations, and whose book *The Imperial Age of Venice* I continually raided. Similarly the books of the late Dr Cecil Roth whose *History of the Jews* everywhere-all-the-time must be invaluable for any creative writer in need of Jewish historical detail. Lastly, the incredible persistence and patience of my friend and German translator, Nina Adler, whose scrupulous intelligence questioned so much that some of the logic and fine detail of the play would not have been as clear without her.

None other of my works have acknowledged such debts – perhaps they should have – but that this one does I'd like taken as a measure of how real and not merely polite this acknowledgement is.

A.W.

PREFACE

(This article first appeared in the *Guardian*, 29 August 1981.)

Once again *The Merchant of Venice* is on school syllabuses. Productions are being mounted around the country. The Royal Shakespeare Company has transferred its version from Stratford to London, though not without some anxiety. Its programme is full of extracts from good and eager Jews with eager good nature defending Shakespeare's humanity and poetry, pointing as always to Shylock's special pleading for his existence – 'Hath not a Jew eyes?' – and carefully getting the play into historical perspective, quite oblivious to the irony in their forgiving the creation of an unforgiving Jew.

Not that their gentle arguments – and bless them! – will stay a few hotheads in the Jewish community from demanding the play be banned from the stage and withdrawn from the school syllabus. But the majority of the Jewish community, if they know what's good for them, will keep quiet. I can't. I have never known what's good for me.

I revere Shakespeare, am proud to write in his shadow, the world is inconceivable without him and I would passionately defend the right of anyone anywhere to present and teach this play. But nothing will make me admire it, nor has anyone persuaded me the Holocaust is irrelevant to my responses. Try though I do to listen only to the poet's lines, yet I find myself seething at his portrait of a Jew, unable to pretend this is simply another Shakespearean character through whom he is exploring greed, or whatever.

No character is chosen arbitrarily by a writer, but for his embodiment of the characteristics the writer wishes to set in opposition to other characteristics. The Jew in Shakespeare's play is meant to embody what he wishes to despise. That he gives

Shylock lines with which to defend and explain himself has more to do with his dramatic instinct for not making the opposition too black, which would lessen credibility and impact, than it has to do with a wish to be kind to a poor Jew.

There is no evidence anywhere else that Shakespeare was distressed by anti-Jewish feeling. The portrayal of Shylock offends for being a lie about the Jewish character. I seek no pound of flesh but, like Shylock, I'm unforgiving, unforgiving of the play's contribution to the world's astigmatic view and murderous hatred of the Jew.

I ceased finally to be a 'forgiver' when, in 1973, watching Laurence Olivier's oi-yoi-yoi portrayal of Shylock in Jonathan Miller's production at The National Theatre, I was struck by the play's irredeemable anti-semitism. It was not an intellectual evaluation but the immediate impact I actually experienced.

Here was a play which, despite the poetic genius of its author – or who know, perhaps because of it! – could emerge as nothing other than a confirmation of the Jew as bloodsucker. Worse, the so-called defence of Shylock – 'If you prick him doth he not bleed' – was so powerful that it dignified the anti-semitism. An audience, it seemed to me on that night, could come away with its prejudices about the Jew confirmed but held with an easy conscience because they thought they'd heard a noble plea for extenuating circumstances.

All the productions I've seen of *The Merchant of Venice* have failed to hide the message which insists on coming through clearly and simply. No matter with what heavy tragedy the actor plays the role, no matter how thuggishly or foolishly the Venetians are portrayed, no matter in what setting – such as Miller's Victorian capitalism to show how everyone was involved in filthy money – the image comes through inescapably: the Jew is mercenary and revengeful, sadistic, without pity.

Nothing will move him from that court with his knife which, to show how cruel he really is, he sharpens on his leather before the assembly. Anybody who conceives of such retribution deserves to be spat upon. It is no wonder Antonio treated him as he did – 'many a time and oft, in the Rialto' – for contained within this arrogant and avaricious man were the seeds of the awful bond. Antonio must have seen it. After all, they demanded the Lord's flesh.

How can it surprise us that this bitter, spitting, conniving and mean little alien in the ghetto of Venice would want a pound of flesh from one of its citizens? Neither in Miller's production, nor in any I've ever seen, could I recognize a Jew I knew. Is being spat upon a reasonable extenuating circumstance for extorting such a savagely conceived death? Shylock is revengeful and insists upon his pound of flesh against all humanity and reason. It is a hateful, ignorant portrayal.

On the other hand perhaps it is impossible to think straight about *The Merchant of Venice*. The Holocaust could be viewed as the ball and chain to all attempts at reason. There are only a few positions to take and each of them is bound to be unnatural.

There are those Christians who are determined not to be intimidated by the history of Jewish persecution throughout the centuries and who, like John Barton, the director of the RSC's current production, will go looking for other themes – 'true and false values', he says in a programme note. And there will be those Jews who will bend over backwards to show how just and tolerant they are. The intelligent Chaim Bermant (gratefully quoted in the RSC programme note) explained in *The Jewish Chronicle* (6 March 1981) that the play 'is a product of its time . . . and in the circumstances his (Shakespeare's) vision of Shylock verges on the sympathetic'.

I don't understand the logic of that argument. If we are presenting the play in 'our times' what is the relevance of pointing out it was a sympathetic vision in past times? We're not living in those times. The vision of Shylock may have been sympathetic then but by no stretch of the imagination can it be viewed as sympathetic now, and anyone producing the play must honestly acknowledge that fact.

'I doubt if *The Merchant of Venice* could induce anti-Jewish feeling in someone who was not already an anti-semite . . .' Bermant continues. Maybe. But it confirms and feeds those whose anti-semitism is latent, dormant. And I would hesitate before suggesting those are an insignificant minority.

It's not only the portrayal of Shylock which offends me. I

don't share the bard's sympathetic view of Portia, and it's foolish of those seeking to whitewash the play to say Shakespeare made her a silly girl. She is not meant to be. She's meant to be a heroine, beautiful and wise and generous, and Bassanio is meant to be handsome and dashing, and Antonio is meant to be attractively melancholy.

But what must we think of Portia, who, in spite of possessing knowledge of the one interpretation of the law which will save Antonio his anguish and Shylock his humiliation, withholds it and prattles on about 'the quality of mercy' which she appears incapable of extending? And what seriousness must we give to Antonio's melancholy and Bassanio's romantic love when they and those other stupid people drone on about love and fidelity and rings who've just witnessed the destruction of a man?

And how lovely Barton makes them in his production, dressed in white, the night gone, early morning birds, a new day dawning for them. And with what glee and satisfaction the audience laughed when Graziano baited Shylock and when finally he was told he must become a Christian. There's real justice for you.

Barton's production goes one better than most. We will ignore the silly *Fiddler-On-The-Roof* rendering of the daughter, Jessica, and her possession of an absurd accent which miraculously her father seems to have lost! We will ignore that Shylock is placed in a setting with scales weighing his silver and gold, just in case one misunderstands the nature of his calling or forgets how he spends his time.

But what we can't ignore is the moment when Shylock, in pain that his daughter and jewels have gone, confronts his friend, Tubal, and cries out '. . . and I know not what's spent in the search . . .' – at which the canny old Tubal presents him with a bill. Ho! Ho! The audience laughed again to be reminded that not only do Jews suck dry Christian blood, they suck each other's as well! Of course! Jews are insensitive to each other's pain. A debt after all is a debt. Why wait till grief is past?

Barton's production echoes the play's contemptuousness very clearly and cleanly. You can hear every word, each action is clearly defined, all motivation cleanly charted. He even seduced the brilliant actor David Suchet, himself Jewish, into re-creating our comfortable and reassuring image of the bent old man, his trousers too long for him, an ever-present false and fawning smile on his face, grimacing through smoke from an uncouthly hanging cigarillo.

Only Suchet's two marvellous moments endow the character with wit and dignity. When Portia asks '. . . which is the merchant here and which the Jew?' the difference is so obvious – Antonio a tall upright Aryan, Shylock stooped, dark and diminutive – that Suchet releases a huge, mischievous laugh at the crassness of the question. And at the end, forced to confront the oppressiveness of the state and his self-inflicted humiliation, Suchet's face reveals a despair which has more to do with concentration camps than anything we've seen till now. In fact his eyes betray the play.

It was while watching the Jonathan Miller production in 1973 that I first began to think of alternatives. When the moment came for Portia to announce that Shylock couldn't have his pound of flesh because it meant spilling blood which was not called for in the contract, I was struck with an insight. The real Shylock would not have torn his hair out and raged against not being allowed to cut his pound of flesh, but would have said 'Thank God!' The point of writing a play in which Shylock would utter these words would be to explain how he became involved in such a bond in the first place.

My first note to myself was that Shylock and Antonio must be friends. My second was that Shylock must be a bibliophile. Gradually, as I researched the history of the Venetian Empire, of the Jews in Italy, of the development of printing – of the entire Renaissance in fact – I realized that my play would not be about bonds for usury but about bonds of friendship and the state laws which could threaten that friendship.

My version of the story – opens in the Jewish Ghetto of Venice, and what an exciting, lively place that was by 1563. Ghetto Nuovo is the old Venetian word for 'new iron-foundry', which is where the Jews – needed but not wanted – were pushed aside to live on the outskirts of Venice. (And from that moment the word entered the world's vocabulary to denote an ethnic slum. The Ghetto Nuovo exists to this day.)

The first scene of the play establishes the relationship, evokes the period. It takes place in Shylock's study, strewn with books and manuscripts. Shylock, a 'loan-banker', and his friend Antonio, a merchant, are leisurely cataloguing. They are old friends, and old: in their middle sixties.

But how could such friends enter into an absurd bond for a pound of flesh? Research showed that no dealings could be entered into with a Jew without contract. This becomes one of the pillars later on in the play. Antonio needs to borrow three thousand ducats to lend to his godson. Shylock would prefer to give him the money without a contract, but Antonio points out that the laws of Venice do not permit this.

The familiar tragedy unfolds. Antonio loses his ships, and Shylock is faced with a quite new dilemma which is spelt out to him by Rivka, his sister:

> Don't you know the court will relieve you of your bond to save a citizen's life? . . . They will even let you bend the law and lend him further ducats for repayment when the hour is passed. . . . But not everyone in the Ghetto will agree to the bending of the law, will they? And that's where your moral problem begins. You can't see that? . . . *Some* may. Some may even beg you to do that rather than have the blood of a Christian on their hands. But others will say, no! Having bent the law for us, how often will they bend it for themselves and then we'll live in even greater uncertainties than before. They'll be divided, as you are, my clever brother. Who to save – your poor people or your poor friend? You can't see that?

The play ends in court. Shylock has no alternative but to safeguard his community and sacrifice his friend and, consequently, himself. Portia comes to the rescue but the state exacts its revenge. He must not merely lose his house and goods but his beloved collection of books, in which, he has enthusiastically claimed, resides the world's wisdom. He's a destroyed man.

Shylock has entered the language. To be called it is to be insulted for being mean like a Jew. A director of Hungarian origin told me he'd seen a production in war-time Hungary when the play's anti-semitic aspects were inevitably exploited to the hilt. Jessica was portrayed as a whore. I can't help feeling there's a certain honesty to such a production, and I would like to think Shakespeare today would be ashamed of his contribution to the world's image of that poor old battered race.

The poet in him is untouchable but I know about Jewish ghetto life, and history has a hindsight which I felt driven to use. All my play offers is a new set of evidence from which a theatre public may choose.

The Merchant received its world première at the Royal Dramaten-theater, Stockholm, on 8 October 1976, directed by Staphan Roos.

It received its English-speaking première at the Plymouth Theatre, New York, on 16 November 1977, with the following cast.

SHYLOCK KOLNER	Joseph Leon
JESSICA	Julie Garfield
RIVKA	Marian Seldes
TUBAL DI PONTI	John Seitz
ANTONIO QUERINI	John Clements
BASSANIO VISCONTI	Nicolas Surovy
LORENZO PISANI	Everett McGill
GRAZIANO SANUDO	Riggs O'Hara
PORTIA CONTARINI	Roberta Maxwell
NERISSA	Gloria Gifford
SOLOMON USQUE	Jeffrey Horowitz
REBECCA DA MENDES	Angela Wood
MOSES DA CASTELAZZO	Leib Lensky
GIROLAMO PRIULI	William Roerick
ABTALION DA MODENA	Boris Tumarin
MAID/SINGER	Rebecca Malka
SERVANTS/SENATORS	Russ Banham
	Mark Blum
	Philip Carroll
	James David Cromar
	Brian Meister
	John Tyrrell

Directed by John Dexter
Designed by Jocelyn Herbert
Lighting by Andy Phillips

N.B. Zero Mostel was originally cast as Shylock but tragically he died after the first night out of town in Philadelphia – 8 September 1977.

The Merchant received its British première at the Birmingham Repertory Theatre on 12 October 1978, with the following cast.

SHYLOCK KOLNER	David Swift
JESSICA	Julia Swift
RIVKA	Hana Maria Pravda
TUBAL DI PONTI	Aubrey Morris
ANTONIO QUERINI	Frank Middlemass
BASSANIO VISCONTI	Tim Hardy
LORENZO PISANI	Greg Hicks
GRAZIANO SANUDO	Timothy Spall
PORTIA CONTARINI	Angela Down
NERISSA	Margi Campi
RODERIGUES DA CUNHA	Teddy Kempner
SOLOMON USQUE	Roger Allam
REBECCA DA MENDES	Judith Harte
MOSES DA CASTELAZZO	Alfred Hoffmann
GIROLAMO PRIULI	Andre Van Gyseghem
MAID/SINGER	Joanna Foster
SERVANTS/SENATORS	Peter Evans
	Christopher Gillespie
	Ian McFarlane
	Raymond Savage

Directed by Peter Farago
Sets designed by Christopher Morley
Costumes designed by Ann Curtis
Lighting by Mick Hughes

Shylock received its first London airing as a reading/workshop production at The Riverside Studios where it played for eight performances from 16 to 22 October 1989. The aim was to attract investment for a future full-scale production. The cast was:

SHYLOCK KOLNER	Oded Teomi
JESSICA	Julia Lane
RIVKA	Anna Korwin
TUBAL DI PONTI	Michael Poole
ANTONIO QUERINI	Frank Barrie
BASSANIO VISCONTI	Pip Torrens
LORENZO PISANI	Richard Lintern
GRAZIANO SANUDO	Hugh Simon
PORTIA CONTARINI	Julie Legrand
NERISSA	Jan Shand
SOLOMON USQUE	Mark Sproston
RODERIGUES DA CUNHA	Brian Mitchell
REBECCA DA MENDES	Kate Percival
MOSES DA CASTELAZZO	Michael Poole
GIROLAMO PRIULI	Michael Cronin

Director Arnold Wesker
Assistant Director Steve Woodward
Lighting Konrad Watson

CHARACTERS

SHYLOCK KOLNER, *a Jew of Venice*
JESSICA, *his daughter*
RIVKA, *his sister*
TUBAL DI PONTI, *his partner*
ANTONIO QUERINI, *a merchant of Venice*
BASSANIO VISCONTI, *his godson*
LORENZO PISANI, *Bassanio's friend*
GRAZIANO SANUDO, *Antonio's assistant*
PORTIA CONTARINI, *an heiress of Venice*
NERISSA, *her maid*
RODERIGUES DA CUNHA, *an architect*
SOLOMON USQUE, *a playwright*
REBECCA DA MENDES, *daughter of Portuguese banker*
MOSES DA CASTELAZZO, *a portrait painter*
GIROLAMO PRIULI, *Doge of Venice*
MAID IN SHYLOCK'S HOUSE*
PATRICIANS AND OTHERS (at director's discretion)

* Who should also be singer at end of play.

ACT ONE

SCENE ONE

[*Venice, 1563. The Ghetto Nuovo.* SHYLOCK's *study. It is strewn with books and manuscripts.*

SHYLOCK *a 'loan-banker', with his friend,* ANTONIO, *a merchant, are leisurely cataloguing.*

ANTONIO *is by the table, writing, as* SHYLOCK *reads out the titles and places them on his shelves.*

They are old friends, and old: in their middle sixties.]

SHYLOCK [*reading out*]: 'Guide to the Perplexed'. Author, Maimonides, Ram-bam, known as the Great Eagle. Cairo. Twelfth century.

[ANTONIO *writes.*]

Hebrew/Hebrew Dictionary. Author, R. David Kimhi. England. Twelfth century. Not too fast for you, Antonio?

ANTONIO: It's not the most elegant script, but I'm speedy.

SHYLOCK: And I'm eager. I know it. But here, the last of the manuscripts and then we'll begin cataloguing my printed books. Such treasures to show you, you'll be thrilled, thrrrrrilled! You'll be – I can't wait . . . just one more –

ANTONIO: Do I complain?

SHYLOCK: – and then we'll rest. I promise you. I'll bring out my wines, and fuss and – the last one. I promise, promise.

ANTONIO: Shylock! Look! I'm waiting.

SHYLOCK: I have a saint for a friend.

ANTONIO: And what does the poor saint have?

SHYLOCK: An overgrown schoolboy. I know it! The worst of the deal. But –

ANTONIO: I'm waiting, Shylock.

SHYLOCK: Deed. Legal. Anglo-Jewish. Twelfth century.

Author – I can't read the name. Probably drawn up by a businessman himself. [*Peering.*] What a mastery of Talmudic Law. I love them, those old men, their cleverness, their deeds, their wide-ranging talents. Feel it! Touch it!

ANTONIO: The past.

SHYLOCK: Exactly!

ANTONIO: And all past.

SHYLOCK: Antonio! You look sad.

ANTONIO: Sad?

SHYLOCK: I've overworked you. Here. Drink. Why should we wait till we're finished? [*Offers wine.*] Drink. It's a special day.

[*They drink in silence.*]

ANTONIO: So many books.

SHYLOCK: And all hidden for ten years. Do you know what that means for a collector? Ten years? Ha! The scheme of things! 'The Talmud and kindred Hebrew literature? Blasphemy!' they said, 'burn them!' And there they burned, on the Campo dei Fiori in Rome, September the 9th, 1553. The day of the burning of the books. Except mine, which I hid, all of them, even my secular works. When fever strikes them you can't trust those 'warriors of God'. With anything of learning? Never! That's what they really hated, not the books of the Jews but the books of men. I mean – MEN! Their spites, you see, the books revealed to them their thin minds. And do you think it's over even now? Look! [*Pushes out a secret section of his bookcase.*] The Sacred Books. The others I can bring back, but still, to this day, the Talmud is forbidden. And I have them, the greatest of them, Bomberg's edition, each of them. Aren't they beautiful?

ANTONIO: So beautiful.

SHYLOCK [*referring to others*]: I've friends who buy for me all over the world. I'm a hoarder of other men's genius. My vice. My passion. Nothing I treasure more, except my daughter. So – drink! It's a special day. Look! A present to cheer you up. One of my most treasured manuscripts, a thirteenth-century book of precepts, author Isaac of Corbeil, with additamenta made by the students. I used to do it myself, study and scribble my thoughts in the margin. We all did it. We had keen minds, Antonio, very profound we thought ourselves, commenting on the meaning of life, the rights and wrongs of the laws, offering our interpretations of the interpretations of the great scholars who interpreted the meaning of the meaning of the prophets. 'Did the prophecies of Daniel refer to the historic events or to the Messianic times, or neither? Is the soul immortal, or not? Should one or should one not ride in a gondola on the Sabbath?' Money lending was never a full-time occupation and the Ghetto rocked with argument – ha! I love it! [*Pause.*] There! I *have* tired you.

ANTONIO: I assure you –

SHYLOCK: Depressed you, then. I've done that.

ANTONIO: Not that either. But –

SHYLOCK: But what? What but, then?

ANTONIO: Those books. Look at them. How they remind me what I am, what I've done. Nothing! A merchant! A purchaser of this to sell there. A buyer-up and seller-off. And do you know, I hardly ever see my trade. I have an office, a room of ledgers and a table, and behind it I sit and wait till someone comes in to ask have I wool from Spain, cloth from England, cotton from Syria, wine from Crete. And I say yes, I've a ship due in a week, or a month, and I make a note, and someone goes to the dock, collects the corn, delivers it to an address, and I see nothing. I travel neither to England to check cloth, nor Syria to check cotton, or Corfu to see that the olive oil is cleanly corked, and I could steal time for myself in such places. It never worried me, this absence of curiosity for travel. Until I met you, old Jew –

SHYLOCK: Not so old *then*, old man, only just past fifty –

ANTONIO: – and I became caught up in your – your passion, your hoardings, your – your vices!

SHYLOCK: Is he complaining or thanking me?

ANTONIO: You've poisoned me, old Shylock, with restlessness and discontent, and at so late a time.

SHYLOCK: He's complaining.

ANTONIO: A lawyer, a doctor, a diplomat, a teacher – anything but a merchant. I'm so ashamed. There's no sweetness in my dealings. After the thrill of the first exchange, after the pride of paying a thousand ducats with one hand and taking fifteen hundred with the other – no skill. Just an office and some ledgers. It's such a joyless thing, a bargain. I'm so weary with trade.

SCENE TWO

[*Belmont.* PORTIA's *estate outside Venice. The estate is in great disrepair.* PORTIA *and her maid,* NERISSA, *both in simple, hard-wearing clothes, have just arrived to view the neglect.*]

PORTIA: Decided! The speculating days of the family Contarini are done. The goods warehoused in our name at Beirut and Famagusta we'll sell off cheaply to cut our losses, I shall raise what I can from the sale of our properties on Crete, Corfu and the Dalmatian towns which are too far from Venice and not worth their troubles, but –

NERISSA: – but agriculture, my lady, what does my lady Portia know of agriculture?

PORTIA: Your lady Portia will learn, Nerissa. The famines are cruel and constant visitors. We must reclaim the land. Besides, the competition for the trade routes is too devious a task for my taste, and –

NERISSA: – and pirates are in the Adriatic, we know all that, my lady, most demoralizing for our sailors, but –

PORTIA: Antwerp! Seville! London! Too far!

NERISSA: – but to leave the city?

PORTIA: I love my city, Nerissa, but I hear rumours. Timber is scarce, the number of ships registered by Venice is dropping. Signs, my dear, the signs are there. It's goodbye to Venice, and into the wheatlands of my estates near Treviso and Vicenza and here, Belmont. We'll become growers! Stock-breeders! Cattle and drainage! that's where our fortunes will go.

NERISSA: When you've realized them, that is.

PORTIA: The land! I've decided! [*Pause.*] Good God! [*Looking around.*] What a mess my father's made of my childhood! [*Pause.*] Is this the room?

NERISSA: Facing the sun at eleven o'clock. This is it.

PORTIA: And *here* we are to find the caskets?

NERISSA [*searching*]: Here, somewhere in all this neglect. Your father's puzzle for picking a spouse. One gold, one silver, one lead. [NERISSA *reveals a dusty corner*.] Found! [*Reading*.] 'By his choice shall you know him.'

PORTIA: What an inheritance! Ten estates in ruin, and a foolish philosophic whim for to find me an idiot husband. Oh father, father, father! What *were* you thinking of? Hear me up there. I *will* honour the one wish you uttered: whom the casket chooses, I'll marry. But your rules for judging men I will forget, and these ruins will be put back again. The material things of this world count. We *have* no soul without labour, and labour I will, father, hear me.

[*She begins to move about the room pulling down tattered curtains, replacing furniture on its feet, picking up strewn books, perhaps rubbing encrusted dirt from a vase till its frieze can be seen, but moving, moving*.]

NERISSA: How your mother would love to be alive now, with all this possibility of work at last.

PORTIA: Perhaps that's my real inheritance, Nerissa: father's marriage to a peasant. My energy is hers.

NERISSA: And such energy, madame.

PORTIA: All stored and waiting for the poor man's death.

NERISSA: Come, be just. He didn't commit you in marriage at the age of seven as my father did. He gave you tutors.

PORTIA: Ah, thank heaven for them.

NERISSA: A very strange collection, I used to think. Why in God's name did you want to learn Hebrew, my lady?

PORTIA: To read the words of the prophets in the language they were spoken, why else? Meanings change when men translate them into other tongues. Oh! Those caskets! Those stupid caskets! Take them out of my sight. I loved him dearly, my father, but those caskets will bring me down as his other madnesses brought down my mother, I feel it.

NERISSA: *Such* energy, madame, you tire me to watch you.

PORTIA: And you must have it too, Nerissa. I demand it. You are not only my help but my friend and I'll have you educated and protected from the miseries of an ill-chosen marriage.

NERISSA: If, that is, you can protect yourself from one.

PORTIA: True! My God, and what suitors have announced they're coming. Why, do you wonder, *is* there such interest in me?

NERISSA: Riches, madame, riches, riches, riches.

PORTIA: But my riches are potential, not realized.

NERISSA: The family name?

PORTIA: My family name is illustrious but somewhat moth-eaten.

NERISSA: Your beauty.

PORTIA: No flattery. I won't have it. My beauty is, well – it *is*, but no more than many such women of Venice I could name.

NERISSA: Why, then? *You* say.

PORTIA: I *think* I know, but I'm not certain. There are simply – mmm – pulses in my veins. I feel, I feel – I feel I-am-the-new-woman-and-they-know-me-not! For centuries the Church has kept me comfortably comforting and cooking and pleasing and patient. And now – Portia is no longer patient. Yes, she can spin, weave, sew. Give her meat and drink – she can dress them. Show her flax and wool – she can make you clothes. But – Portia reads! Plato and Aristotle, Ovid and Catullus, all in the original! Latin, Greek, Hebrew –

NERISSA: With difficulty!

PORTIA: She has read history and politics, studied logic and mathematics, gazed at the stars, scrutinized maps, conversed with liberal minds on the nature of the soul, the efficacy of religious freedom, the very existence of God!

NERISSA: Why! Her brain can hardly catch its breath!

PORTIA: She has observed, judged, organized and – crept out of the kitchen. Knowledge may have lost her sweet innocence but – the fireside chair rocks without her now, and what she will do is a mystery. Portia is a new woman, Nerissa. There is a woman on the English throne. Anything can happen and they are coming to find out.

SCENE THREE

[SHYLOCK'S *study. He and* ANTONIO *have been drinking.*]

SHYLOCK: I gave you wine to cheer you up. It's cheered me down!

ANTONIO: The work's done. You should be happy! I've lost the use of my hand, but what of that? Look, order! Filed, catalogued, all that knowledge. You could save the world.

SHYLOCK: When I can't be certain of saving myself? What a thought! Not even the sages with all their wisdom could save themselves. Here, read this elegy on the Martyrs of Blois by the Rabbi Yom Tov of Joigny. What a lovely old man he must have been. To a question once about whether or not to use a stove on the Sabbath, he replied 'May my lot be with those who are warm, not those who are stringent!' Poor sage. They were all poor sages. Constantly invited to run educational establishments here and there, and never certain whether they were running into a massacre. From the massacre of Rouen they fled into the massacre of London; from the massacre of London into the massacre of York, and from the massacre of York no one fled! [*Pause.*] Travelling wasn't very safe in those days!

ANTONIO: Are you a religious man, Shylock?

SHYLOCK: What a question. Are you *so* drunk?

ANTONIO: You *are* religious, for all your freethinking, you're a devout man. And I love and envy you for it.

SHYLOCK: You are *so* drunk. Religious! It's the condition of being Jewish, like pimples with adolescence, who can help it? Even those of us who don't believe in God have dark suspicions that he believes in us. Listen, I'll tell you how it all happened. Ha! The scheme of things! I love it! Imagine this tribe of semites in the desert. Pagan, wild, but brilliant. A sceptical race, believing only in themselves. Loving but assertive. Full of quarrels and questions. Who could control them? Leader after leader was thrown up but, in a tribe where every father of his family was a leader, who could hold them in check for long? Until one day a son called Abraham was born, and he grew up knowing his brethren very, very well indeed. 'I know how to control this arrogant, anarchic herd of heathens, ' he said to himself. And he taught them about one God. Unseen! Of the spirit! That appealed to them, the Hebrews, they had a weakness for concepts of the abstract. An unseen God! Ha! I love it! What an inspiration. But that wasn't all. Abraham's real statesmanship, his real stroke of genius was to tell this tribe of exploding minds and vain souls: 'Behold! An unseen God! God of the Universe! Of all men! and –' wait, for here it comes, '– and, of all men you are his chosen ones!' Irresistible! In an instant they were quiet. Subdued. 'Oh! Oh! Chosen? Really? Us? To do what?' 'To bear witness to what is beautiful in creation, and just. A service, not a privilege!' 'Oh dear! Chosen to bear witness! What an honour! Ssh! Not so loud. Dignity! Abraham is speaking. Respect! Listen to him. Order!' It worked! They had God and Abraham had them. But – they were now cursed. For from that day moved they into a nationhood that had to be better than any other and, poor things, all other nations found them unbearable to live with. What can I do? I'm chosen. I *must* be religious.

ANTONIO: I love you more and more, Shylock. You have a sanity I could not live without now. I'm spoiled, chosen also.

SHYLOCK: But sad, still. I can see it. I've failed to raise your spirits one tiny bit.

ANTONIO: *I'm* not a religious man. I had a letter today, from an old friend, Ansaldo Visconti of Milan, a rich merchant, and well-loved in my youth. But I'd forgotten him. And in this letter he talked of his misfortune, his downfall into ruin through strange and cursed events which I couldn't make any sense of, it was so wordy and maudlin and full of old times. And in the end he commends to me his only son, Bassanio, my godson it seems. And I'd forgotten him also. Poor young Bassanio. Probably a very noble young nobleman. His father was born in Venice, if I remember, of patrician stock, if I remember. No, he's probably a swaggering young braggart! Coming to see me in the hope I'll put trade his way, or put him in trade's way, or keep him by me as an assistant, passing on wisdom, or something. [*Pause.*] Here, Bassanio, a little piece of wisdom, here, in my pocket. [*Pause, mock pomp.*] I am now going to be wise! [*Pause. Then as if calling a dog.*] Here, wisdom, here, boy. Sit. Still. Quiet now. There, Bassanio, sits wisdom. [*Pause.*] I don't want to be wise, or to talk about trade, or to see him. Ungodly man! Doesn't that make me an ungodly man? I should never have had godsons. Not the type. Bachelor merchant. On the other hand I suppose that's just the type.

SHYLOCK: When do you expect him?

ANTONIO: Oh, tomorrow, or the next day, or is it next week? Can't remember which. Bassanio! Humph! [*Shouting out.*] I'm not a religious man, Bassanio.

SHYLOCK: Antonio, my friend, it's late. In ten minutes they lock the gates of the Ghetto and all good Christians should be outside.

ANTONIO [*still shouting*]: I may be your godfather, Bassanio, but I'm not a religious man.

SHYLOCK: I have a suggestion.

ANTONIO: Bassanio, Bassanio!

SHYLOCK: Stay the night.

ANTONIO: Stay the night?

SHYLOCK: It's not permitted, but with money –

ANTONIO: What about Bassanio, in search of wisdom?

SHYLOCK: We'll send a message in the morning to say where you can be found. Stay. You know my house, lively, full of people in and out all the time. My daughter, Jessica, will look after you – if she deigns to talk that is.

ANTONIO: Very haughty, your Jessica.

SHYLOCK: And free and fractious but – cleverer than her illiterate old father. Gave her all the tutors I couldn't have. But soon I will have one of my own.

ANTONIO [*trumpeting*]: Abtalion da Modena the illustrious!

SHYLOCK: My very own scholar.

ANTONIO: Arriving any day now, as he keeps assuring us.

SHYLOCK: Any day now.

ANTONIO [*still trumpeting*]: On his very own pilgrimage from Lisbon to the holy Jerusalem, financed by his very own pupil here, Shylock Kolner, in return for his very own wisdom. [*As if calling a dog.*] Here, wisdom, here, boy!

SHYLOCK: Stay! You know how the Ghetto is constantly filled
with visitors. In the morning Solomon Usque the writer is
coming with the daughter of the Portuguese banker Mendes,
and in the afternoon we'll go to the synagogue to hear the
sermon of a very famous rabbi from Florence, preaching on
the importance of the Talmudic laws on cleanliness, with
special reference to Aristotle! Stay. It'll be full of Venetian
intelligentsia, they're always coming to attend the festivals,
listen to the music. Very exotic we are. We fascinate them all,
whether from England where they've expelled us, or Spain
where they burn us. Stay [*Pause.*] He's asleep. He'll have to
stay. [*Taking the arm of the now half-asleep* ANTONIO, *he
struggles with him towards a bedroom.*] And if the gatekeepers
remember and come looking don't worry, I'll keep them
happy. Happy, happy, happy.

SCENE FOUR

[SHYLOCK's *main room. Next morning. An atmosphere of great
activity.* JESSICA, *helped by* SHYLOCK's *old sister,* RIVKA, *and a*
MAID, *is supervising the comings and goings, in preparation for the
midday meal.* TUBAL, *his partner, is going through accounts.*]

JESSICA: We shall be six to eat at midday. Yesterday it was
eight, the day before seven, and tomorrow, no doubt, more
again. And is he up? He's not even awake yet. Eleven o'clock
and he sleeps.

RIVKA: Yesterday was a very special day for him, Jessica. The
books, remember, came out of hiding.

JESSICA: He dusted his dusty books! Heaven help me, Aunt Riv-
ka, I have to look at those books again. From my earliest days
I remember nothing but this madness, this illness for books.
And at fifteen I thanked God that they had to be hidden away.

RIVKA: That's a sinful thing to say, niece. Your father would
be ashamed to hear you talk like this.

JESSICA: My father is an intellectual snob. Every passing scholar or rabbi, or eminent physician has to dine at his table.

Some men fawn before crowns, he before degrees. And soon
he'll have his very own scholar to come and stay and stay and
stay and stay and –

RIVKA: When Abtalion da Modena comes –

JESSICA: 'When Abtalion da Modena comes! Wait till Abtalion da Modena comes!' My father promises him as some
men promise the Messiah!

RIVKA: This is not worthy of you, Jessica. Scholarship must
be respected.

JESSICA: Oh, I respect scholarship, but there is a world outside
the covers of a book, isn't there? Men don't always behave as
the philosophers fear, do they? I have the sayings and warnings
of sages ringing in my ears so loudly that music, which I adore
above all things, can hardly make sense in my head any more.

TUBAL: Your father is a special man, Jessica. He's animated by
ideas. 'Keep me moving,' he cries, 'don't let the dark overtake
me, it's my only hope.' A man not afraid to have his mind
changed? That's rare. I wish I had such courage.

JESSICA: But he bullies with it all, Uncle Tubal. My father's
cruelty is to diminish whoever can't recall a name, a date, an
event, or argument. 'Patterns! The scheme of things.' Well, I
do not believe there is a scheme of things, only chaos and
misery, and –

RIVKA: That's wanton!

JESSICA: – and in it we must carve out just sufficient order for
an ounce of happiness.

RIVKA: Wanton!

JESSICA: Nothing too ambitious. A little modest sweetness, at
any price.

RIVKA: At any price?

JESSICA: At almost any price. We have no choice. There are
madmen at large in the world. All writing books! Men fired by
this ideal, that passion, full of dogma about the way other men
should live, assuming moralities for us, deciding the limits of
our pleasure, our endeavour, our abilities, our pain. Decreed
by whom? By what right? My father is full of them and I am
oppressed by them and I think my time is done for them. [*She
leaves.*]

RIVKA: She exaggerates. My brother's not a tyrannical father.

TUBAL: Of course not. When their quarrels are over, Shylock makes light of it. But I fear he confuses her frustrations for her originality.

RIVKA: He wanted to prove that daughters could achieve the intellectual stature of sons.

TUBAL: A wilful thought I've always thought. But there you are, you can't discuss children with parents, you offend them where they've placed their most cherished endeavour.

[*A young man,* RODERIGUES DA CUNHA, *rushes in. He carries rolls of plans.*]

RODERIGUES: Shylock! Shylock! The plans of the new synagogue! No Shylock?

RIVKA: Asleep still.

RODERIGUES: Asleep still. My appointment was for eleven.

TUBAL: As was mine. 'The accounts,' he cries, 'the accounts are in disorder.'

RODERIGUES: 'The plans,' he cries, 'the plans! You want me to contribute to the building of a new synagogue? Let me see the plans first.' So I stay up all night to draw a new set of plans, and he sleeps!

RIVKA: Go into the kitchen, Roderigues, Jessica is there.

RODERIGUES: All night!

RIVKA: Calm yourself –

RODERIGUES: Well, not *all* night.

RIVKA: – take mid-morning refreshment but don't complain to her, she's a little – heavy. My brother will be with us soon.

[RODERIGUES *nearly succeeds in leaving but is forced back into the room by a storming* JESSICA.]

JESSICA: Did you know they were coming *now*?

RIVKA: Who, my dear, who?

JESSICA: Solomon Usque and Rebecca da Mendes.

TUBAL: But these are honours, Jessica.

JESSICA: Honours for you, work for me, and overcrowding for the Ghetto. Suddenly Venice is alive with Portuguese Anusim.

RIVKA: Fleeing the Inquisition, child, what are you saying?

JESSICA: They will be welcome, but I'm not told, I'm not told.

[*Enter* SOLOMON USQUE *and* REBECCA DA MENDES.]

USQUE: Solomon Usque, playwright of Lisbon, otherwise known as Duarte de Pinel. May I present the Signora Rebecca da Mendes, daughter of the late Francisco Mendes, banker of Lisbon. Peace be unto you, Signor Shylock.

TUBAL: You're both known and welcome, but I'm not Shylock. Tubal di Ponti, his friend and partner, and honoured.

REBECCA: He's always greeting the wrong person –

USQUE: – pushing the wrong door –

REBECCA: – drinking from the wrong shaped glass!

USQUE: When artists aspire to elegance they end by being ridiculous. Please, when will friend Shylock appear?

[SHYLOCK *enters accompanied by* ANTONIO.]

SHYLOCK: He appears, he appears! Friend Shylock appears! Signora Mendes, Signor Usque, I'm ashamed to have had no one waiting for you at the door. May I present my daughter Jessica; my sister Rivka; my good friend Antonio Querini, a merchant of Venice whose head is not his own this morning, and my partner, Tubal di Ponti. Oh yes, and Roderigues – er –

RODERIGUES: – da Cunha.

SHYLOCK: – da Cunha, architect. They're building a new synagogue for the Spanish and Portuguese refugees. Of all people you must know of the plans. Your father, Signora, renowned! Renowned!

REBECCA: There are so many –

SHYLOCK: No, no! We are all indebted. No comparison: benevolence! statesmanship! Whatever I can do for you will be nothing in return. Nothing.

JESSICA: I must attend to the food. Please excuse me.

RODERIGUES: I will join you. Forgive me, everyone, I'm dying of thirst.

SHYLOCK: Thirst! My goodness. Look at me! Jessica, the citronade.

JESSICA [*leaving*]: It's on the table, father.

SHYLOCK: Soon, dear Roderigues, I'll be with you soon.

RODERIGUES [*leaving*]: Beautiful! Beautiful plans!

[*They go.* SHYLOCK *pours drinks which he gives to* RIVKA *to hand out.*]

SHYLOCK: Everything is beautiful to him.

RIVKA: Especially my niece.

SHYLOCK: But not he to her! Stop match-making! He's a sweet boy but not her match. She always match-makes. And always the wrong one. She'll marry the wrong man without your help, push not! [*To his guests.*] Now, what news do you bring?

USQUE: The news is not 'beautiful' either.

SHYLOCK: Tell us.

USQUE: What point in the details, their awfulness is monotonous.

REBECCA: We need help, let's talk about that.

SHYLOCK: Tell us.

USQUE: In the last year the Coimbra Tribunal, which has jurisdiction over the Northern provinces of Portugal, has held thirty-five autos-da-fé drawn from different towns and villages of Trás-os-Montes and Beira alone.

REBECCA: In addition to which the Lisbon and Evora Tribunals have tried Anusim from the Eastern department of Braganza.

USQUE: Fifty people burnt at the stake.

REBECCA: Old women, young men, relatives, friends.

USQUE: Marian Fernandes, a cousin from Lisbon.

REBECCA: Maria Diez, my old aunt from Guarda.

USQUE: Sebastian Rodrigo Pinto, a friend from Lamego.

REBECCA: Diego Della Rogna, his wife Isabelle Nones, their four daughters and two sons.

USQUE: An entire family burnt.

REBECCA: Facing each other.

    [*Silence.*]

    But there are survivors. It's to those we must attend. Signor Shylock, we are among friends?

SHYLOCK: Everyone, inseparable.

REBECCA: I have been told that you are a courageous man –

SHYLOCK: Please! A fool with my chances, perhaps –

REBECCA: During the next months, a steady stream of the Portuguese community will be making their way to Ancona before leaving for Salonika. Though not easy, Venice is the least dangerous place for them to stop en route and rest. We would like you to arrange places for them to stay, families who would put them up, and a fund started to assist their journey.

RIVKA: And who else but my brother!

SHYLOCK: Who else! I'd have been offended had anyone else been approached. You knew who to come to, didn't you?

REBECCA: We'd been told.

SHYLOCK: They talk, you see, Antonio! I'm a name in my community. From nobody to somebody, a name! Now, you'll stay for food, you must eat with us.

RIVKA: Of course they'll stay and eat with us. You imagine I wouldn't ask them to stay and eat.

SHYLOCK: Say you'll stay, please, please, I insist.

RIVKA: We all insist.

SHYLOCK: We all insist. And you must allow me to show you my collection of manuscripts, come.

USQUE: Signora Mendes is the collector, I only write them.

SHYLOCK: You must persuade him to sign one of his books for me.

USQUE: Ha! they hardly perform me let alone print me.

REBECCA: Fortunately he has other skills.

USQUE: Self-appointed plenipotentiary for refugees.

REBECCA: A constant occupation but one giving him great opportunity for travel – from Constantinople to London.

SHYLOCK: To London?

RIVKA: Are there still Jews in England?

REBECCA: Hardly any. A clandestine existence. But we go back and forth for trade.

SHYLOCK: Then you must look out for a rare manuscript for me – *The Fox's Fables*.

REBECCA: What's your special interest?

SHYLOCK: There's an edition in the library of Exeter Cathedral written by the author *himself* in which he complains about his life in England and the indifference of its wealthy Jews to intellectual and literary activities.

USQUE: Perhaps *that* accounts for the massacre of London.

[SHYLOCK, REBECCA *and* RIVKA *prepare to leave.*]

REBECCA [*to* SHYLOCK *as they're leaving*]: I shall never understand this habit of using our misery to feed our wit.

USQUE [*parting shot as they go off*]: What else is left to feed it, Signora?

SHYLOCK: And the plans for the synagogue! We simply must look at the plans for the new Spanish synagogue together.

[*Exit with* REBECCA *and* RIVKA.]

USQUE: Is that how it is every day?

TUBAL: Every day! Brother and sister rivalling one another in hospitality, and daughter pushing the other way. A house never still.

ANTONIO: When he's not negotiating loans, he's dispatching men around the world to buy him books, or opening the sights of the Ghetto to visiting dignitaries. Wait till his very own scholar arrives, there'll be time for nothing but tutorials and debate.

TUBAL: Though in time you'll find he's a very melancholy man, will you agree, Signor Antonio?

ANTONIO: In my warehouse is a young man, Graziano Sanudo, in charge of the import of spices. Now *he's* a happy man, no melancholy in him, and I don't know that I can stand him around. He has no real opinions, simply bends with the wind, quickly rushing to agree with the next speaker. He's a survivor, not defiantly, which is honourable, but creepily, like a chameleon, blending with everyone to avoid anyone's sting. He laughs when every idiot farts out thin wit, fawns on the tyrannical, is reverential before the papal, and manifests the most depressingly boisterous happiness I know. Give me Shylock's melancholy, gentlemen, and take away my man's smiles.

TUBAL: But Jessica is right. Shylock's kind of intelligence *is* an illness.

ANTONIO: Aye! You die from it in the end.

USQUE: I see he has an eternal friend in you, Signor Antonio.

ANTONIO: And I in him. Now, gentlemen, excuse me. I've been expecting a young man to call for me here in search of wisdom, and I fear he's lost.

TUBAL: The message went to your offices, Antonio, first thing this morning. Come at once to the Ghetto Nuovo between the German Synagogue and the Association for the Jewish Poor. Ground floor, ask if lost.

ANTONIO: Thank you, but I've no knowing what kind of soul he is, simple or bright. And in case the former, I'd better go out in search. I think I need the air, besides. [*Leaves.*]

USQUE: Your community lives well, I see. You can build your synagogues and depend upon Gentile friends.

TUBAL: Personally I depend upon no Gentile but, misery is difficult to wear all weathers. We survive from contract to contract, not knowing if after five years it will be renewed, and if renewed whether it will be for another five, or ten or three but –

USQUE: – Trade is trade:–

TUBAL: – Trade is trade and they know it also, and we pay! An annual tribute of twenty thousand ducats; another twenty thousand for renting these squalid walls; fifteen thousand more to the Navy Board – for God knows what; another hundred for the upkeep of the canals, which stink! And, on top of all that, ten thousand more in time of war which, since our beloved and righteous republic seems constantly fighting with someone or other, ensures that sum too as a regular payment. Why, sometimes there's barely pennies in the Ghetto. For days we're all borrowing off each other, till new funds flow in. Only fourteen hundred souls, remember. We're no more than that, trapped in an oppressive circus with three water wells and a proclivity for fires.

[SHYLOCK *enters.*]

SHYLOCK [*calling*]: Roderigues! In here! Bring the plans in here, the light's better.

[RODERIGUES *struggles in with rolls of plans.*]

The entrance, why so plain? Why no wrought-iron gates? They're Spanish, come from a highly cultured background! Signor Usque, *you* must look at these plans for the Spanish synagogue.

[ANTONIO *and* BASSANIO *enter at this point but hold back to watch and listen.*]

TUBAL [*continuing to* USQUE]: And I make no mention of special demands in times of 'special distress', nor of the unreturned 'loans' to the treasury which bring in no more than a four per cent rate of interest. And did I leave out the cost of upkeeping our own community services and our own streets? I did, I did!

RODERIGUES: And did you leave out the bribes demanded by petty officials?

TUBAL: I did! I did!

RODERIGUES: And payments to the local church? the local police?

SHYLOCK: He did! He did! But never mind about politics. Why is the façade so dull? Is the new mint dull? Or the library and museum of antiquities? And the windows! There's no light!

RODERIGUES: Give me the taxes of Venice and I'll give you light!

SHYLOCK: You don't need money to be bold. You need boldness! Take them away and think again. Bolder! Be bolder!

ANTONIO: [*finally making himself known*]: Gentlemen, allow me to introduce my godson, Bassanio Visconti.

SHYLOCK: Ah, Antonio. You found him. Welcome, young man, welcome. You'll stay to eat with us, won't you? Do you know anything about architecture? We're building a new synagogue, look. We don't have a Palladio to build us a San Giorgio Maggiore, but with our modest funds. . .

ANTONIO: I don't think Bassanio plans to stay, but we would like to talk together, and if –

SHYLOCK: But of course, friend Roderigues is leaving.

RODERIGUES: To be bolder!

TUBAL: And I have sights to show Signor Usque.

SHYLOCK: The first time godfather and son meet is a special and private time. [*To* TUBAL *as he and* SHYLOCK *prepare to leave.*] Tubal, you *should* look at these plans for the new synagogue before they're folded away. It's your money too, you know.

TUBAL: I'm plan-blind, Shylock. They mean nothing to me. *You* spend my money.

[*They leave.*]

BASSANIO: And *that* is a Jew?

ANTONIO [*reprimanding*]: *He* is a Jew.

BASSANIO: I don't think I know what to say.

ANTONIO: Have you never met one before?

BASSANIO: Talked of, described, imagined, but –

ANTONIO: Shylock is my special friend.

BASSANIO: Then, sir, he must be a special man.

ANTONIO [*suspicious and changing the subject*]: Your father speaks highly of you and begs me to help where I can.

BASSANIO: My lord Antonio –

ANTONIO: I'm not a lord, I'm a patrician – lapsed and indifferent to their politicking but a patrician nonetheless.

BASSANIO: Lord, patrician – you are my godfather.

ANTONIO: I'd forgotten.

BASSANIO: Oh, understandably, understandably! The early years were so full of my father's talk of you and your goodness and your good time together, but – he made no effort to make us known to one another. It was a cause of distress between us.

ANTONIO: There were good times together, were there?

BASSANIO: He spoke of little else. What he shared with you, I shared. What happened between you, I saw happen. If I did wrong he'd say, your godfather would not approve of that. And as I grew I did what I did, thought what I thought, saying to myself – what would the good Antonio do now, how would the wise Antonio decide?

ANTONIO: Ah, wisdom! I feared it.

BASSANIO: You must surely have experienced this yourself, sir, that in your mind there is always one person, a vivid critic, whose tone of voice and special use of words is there in your brain, constantly.

ANTONIO: They call him God, Bassanio.

BASSANIO: I think you're mocking me. Have I come at a wrong time? Perhaps I shouldn't have come at all. To be honest, I hate arriving behind letters of recommendation. What can the poor host do but be courteous, obliging. Forgive me, sir. You know nothing of me. I'll go. But I'll find ways of making myself known to you, and useful, and in the coming months I'll try to earn your trust. Goodbye, sir.

ANTONIO: No, no, no. Don't go, young man. I've been rude and discourteous, forgive me. Bachelors have special dreads. Old age, loneliness, too much noise, too many requests; we fear opportunists and women. Forgive me. Sit and talk about yourself and what you want of me. Of course I remember your father. We were good for one another in lean years. Talk. I'll help his son. Without question. Trade? Tricks of the trade? Contracts? To represent me? Tell me what you want.

BASSANIO: In Belmont, sir, there is a lady.

ANTONIO: Ah, love!

BASSANIO: Her father's family goes back to the time when Venetians were fishermen, and –

ANTONIO: And would now prefer to forget it!

BASSANIO: – and, like all of those ancient families, became wealthy. These, the Contarinis, added to their wealth with – what shall I call it? – not madness, but – unorthodoxy. The father of my lady, whose name is Portia, was – well – odd! A philosopher.

ANTONIO: Oh, very odd.

BASSANIO: He evolved, it seems, a strange theory that men's character could be learned by tests, and to this end he devised a huge chart divided into the most important aspects of a man's character. Honour, common sense, loyalty, stamina and so on. And for each virtue and its opposite he devised their tests. His entire estates became manned by men he'd chosen based upon these philosophically evolved examinations. All, with one exception, fell into ruin.

ANTONIO: What an incredibly sad story.

BASSANIO: There is a happy side. The daughter –

ANTONIO: Beautiful?

BASSANIO: Well, not beautiful perhaps, but – striking, vivid. Compelling. Intelligent eyes, mobile features – handsome. In fact, if I must be blunt, determination and strength of will give her face a masculine aspect. She's feminine to the extent that she doesn't deny her sex, yet misleading because she doesn't cultivate, exploit, abuse it.

ANTONIO: Just such a woman I'd like to have met in my youth.

BASSANIO: You'll understand, then, the reason for my agitation.

ANTONIO: But not yet how it concerns me.

BASSANIO: Three caskets rest at Belmont. One gold, one silver, one lead. Who chooses the correct casket wins the daughter.

ANTONIO: Aha! The final test. And my role in this?

BASSANIO: I've lived a stupid, wasting life, Signor Antonio. I possess nothing and can lay my hands on nothing. I had hoped to marry wealth but now I've fallen in love with ruins. I mean to choose the right casket, marry that extraordinary woman and work to restore her property to profit. But I'm without means either to dress myself or reach her.

ANTONIO: It will cost?

BASSANIO: To present myself without insult? Three thousand ducats.

ANTONIO: Three thousand ducats!

BASSANIO: I believe no claim was ever made on your godfathership before.

ANTONIO: None.

BASSANIO: And none will be again.

ANTONIO: Bassanio, you come at a bad time. I've ships to sea but no cash to hand. More, I plan retirement, and all my wealth lies in their cargoes. The small change I need for daily living is easily got on credit from friendly traders, but the eyes of the Rialto are on me and I know no one who'll lend me so large a sum except –

BASSANIO: Who?

ANTONIO: Shylock.

BASSANIO: The Jew?

ANTONIO [defying his contempt]: Shylock.

BASSANIO: But the interest rate, the conditions.

ANTONIO: Whatever the conditions! It's more than I've ever borrowed in my life, but for the good years of my youth with your father, done!

BASSANIO: With a Jew!

ANTONIO: I've told you, young man, the Jew is my special friend.

BASSANIO: Of course. Forgive me, sir. And now, I'll go. If there's anything I can do for you in the city?

ANTONIO: Yes, take a message to my assistant, Graziano Sanudo. Tell him I won't be in today, but to arrange for dinner on Wednesday. I'm entertaining my friend, Shylock, so no pork. Join us, Bassanio, I keep a good wine cellar.

BASSANIO: With the greatest of pleasure, and honoured. May

I bring with me an old friend I've recently met again? A sort of philosopher.

ANTONIO: 'Sort of'?

BASSANIO: Writes poetry occasionally.

ANTONIO: A 'sort of philosopher' who 'writes poetry occasionally'! Good! Old Shylock might enjoy that. What's his name?

BASSANIO: Lorenzo Pisani.

ANTONIO: Ah! The silk manufacturers.

BASSANIO: You know them?

ANTONIO: The fabric, not the family.

BASSANIO: You won't regret this trust, signor.

ANTONIO: I hope to God I do not, Bassanio.

> [BASSANIO *leaving, meets* SHYLOCK *on the way out.* SHYLOCK *bows but is ignored.*]

I hope to God.

SHYLOCK: And what was that like?

ANTONIO: I'm not certain. He'd not met a Jew before.

> [SHYLOCK *goes into fits of laughter.*]

ANTONIO: What is so funny?

SHYLOCK: That's not a sin. There are a hundred million people in China who've not met a Jew before!

ANTONIO: Still he worries me for other reasons. There was too much calculation in him. You'll be meeting him on Wednesday and can judge for yourself. I've invited him for dinner. With a friend of his, Lorenzo Pisani.

SHYLOCK: Pisani?

ANTONIO: You know him?

SHYLOCK: I know him. He wrote a poem once, too long, 'The Ruin of the Nation's Heart'. A murky thing, full of other people's philosophy. Jessica showed it to me. She seemed very impressed because it called for a return to simplicity . . .

ANTONIO: Of course! My assistant Graziano showed it *me*. Seems it set our youth on fire, full of disgust with the great wretchedness of the world and the sins of men. It had a sense of doom which the poet seemed to enjoy rather more than he was anxious to warn of.

SHYLOCK: That's the one! Ah, children, children! [*Which reminds him, so he calls.*] Children! Children! Let's eat. [*To*

ANTONIO.] You must be starving, and the Portuguese must be bored to death with my books by now, and we must be finished eating in time for a sitting. [*Calling again.*] Jessica. [*To* ANTONIO.] I'm having our portrait painted. It's the day for a sitting. A great painter, an old man now, but exquisite, Moses da Castelazzo. Renowned!

ANTONIO: Shylock?

SHYLOCK: My friend!

ANTONIO: I have a great favour to ask of you.

SHYLOCK: At last! A favour! Antonio of Shylock!

ANTONIO: To borrow three thousand ducats.

SHYLOCK: Not four? Five? Ten?

ANTONIO: I'm not making jokes, Shylock.

SHYLOCK: And why do you think I make jokes?

ANTONIO: For three months?

SHYLOCK: Your city borrows forever, why not three months for you?

ANTONIO: You know my position?

SHYLOCK: I know your position. Your fortune in one voyage, insane. Still.

ANTONIO: You're a good man, old man.

SHYLOCK: Old man – forever! Good – not always. I'm a friend.

ANTONIO: What shall you want as a surety in the contract?

SHYLOCK: The *what*?

ANTONIO: The contract, Shylock. We must draw up a bond.

SHYLOCK: A bond? Between friends? What nonsense are you talking, Antonio?

ANTONIO: The law demands it: no dealings may be made with Jews unless covered by a legal bond.

SHYLOCK: That law was made for enemies, not friends.

ANTONIO: Shylock! The law says, in these very words, 'It is forbidden to enter into dealings with a Jew without sign and sealing of a bond, which bond must name the sums borrowed, specify the collateral, name the day, the hour to be paid, and –

TOGETHER: – and be witnessed by three Venetians, two patricians and one citizen, and then registered.'

ANTONIO: Be sensible! The French markets are gone, the

English are building faster and better ships and there are fools talking dangerously about protectionist policies. We are a nervous Empire with a jealous law. No man may bend it.

SHYLOCK: Sensible! Sensible! I follow my heart, my laws. What could be more sensible? The Deuteronomic Code says 'Thou shalt not lend upon usury to thy brother'. Let us interpret that law as free men, neither Christian nor Jew. I love you, therefore you are my brother. And since you are my brother my laws say I may not lend upon usury to you. Take the ducats.

ANTONIO: But law in Venice is sacrosanct, dear Shylock, dear brother.

SHYLOCK: My dealings with you are sacrosanct.

ANTONIO: The city's reputation thrives on its laws being trusted.

SHYLOCK: I thrive on my reputation being trusted.

ANTONIO: I would trust you with my life but you must not bend the law of Venice.

SHYLOCK [angry with the law]: You can have three thousand ducats but there will be no bond, for no collateral, and for no time-limit whatsoever.

ANTONIO: I understand. And it brings me closer to you than ever. But the deeper I feel our friendship the more compelled I feel to press my point, and protect you. You are a Jew, Shylock. Not only is your race a minority, it is despised. Your existence here in Venice, your pleasures, your very freedom to be sardonic or bitter is a privilege which has to be negotiated every five or seven or ten years. It is not a right. Your lives depend upon contract. Do you want the city councillors to respect *their* contract? Then you of all people must respect their *laws* behind contract. The law, Shylock, the law! For you and your people, the bond-in-law must be honoured.

SHYLOCK: Oh, you have really brought me down. That's earth I feel now. Solid. [Pause, not losing his good humour.] We'll cheat them yet.

ANTONIO: You mean you're still not persuaded?

SHYLOCK: I'm persuaded, oh yes, I'm very persuaded. We'll have a bond.

ANTONIO: Good!

SHYLOCK: A nonsense bond.

ANTONIO: A nonsense bond?

SHYLOCK: A lovely, loving nonsense bond. To mock the law.

ANTONIO: To mock?

SHYLOCK: Barbaric laws? Barbaric bonds! Three thousand ducats against a pound of your flesh.

ANTONIO: My flesh?

SHYLOCK: You're like an idiot child suddenly. [*Mocking.*] 'A nonsense bond? My flesh?' Yes. If I am not repaid by you, upon the day, the hour, I'll have a pound of your old flesh, Antonio, from near that part of your body which pleases me most – your heart. Your heart, dearheart, and I'd take that, too, if I could, I'm so fond of it.

   [*Pause as* SHYLOCK *waits to see if* ANTONIO *accepts.*]

ANTONIO: Barbaric laws, barbaric bonds?

SHYLOCK: Madness for the mad.

ANTONIO: Idiocies for the idiots.

SHYLOCK: Contempt for the contemptuous.

ANTONIO: They mock our friendship –

SHYLOCK: – we mock their laws.

ANTONIO [*pinching himself*]: Do I have a pound of flesh? I don't even have a pound of flesh.

SHYLOCK [*pinching him*]: Here, and here, and here, one, two, three pounds of flesh!

   [*He's tickling him;* ANTONIO *responds. Like children they're goosing each other and giggling, upon which note* JESSICA *and* RIVKA *enter with food,* RODERIGUES *also.*

   TUBAL, REBECCA *and* USQUE *enter deep in animated conversation. A meal is to be eaten, the sounds and pleasures of hospitality are in the air.*]

SCENE FIVE

[ANTONIO's *warehouse. Bales of coloured cloth, some from* PISANI *factories. Sacks of spices.*

GRAZIANO, *throwing cloth over* BASSANIO *to see which suits him.*

213

He tends to have conversations with himself, ignoring what others are saying.

LORENZO, *plunging his hand in a sack drawing spice pebbles which run back through his fingers.*]

BASSANIO: I was amazed. 'And *that* is a Jew?' I asked. 'He is a Jew,' my godfather corrected.

LORENZO: I don't like it. A world turned upside down.

BASSANIO: They were all Jews! His friends!

GRAZIANO: But a loan of three thousand ducats? I don't like it!

BASSANIO: You should have heard them, discussing Venice as though the city *cared* for their voice, existed for their *judgement!*

LORENZO: Money is a dead thing, with no seed, it's not fit to engender.

GRAZIANO: Well said.

BASSANIO: What could I do, Lorenzo? 'The Jew is my special friend,' he said.

GRAZIANO: Ah, now that *is* understandable.

LORENZO: Is it?

GRAZIANO: Well –

LORENZO: Shylock dares play God with a dead thing, and Venice has only a tired language to answer him with. Of course his usury flourishes. A nation that confuses timidity for tolerance is a nation without principle.

GRAZIANO: A nation turned upside down.

BASSANIO [*to* LORENZO]: Do you know Shylock well?

LORENZO [*moving from sack to sack, the spices trickling through his hands*]: I know him.

GRAZIANO: [*pursuing his own conversation with* BASSIANO *while winding cloth round him*]: Who do you know asserts authority?

LORENZO: A loud, enthusiastic man.

GRAZIANO: Men fear earning hatreds! No leadership! No God!

LORENZO: I've stood by him in the Ghetto when he's showing visitors its sights.

GRAZIANO: Not even the priests have time for God and our painters paint their Virgin Marys like whores.

LORENZO: Thin achievements in stone which he's magnified more from relief they've any stones at all than from their real worth.

GRAZIANO: The aged are in control of Venice, my friends.

LORENZO: There's hysteria in his description of things. His tone is urgent –

GRAZIANO: A burning issue.

LORENZO: – excited –

GRAZIANO: I burn whenever it comes up.

LORENZO: – excited, ornate and proudly erudite.

GRAZIANO: It comes up burning and I burn.

LORENZO: That's his sin: intellectual pride. His daughter can't bear it.

BASSANIO: You know Shylock's daughter?

GRAZIANO: A friend of yours?

LORENZO: You'd not think they're of the same blood. He's proud, she's modest. He imagines knowledge is all, she lives in the world. His voice is metallic with contempt, hers is sweet with reason. And she listens to music.

BASSANIO: And poetry perhaps?

LORENZO: And poetry, perhaps.

BASSANIO: Even praised some?

LORENZO: Even that.

BASSANIO: Good God, Lorenzo, are you in love?

LORENZO: Love? Who knows about love? She admired the poem and those who admire us must have merit we think. Can that be love? Respect perhaps.

BASSANIO: What an uncertain young man! Is this the 'he' who wrote 'The Ruin of the Nation's Heart'?

LORENZO: You're right! My nature can't decide itself. I feel passionate appetites within me but for what? I despise power yet so much offends me that I want power to wipe out the offence. And where does it lie? In trade or moral principle? The spirit of the trader is in me as in every Venetian but there is such a frenzy of avarice and unbridled ambition that I feel the end of the world must be near, a world which one moment I want to renounce, the next help save from itself.

BASSANIO: Beware, young man, beware. Help the poor world

save itself? Would you preach like Savonarola? The trap is that preachers intoxicate themselves so, come to deem themselves lords of life and earth, abuse their powers and weary men by perpetual admonitions. Beware, young man, beware.

GRAZIANO: Beware, nothing! Lorenzo's right. Horrible times. There's little for young men of character here.

BASSANIO: Nonsense! Everywhere I turn I hear of young patricians being schooled for trade, diplomacy, the Council's work.

LORENZO: But can those young patricians vote for the Doge if they're under thirty, or become senators before forty? Power doesn't reside in principle but in the hands of a few families.

BASSANIO: Who trade with the world! Come, what are you saying? Venice is a free city. Her doors are open, open!

LORENZO: Her legs are open, open! Venice – brothel of the Mediterranean. And all so that we can boast to everyone of our local codes and a freedom which tolerates corruption.

BASSANIO: Steady there, Lorenzo. Not too far. The toleration of Jews may be unpalatable to us, but trade, I sometimes think that men in trade have kept our mad world sane, preserved us from destructive politicians. Venice built its glory on its ancient trading families, after all.

GRAZIANO: And that's where the power lies, in the long ancient families who trade. I should know, coming as I do from one of them.

BASSANIO: *Long* ancient families? You?

GRAZIANO: Don't be surprised, my friends, not all Venetian aristocracy is bright, you see. Least of all I. Me. Least of all me. Or is it 'I'? I'm what they call an academic failure, expect nothing of me. My family are wealthy but not illustrious. They hoped I'd rise to be a statesman and add honour to their fortune, but I've neither tact nor memory, and in shame my family apprenticed me to trade. Personal assistant and happy!

BASSANIO: But what is a 'long family'?

GRAZIANO: A long family it is us, jealously listed in the chronicles and lists of our nobility as one of the twenty-four families. Of old. Who began it all. Or rather, there are twelve, from which I come, who claim the greatest nobility because they go back before 762, or is it 726? When the first Doge was elected, whose name was Orso, a military man, or was that Anafesto? Because some say the first Doge was elected in 679, or was it 697? And that *his* name was Anafesto, or was *his* name Orso? Whoever, my family goes back beyond then. The other twelve families only claim to have elected him. But both are long families. So called. As you see.

BASSANIO: And all were fishermen?

GRAZIANO: No! I mean, yes! I mean, the point is, we don't think of ourselves as descended from fishermen. It's just that we're – old. Go back a long way. The Roman Empire. Venice as a second Rome. Ancient.

BASSANIO: To be ancient is to be noble, you mean?

GRAZIANO: Exactly what I'm trying to say.

BASSANIO: So, a peasant family if it had the memory and evidence of a long past would be noble too?

GRAZIANO: Ah, no.

BASSIANO: So that's *not* exactly what you're trying to say?

GRAZIANO: That's what I'm saying, not exactly.

BASSANIO: Something more is needed to be a noble family?

GRAZIANO: Power!

BASSIANO: Which comes from where?

GRAZIANO: Stop teasing me, Bassanio. The question of Venetian nobility is an anxious one, my family quibble about it constantly.

LORENZO: And pointlessly. The question remains. What's to become of Venice? Does strength lie in trade or moral principle?

BASSANIO: Now you talk of strength. I thought we were talking of power.

LORENZO: You're right. We must distinguish our words or the concepts behind them will become entangled also.

BASSANIO: And strength may lie in moral principle but power resides in trade. See this pebble of pepper – it's this has the power to push men across seas. Three million pounds passed through Venice this year. Do you know what amount of gold that represents? Kings monopolize the spice trade for themselves.

LORENZO: But religious principle is constant, trade is not. A Portuguese sailor circumnavigates the Cape? The spice trade of the Mediterranean dies!

BASSANIO: And who takes over? The Portuguese! Another Catholic nation! And where is religious principle then?

LORENZO: More reason to defend it! For it would then have power to bind the trade of nations who would otherwise fight.

BASSANIO: Precisely! As I said! Trade keeps the world sane while the wild men rant on about their principles. Gentlemen, it's my time to go. I must cut my suits and sharpen my wits for Belmont. I chase a woman there they say has intellect.

LORENZO: And what is *her* inheritance? Ruins!

BASSANIO: Which she will rebuild.

LORENZO: If the elders will allow her.

BASSANIO: Despite them she will.

LORENZO: If their laws don't cripple her.

BASSANIO: I know her. She will.

LORENZO: If she has cunning and connections and the facility to fawn.

BASSANIO: She will, she will! Rebuild! As youth does, ignoring the evil within, defying the past. With my help of course. We're young! Don't be so solemn, Lorenzo. We'll meet at Antonio's for dinner and talk more. Perhaps we'll get to know you better, Graziano.

GRAZIANO: You'll love me, I promise you.

BASSANIO: And old Shylock too. What more will he be made of, I wonder?

LORENZO: Nothing much for loving there.

GRAZIANO: I know what he means, I know what he means.

SCENE SIX

[SHYLOCK's *main room.*
Chairs and easel are being set up for a portrait sitting.
SHYLOCK *enters with* USQUE, *followed by a bustling* RIVKA, *and* RODERIGUES *who is planning to do his own sketch of* JESSICA.
The old Jewish portrait painter MOSES DA CASTELAZZO *arrives.*]

SHYLOCK: Ah! Moses, you're here!

MOSES: No! I'm not here!

SHYLOCK: Signor Usque, playwright, allow me to introduce you to the renowned Moses da Castelazzo, painter!

MOSES [*ignoring the niceties of introduction and going straight to the easel*]: Renowned! Renowned! Who cares about renown at eighty!

   [SHYLOCK *and* RIVKA *take up positions.*]

RODERIGUES: And where's Jessica? How can I draw a subject who's not there?

MOSES [*mocking*]: And where's Jessica? How can I draw a subject who's not there! Look at him! If you must be in love don't show it. If you must show it don't draw it! Let me see. [*Snatches sketch book.*] You can't draw! Why are you trying to draw when you can't draw? Suddenly everybody imagines he's an artist!

RODERIGUES: The very old like him should be kept apart from the very young like me. I can see it now.

SHYLOCK: Stop squabbling. Moses can begin without Jessica, and Signor Usque has promised to tell us about his new play.

MOSES: Another one! Suddenly! Everyone! An artist!

USQUE: It will be a debate.

SHYLOCK: Between whom?

USQUE: Between rabbis who were interpreting –

SHYLOCK: – the interpretations of the interpretations of the great scholars who interpreted the meaning of the meaning –

USQUE: Precisely! You will remember that Catherine of Aragon had been the widow of Henry the Eighth's brother, Arthur, and now Henry wanted his marriage with her annulled. The Pope would probably have said yes, but was worried about Catherine's nephew, Charles the Fifth. Both – Henry and the Pope, that is – found support for their views in the Bible.

SHYLOCK: Naturally!

USQUE: Henry's wishes were supported by the book of Leviticus which said marriage to the widow of a dead brother was forbidden. While Rome's refusal supported itself with Deuteronomy which allows such a marriage in the case of a previously childless match.

SHYLOCK: Sons! Sons must be born to perpetuate the man's name! Power. Lineage. Lust – and all rushing for succour to the Bible.

USQUE: But the problem of interpretation was perplexing.

SHYLOCK: Naturally!

USQUE: And so to whom did they turn for guidance?

SHYLOCK: We can't wait to hear.

MOSES: To the bickering old Jews of Venice.

SHYLOCK: *You* know?

MOSES: Around 1530. Big quarrels.

RIVKA: Old fools of Venice, more like.

MOSES: And all a lot of nonsense. There was a man I remember came all the way from England to get the opinions of the Italian rabbis –

RIVKA: Who immediately formed different camps!

MOSES: Now what was his name – er – er –

USQUE: Richard Croke.

MOSES: Croke. Yes. Names! Why can't I remember names?

RIVKA: They didn't know the King of England or the Pope but they fought for them!

MOSES: I used to remember everybody's names. Age!

RIVKA: Old fools!

MOSES: Damn age!

USQUE: But, who do *you* think was right, Shylock? Remember my play will not be seeking interpretations of history, but of the Scriptures.

[JESSICA *enters and takes up her pose the other side of* SHYLOCK.]

SHYLOCK: You're late.

JESSICA: This is the last time I sit, father.

SHYLOCK: Don't you understand how insulting it is to be late for an appointment?

JESSICA: Signor Castelazzo was not held up by me.

SHYLOCK: This is my house, and while under my roof –

JESSICA [*challengingly*]: While under your roof, *what*?

SHYLOCK: An appointment is sacred.

JESSICA: You exaggerate.

SHYLOCK: To keep another waiting is to say to him you don't care for him.

JESSICA: Or that you care more for what you've left. Or that what you've left presented problems unanticipated. Or that what you've left was a dying man, you were needed, or you were compelled, or forced – really! Father! You're so full of tight, restricting little codes.

SHYLOCK: An appointment is a bond. Between two people. They depend upon each other honouring it, and if it's broken – lives can be affected, deals fall through, hearts broken, disappointment –

JESSICA: The scheme of things! The scheme of things! Stop lecturing me with your scheme of things.

MOSES: I have a painting to paint. Please.

USQUE: You've not answered my question, Signor Shylock.

SHYLOCK: Ask my daughter. She's the clever one.

USQUE: My new play, about a quarrel between rabbis, some interpreting Deuteronomy on behalf of the Papacy, others Leviticus on behalf of Henry the Eighth. The positions were this –

JESSICA: With respect, Signor Usque, I don't need to have their relative positions described. The idea is offensive. To scurry backwards and forwards in and out of the Bible's pages for such an obscene quarrel – the rabbis should have been ashamed of themselves. The cause doesn't interest me.

USQUE: The cause doesn't interest me, either, but the nature of interpretation does.

SHYLOCK [*but proud*]: Forgive her. She's had good tutors to exercise her mind but no mother to shape her manners.

RODERIGUES [*sketching furiously*]: But keep her angry, she looks beautiful when she's angry. Beautiful!

MOSES: Idiot!

RIVKA: I thought women today only looked beautiful when they were in love, Roderigues.

JESSICA [*topping her*]: This is the last time I pose, father.

SHYLOCK: You've told me already.

JESSICA: As you've told me a thousand times that this is your house and your roof.

SHYLOCK: Under which you are deprived of nothing.

JESSICA: Except the sweetness of feeling that it is *my* house and *my* roof also. You want a debate for your play, Signor Usque? Then debate this question: to whom does a house belong? Only the father? Not even the mother? And if not the children and the mother, then how must their relationship be described? As temporary occupants? As long standing visitors? At what point is the child's right of movement and taste taken into consideration? Does she only become whole when taken from the possession of her father to the possession of her husband? What do Leviticus and Deuteronomy have to say on those things? Look how my father swells with pride at his daughter's intellect. He's given me teachers to nourish and exercise my mind, while he continues to exercise control.

SHYLOCK: If she is talking about control and the child's right it can only mean she wants to go out again one day soon. I feel her tremors long before she erupts.

JESSICA: He talks as though the world elected him.

SHYLOCK: *She* talks as though the tutors' fees were well spent!

JESSICA: Tell him his daughter must be taken seriously.

SHYLOCK: Tell her she should not be neglecting her music studies.

JESSICA: Tell him you can be oppressed by study.

SHYLOCK: Dancing, singing, the instruments I bought for her – tell her.

JESSICA: Tell him not everyone wants to perform, some are content to listen.

SHYLOCK: Tell her –

JESSICA: Tell her, tell her! Tell her nothing more –

[*She storms out.* SHYLOCK *is shocked.*]

RIVKA: Mean! Mean! To withhold praise from your daughter, mean. From your own daughter.

SHYLOCK: The Talmud says: praise not a man more than ten per cent of his worth.

USQUE: Forgive me, Signor Shylock, I do not think you've judged well. You'll drive her into a hasty marriage.

RIVKA: He doesn't *want* her to marry.

[USQUE *turns to* SHYLOCK *for a response.*]

SHYLOCK: The *Pope* calls for the vows of chastity, but *God* only ever ordained matrimony. To whom should I listen?

[*But he is thinking of other things.*]

SCENE SEVEN

[ANTONIO'*s house.*

Present are BASSANIO, LORENZO *and* GRAZIANO. *They have just eaten.*

SHYLOCK *has been with them but is out of the room, unwell, accompanied by* ANTONIO.

Contented pause of men who've eaten, drunk and conversed well.]

GRAZIANO: Well, the poor Jew is very sick, for sure. He's been gone a quarter of an hour.

BASSANIO: I think you gave him too much wine.

LORENZO: Or the food was too rich for him.

BASSANIO: The man looked anxious. Worried. Sad.

GRAZIANO: I must say, he did drink fast. Very nervously. He came in and at once downed two glasses of wine.

LORENZO: It was not that. He eats and drinks and talks at the same time. There's no grace in the man.

BASSANIO: I find him most interesting. *You* see many Jews in Venice – at least ten thousand, I'd say –

GRAZIANO: Fourteen hundred.

BASSANIO: Really? As few as that? Well, they seem more. But where I lived, just outside Milan, we saw none. Everyone talked about them, but I'd never actually met one. So for me – interesting.

[SHYLOCK *and* ANTONIO *enter.*]

SHYLOCK: Oh, I love Venice.

GRAZIANO: A noble city, Signor Shylock, you're right.

LORENZO: You were born here, of course.

SHYLOCK: Yes, I was born here, of course.

LORENZO: I ask because so many of you come from here and there and everywhere.

SHYLOCK: I know why you ask.

LORENZO: It must be very difficult for your tribe to produce much of art or thought, as civilized nations do who have roots in territory.

SHYLOCK: Very.

LORENZO: Would you not agree that –

[SHYLOCK, *bored and despising* LORENZO, *turns aside to talk with his friend,* ANTONIO. *He's still a little drunk.*]

SHYLOCK: I love Venice, Antonio, because it's a city full of men busy living, and passing through, and free to do both as their right, not as a favour.

ANTONIO: Venice is distorted through your gratitude, Shylock, you've forgotten your yellow hat.

SHYLOCK: If I'd been a damned physician, I'd not have to wear this damned yellow hat every time I took a walk. Physician! Now *there* was a profession to belong to instead of my own seedy lineage. Failures! [*Pause.*] I descended from German Jews, you know. My grandparents. Grubby little things from Cologne. Came to Venice as small-time money lenders for the poor. But my parents – they tried a new profession. Very brave. Second-hand clothing! My mother went blind patching up smelly old clothes and my father became famous for beating out, cleaning and reconditioning old mattresses. Bringers of sleep – not a dishonourable trade don't you think, gentlemen? Mattresses: bringers of sweet sleep.

LORENZO: And sweet plagues.

SHYLOCK [*hisses*]: Yes! I know! Better than you, I know! [*Relaxing again.*] But he was not an ambitious man, my father. Had no confidence in himself. Not like the really big pawnbrokers, men who built up huge stores of carvings, furniture, paintings. For their banquets the Doges could always be certain of hiring dazzling tapestry in the Ghetto. Except from my father. Verminous vests you could get from him.

LORENZO: It's true. The Ghetto *is* notorious for its smells.

ANTONIO: I will not have discourtesies in my house.

LORENZO: You must forgive me, Signor Antonio. But I too am a guest, and we can't pretend that animosity doesn't exist between your guests. You ask me to respect your Jewish friend but what respect has he shown for me? Respect has no merit if it's unilateral. And disputation is a sacred right in our city. On several occasions this evening I've attempted to engage Signor Shylock in a theological discussion. He's turned away. If courtesy is esteemed then such a manner is not an efficacious way to achieve it.

SHYLOCK: Efficacious! Unilateral! Disputation! What a rich vocabulary! Perhaps I'm too frightened to dispute with you, friend Lorenzo. Yours is a university-trained mind. Mine is the Ghetto's.

BASSANIO: You must not be surprised if with such scorn you attract hostility.

LORENZO [*with evangelistic fervour*]: 'They are not humbled even unto this day, neither have they feared, nor walked in my law, nor in my statutes, that I have set before you and before your fathers.' Thus sayeth Ezekiel.

SHYLOCK: It was Jeremiah. Oh dear. You want theological disputation? Listen. You have us for life, gentlemen, for life. Learn to live with us. The Jew is the Christian's parent. Difficult, I know. Parent-children relationships, always difficult, and even worse when murder is involved within the family. But what can we do? It *is* the family! Not only *would* I be your friend but I *have* to be your friend. Don't scowl, Signor sweet Christian. For life. Old Shylock, Jew of Venice. For ever!

[*Long embarrassed pause.*]

GRAZIANO: Yes. Well. A very noble city. You are absolutely right, Shylock. We were discussing nobility the other night.

SHYLOCK: Now what is *he* talking about?

GRAZIANO: Nobility and power. What *is* the nature of nobility and in what does power reside?

SHYLOCK: Power? Were we talking about power?

GRAZIANO: Bassanio here believes that power resides in our ability to trade.

BASSANIO: Lorenzo-the-silent on the other hand believes power resides in the strength of moral superiority. Only Christian principle should activate our republic.

SHYLOCK: Good God! There was no one in the room when I was talking!

BASSANIO: While Graziano here believes power resides in the family who trades, which power in turn gives the family nobility.

GRAZIANO: Exactly! The *accumulated* knowledge of superiority *gives* one superiority: Venice is as a second Rome.

ANTONIO: Venice as a second Rome is nonsense. We're a commercial enterprise and no more.

BASSANIO: Come, Antonio, that's cynicism. I agree in part but that's not the whole truth. What about Venetian rule of law? Her Christian pride and fervour? All vital organs of the Empire.

ANTONIO: The most vital organs of our Empire are warehouses, ships' holds, barges and pack-horses. We're not even honest industrialists, we're simply importers and exporters, rich because the commerce of other people flows through us, not because we produce it ourselves. And as for Venice's sense of justice, it's to retain for her patricians the best opportunities for long-distance trade. Our motives are opportunist and our power rests on a geographical accident, so let's have no nonsense about Venice being a second Rome.

SHYLOCK: No, no, friend Antonio. Forgive me, I must quarrel with you as well. Oh, this is terrible. You defend me and I cross you. But I must. You both miss the point of Venice, of all Italy. Venice as Rome or not, as a commercial enterprise or not is irrelevant. What you say may be true but there is a scheme of things much grander. Let me remind you of three distinct developments affecting the history of this extraordinary land of yours and let's see where real power resides.

LORENZO: Are we now to be given a history lesson about our own lands by a German Jew?

SHYLOCK: Don't be offended, Lorenzo-the-silent. Remember, the synagogue existed in Rome before the Papacy.

GRAZIANO [incredulous]: The rabbi before the Pope?

SHYLOCK: The Roman wars. Jewish slaves. The captured princes of Israel. Now ssssh! And listen. It's a very thrilling story. Three developments! But first, who said: 'Religionem imperare non possumus –

ANTONIO: – quia nemo cogitur –

SHYLOCK: – ut credat invitus'? Mmm? How do you like my pronunciation of Latin, eh?

GRAZIANO: 'We cannot enforce acceptance of a creed, since no one can be compelled to believe against his will.'

SHYLOCK: Excellent, Graziano, bravo!

GRAZIANO: Had to learn it by heart at school.

SHYLOCK: But who said it?

[*Pause.*]

ANTONIO: Cassiodorus!

SHYLOCK: The last and lovely link between Imperial Rome and Gothic Italy.

ANTONIO: Born 479, died 575.

[*Then* SHYLOCK *tells his story with mounting excitement and theatricality, using whatever is around him for props, moving furniture, food, perhaps even people, like men on his chessboard of history.* ANTONIO *is singled out to be 'Cassiodorus'.*]

SHYLOCK: A sweet and intellectual man. Dubious elasticity of conscience, perhaps – always able to make himself necessary to the different rulers of the country, but still. A statesman! A scholar! And for what is this man remembered most? His administrations on behalf of monarchs? Never! During his life he'd succeeded in preserving through all the devastations of civil wars and foreign invasions a great collection of Greek and Roman manuscripts, and – here is development one.

At sixty he retires to Brutti taking with him his library of classics which he makes certain are scrupulously copied by the monks. *What* a work! What a faith! But why? Why should he have bothered? What makes one man so cherish the work of others that he lovingly guards it, copies, preserves it? And a Christian, too, preserving the works of pagans! From monastery to monastery, busy, busy, scribbling, for centuries, until the book trade creeps from the monasteries into the universities. The scholars take over from the monks. The pattern takes shape.

Development number two: the destruction of the Roman Empire! Italy breaks into three pieces. The north goes to the German Holy Roman Empire, the centre becomes dominated by the Papacy, and the French house of Anjou takes over the South. Look how fortunes change, rearrange themselves.

LORENZO: Your pleasure in history is superficial, Signor – playful. Its *patterns* please you but not its *meanings*. Such delight in chance is spiteful. You'd have us believe there was no cause and effect. I have no sympathy with such approaches.

SHYLOCK: Aha! Spirit! I might even come to respect you, young man, but –

LORENZO: And don't play with me, either, Signor.

SHYLOCK: But – you read me wrong if you believe I read history so carelessly. I'm perfectly aware how causes work their effects – but *within their time*. The line *I* stretch joins together men and moments who could never possibly have forecast one another's acts. Did old Cassiodorus working a thousand years ago see how Italy's development would shape a thousand years later? Hear me out. It's thrilling, thrilling – believe me.

The land in three pieces, then. But does everything stand still? Impossible! Watch in the north how the German Holy Roman Empire disintegrates; in the centre how the families of Rome brawl among themselves; in the south how the French house of Anjou fights the Spanish house of Aragon. Nothing stands still! And as the dust of war and madness settles what, gentlemen, is revealed? City States! The magnificent City States of Milan, Genoa, Florence, Venice! The Empires have broken up, and suddenly – every city is left to its own government. What can it do? How *does* one govern? Industry and trade grows. Can't help itself. What! The centre of the Mediterranean basin and *not* trade? So – the Italians invent partnership agreements, holding companies, marine insurance, credit transfers, double-entry book-keeping! Progress! But listen! Listen what else happened, and don't forget old Cassiodorus lurking away patiently down there in the sixth century. More business meant more complex agreements, which meant more law, which complicated the business of government, which meant men of greater education were needed, which meant a *new* kind of education, more practical, more – ah! worldly! And where, where I ask you, could that worldly, new education come from to produce that new law, the new government? Tell me. [*Pause.*] Why, from books! Where else? And where *were* the books? Old Cassiodorus! In the monasteries! He'd preserved the ancient manuscripts of Rome and Greece, hallelujah! Praise be to wise old men! Aren't you enjoying it? Admit it, doesn't it thrill you to watch it take shape! Be generous. Let yourselves go, for here comes development three.

The year 1450. Two beautiful births: a wily old German

from Mayence named Gutenberg gives birth to an extraordinary invention called – the printing press; and a great classical scholar named Aldus Manutius is born. Here! In our very own city of Venice, at the age of forty-five, less than a hundred years ago, the great Manutius sets up his divine press and produces the incredible Aldine Editions. Suddenly – everybody can possess a book! And what books! The works of – Plato, Homer, Pindar and Aristophanes, Xenophon, Seneca, Plutarch and Sophocles, Aristotle, Lysias, Euripides, Demosthenes, Thucydides, Herodotus, and all printed from manuscripts kept and preserved in monasteries as far apart as Sweden and Constantinople which Italians were now bringing back home. Amazing! Knowledge, like underground springs, fresh and constantly there, till one day – up! Bubbling! For dying men to drink, for survivors from dark and terrible times. I love it! When generals imagine their vain glory is all, and demagogues smile with sweet benevolence as they tighten their screws of power – up! Up bubbles the little spring. Bubble, bubble, bubble! A little, little lost spring, full of blinding questions and succulent doubts. The word! Unsuspected! Written! Printed! Indestructible! Boom! I love it!

[*Bells ring. Time to return to the Ghetto.* ANTONIO *rises to give* SHYLOCK *his yellow hat. He looks at* ANTONIO *and shrugs sadly, as though the hat is evidence to refute all he's said.*]

ANTONIO: What little lost spring can help you now?

[*And yet . . . he defiantly places it on his head, embraces* ANTONIO, *bows to the other three and goes off chuckling and mumbling . . .*]

SHYLOCK: Bubble, bubble, bubble! Bubble, bubble, bubble! Bubble, bubble . . .

ACT TWO

SCENE ONE

[*A room in Belmont. Time has passed. Some order is restored.* PORTIA *and* BASSANIO *in conversation.* NERISSA *reading.*]

BASSANIO: Wrong, madame, wrong! It may be true that trade in spices and the old wares is less profitable and safe these days, but land and agriculture are not where the fortunes lie. Precious metals! Trade in those. Gold! A bank! The bank of Contarini! – doesn't that thought dazzle you? Besides, where will you obtain your capital for implements?

PORTIA: I've sold estates, and will perhaps sell even more with your help, but now dear friend, you must choose. Choose wisely. None of the others did. Some chose swiftly, some with pride. Others stood thinking for so long they terrified themselves out of the simple ability to choose at all. So take your place and take your time. I'll talk with Nerissa. She's reading the letters of Seneca and I've asked her to select a favourite one. I think I know which one it will be.

[BASSANIO *takes up his place by the caskets.* NERISSA *approaches* PORTIA.]

NERISSA: This one, my lady, letter forty-seven. [*She begins to read.*] 'I'm glad to hear, from these people who've been visiting you, that you live on friendly terms with your slaves. It is just what one expects of an enlightened, cultivated person like yourself . . .'

[*Her voice lowers as the main melody takes over. Attention must be focused upon* BASSANIO.]

BASSANIO: What an eccentric test of love. Whose mind constructed this? 'By his choice shall you know him.' [*Contemptuously, and gradually drawn into a conversation with*

230

PORTIA'S FATHER *'up there'*.] What shall you know of him? That if he choose gold he will be a man without a soul, with a purse where his heart should be? But a man without a soul may have cunning, surely? Greed does not preclude perception, and a greedy man may cunningly perceive misfortune where his instinct leads. Suppose an even more human condition: the man who loves gold has plagues of guilt and may be ripe for self-disgust? Now there's a man who'd shy away from the shiny stuff. No, I don't see the point of such a simple trick. And silver? What's one supposed to think of that, stuck between gold and lead? Oh, here's the mediocre man! Here's the man plays safe with life and neither dares much nor achieves! Or is silver the test of the temperate man, the sober man? Perhaps the diplomat is being looked for here? The statesman? The judge? Not unworthy men! Yet I'm hardly any of those. A little bit of each in me I'd like to think, but – I hardly riot in those qualities. Still, if such a man is wanted for that extraordinary lady, and that extraordinary lady is what I want, then perhaps the statesman, diplomat and judge in me had *better* blossom. Hm! Not such a simple test after all. Come on now, Bassanio, use your wits. You've not survived this far without an arsenal of guile. Think! Think! What father, wanting his daughter to marry a statesman, diplomat or judge would devise such a scheme? A very wise father I'd say, if I didn't know that he was very stupid. Perhaps, then, a better question would be: does Portia look the kind of a daughter who'd have the kind of father who would *want* her to marry a statesman, diplomat or judge? [*Pause.*] I will go mad.

The wrong approach! These caskets can't be a test for a profession but – a sort, a kind, a spirit. The question then is: what kind of, sort of spirit would such a woman's father want for her? The father! Look to the father. He's the key. Good! That's something. So. The father descends from a long illustrious line. An aristocracy. But by the time the blood of rulers reached her father it had been watered down to the blood of a philosopher. And now, abundant though the estates' possibilities are, yet they're in ruin. Very decorous ruin, but – ruin. What metal would a ruined ruinous philosopher choose? [*Long pause, smile, he's seen through the strategy, but at first cunningly misleads.*] There can only be one answer. Simple! The end of philosophy is despair. He looked around him, saw the constant battles being fought, the waste, disintegration and decay, and he concluded: for my daughter, none of that! Gold! The hard, determined, merciless pursuit of gain, security and comfort. Gold! With gold is bought beauty, art, obedience, the power for good. Gold! For my daughter shall be trapped a man of gold. The sun is golden, the harvest too – energy and sustenance. These things I will, for my only child, these things which I with my engagement in philosophy neglected to provide. Gold! [*Pause.*] And then he changed his mind! For who can change the habits of a foolish lifetime? [*To* PORTIA.] Lead, my lady. Lead I choose. My brain has battled. There's its choice.

PORTIA: Your brain, Bassanio? Not your heart? Still, heart or brain, you've chosen as my father wished.

BASSANIO: Not you?

PORTIA: I? You must forgive me. It *is* possible for eyes to meet and feel their love at once, I know. But I'm not made that way. Love grows with me. My mother taught love ripens on the mind, is made of passions, laughter, all the minutiae of living *shared* rather than surmised. Is that pedantic, you think? Would you rather I embrace you now and say, with routine ardour, that *your* choice decides? Don't think from my response that I'm a calculating woman, though sometimes I wish I were. The truth is I'm impulsive. My responses shape at once. I know a man, a situation at a glance, but my mother said 'humility, your impulse may be wrong'. You'd rather have my love relaxed and confident, Bassanio? Be patient. We will live together. All I have is yours, you know that. Settle here. Rehearse the role of husband. We'll work together, find each other carefully. We *may* be born for one another, part of me believes we are. I want my *all* to know it though. See, I'm trembling as I talk. I think you must embrace me after all.

[*They embrace.*]

Now leave. I must arrange and scheme for you.

BASSANIO [*facilely*]: I have no words.

PORTIA [*catching the tone, cools*]: I'm touched.

> [BASSANIO *leaves.*]

> Perhaps I should be his mistress only. That gives him no holds over me then. As his wife the State chains me. *There's* something to exercise your logic on, Nerissa.

NERISSA: You're uncertain?

PORTIA: Oh, I am that.

NERISSA: You should not love someone you don't like.

PORTIA: What a ridiculous carrier of passion – a casket. I'm uncertain all right. What if I should tire of him? God forbid a woman should tire of a man. Of his vanities and little faults which always, always magnify with time. He has such a blindness for his image, such an incredible satisfaction with his long-considered thimbleful of thoughts, his firm decisive manner over that which should be racked with doubts, his silly coloured feathers which he feels to be his masculinity. Oh! his masculinity!

NERISSA: Have you watched the way a man walks? Careful that the width of him is seen? As though his shoulders balanced cannon-balls?

PORTIA: Such presumption! Such an air of arrogance! What else could woman be but his rib, a mere bone of his body? After all, my dear, men have won battles with a bone missing!

NERISSA [*lasciviously*]: And lost them even with one there!

> [*Great laughter between them.*]

PORTIA: Heaven help us, but there are so few poets among them!

NERISSA: They are such clumsy things. So weighed down with dull earthiness.

PORTIA: And worse at wooing-time! Then, ah! then – note that collapse of features which they feel is tenderness? That slow softening of the eyes into a milky melancholy they think is love-sick helplessness?

NERISSA: That sudden clenching of the jaw and fist which struggles to be passion?

PORTIA: What feeble and pathetic arts they have. And we must pretend! Poor gimcrack men! Oh! There are such stirrings in me. Such untried intellect. Such marvellous loves and wisdom. I could found cities with my strengths, Nerissa, cities undreamed of by any man.

[*Bells peal out as we change to –*]

SCENE TWO

[*The 'loggetta' beneath the campanile of St Mark's. Normally a meeting-place for patricians.*

TUBAL *and* RODERIGUES *approach from different parts. It is night.*]

TUBAL: Nothing?

RODERIGUES: Nothing!

TUBAL: You've asked discreetly?

RODERIGUES: Discreetly and indiscreetly. What do I care now!

TUBAL: The entire Ghetto is out looking for her, taking risks. Foolish girl.

RODERIGUES: 'I know your daughter,' I told him, I warned him.

TUBAL: You warned? I warned! Who didn't warn?

RODERIGUES: 'She's too intelligent to be constrained, too old to be teased and too hot to be predictable,' I told him.

TUBAL: Foolish girl!

RODERIGUES: But he understands nothing. 'If I'd beaten her, been a drunkard, gambled my money away like those other old men, playing cards and dice all day between synagogue services . . . But we loved one another!' As if loving helps!

TUBAL: Nor is that to be his only tribulation. There are other calamities in the wind. The sea's wind. Your clever patron signed a bond with his best friend, Antonio. It was to be a joke, to mock the laws of Venice: a loan of three thousand ducats with a pound of flesh as bond if, within three months, the loan was not repaid. And now –

RODERIGUES: A pound of flesh?

TUBAL: And now his ships are threatened.

RODERIGUES: A pound of flesh?

TUBAL: A pound of flesh, his ships in threat, the Ghetto penniless, and the time is up at six the evening after tomorrow.

RODERIGUES: A pound of *human* flesh?

TUBAL: Yes, yes, yes, YES!

RODERIGUES: But, of course, the ships are not sunk.

TUBAL: No! Captured only! By pirates. The market is buzzing with the news.

RODERIGUES: And the bond is a joke.

TUBAL: There are no more jokes left in this world, Roderigues. The next, perhaps – ach! I am so loath to lend and deal in this trade any more.

[*Enter* GRAZIANO.]

GRAZIANO: Ah, Signor Tubal, if anyone knows where Antonio is, it will be you.

RODERIGUES: Here comes everyman's everything and I'm in no mood for him.

TUBAL: What's the news of Antonio's ships?

GRAZIANO: Bad, bad, bad, oh bad.

TUBAL: Bad, we know. Facts we want.

GRAZIANO [*cheekily*]: The facts are that the news is bad.

TUBAL [*with powerful anger*]: No courtesies and games. Tell us the news.

GRAZIANO [*portentously*]: Grave. The news is grave. In view of how huge the cargo is the maritime office have ordered armed ships to the rescue.

TUBAL: Good, that's news worth taking back. Come, Roderigues.

GRAZIANO: But the damn winds are not helping, they fear a storm. The armed ships are paralysed.

TUBAL: Oh, Abraham! Abraham! Someone's God is angry. I'm too old for all this, too old, too old . . .

[TUBAL *and* RODERIGUES *leave*.]

GRAZIANO [*mocking as he, too, leaves*]: Oh Abraham, Abraham! I'm too old for all this, too old, too old . . .

[LORENZO *and* JESSICA *who have been looking for each other now meet, clutch one another in relief. She is agitated.*]

LORENZO: You're trembling.

JESSICA: I'm frightened and I'm ashamed, so I'm trembling.

LORENZO: Oh, those eyes. Those sad, sad eyes.

JESSICA: Forget my eyes, Lorenzo, and tell me what is to happen next.

LORENZO: First be calm, if for no other reason than not to command the staring of others.

JESSICA: I've spent so much, you see. It's cost so much.

LORENZO: I know, I know.

JESSICA: The decision to break away. You can't imagine. To be cut off.

LORENZO: I know.

JESSICA: So I'm drained. I'll be all right soon but for the next hours my reason is numb and you must do it all.

LORENZO: Trust me.

JESSICA: Kiss me.

[*He hesitates.*]

All these months of meetings and you've not kissed me.

[*He hesitates again.*]

Haven't you kissed a woman before?

LORENZO: A hand, a cheek.

JESSICA: Not lips?

LORENZO: Not lips.

JESSICA: Then mine will be the first for you.

LORENZO: And mine?

JESSICA: Will be the first for me.

[*They kiss.*]

Oh, I have known that kiss all my life.

LORENZO [*lifting her and whirling her round*]: Now, I would like to nail your name, proclaim you, claim you!

JESSICA: And say this is mine, and this, and here I've been before, and that skin, that smell, that touch so belongs, belongs, belongs that surely I was born the twin to it.

LORENZO: Nail your name and claim your strength!

[*They kiss as* SHYLOCK's *voice is heard.*]

SCENE THREE

[SHYLOCK's *study. He's trying to read a letter from his daughter.*]

SHYLOCK: 'Dear Father. I am not what you would like me to be, and what I am, brings me to this. To write more will urge

236

upon me the necessity to think more. I have thought and reassured enough, not conclusively, but sufficient to drive me out. Reflect on our quarrels. They have said all. Your daughter, Jessica.'

[RIVKA enters.]

RIVKA: And where has your joking got you?

SHYLOCK: I have a letter from my daughter, now be silent, Rivka.

RIVKA: Have you asked yourself why she's gone?

SHYLOCK: I'm trying to find out, don't nag at me.

RIVKA: Are you certain there was no wrong in *you*?

SHYLOCK: You're the only person I know who *asks* accusations.

RIVKA: Please, Shylock, I beg you. Be a kind man, be a considerate brother. I've no health for laughter. Be finished with joking.

SHYLOCK: I have a letter from my daughter.

RIVKA: You've read it seven times, already. Talk with me. I'm not a fool.

SHYLOCK: What would you have me talk about, sister?

RIVKA: The meaning of your bond.

SHYLOCK: It has meanings? Clauses, perhaps, but meanings?

RIVKA: Clauses, meanings, meanings, clauses! If *you* won't read the meanings like a man, then this old woman will. What you wanted to mock now mocks you! That's what your bond means.

SHYLOCK: I don't see what meaning that meaning means.

RIVKA: Oh yes you do.

SHYLOCK: I see problems. I see possibilities. I see maybes and perhapses. The problem of Antonio's ships captured, the possibility of rescue, though maybe the wind will delay it or perhaps Antonio's creditors will advance him more money and there'll be no problem because he'll have the possibility to repay me in time.

RIVKA: In time? What time? The clocks will soon strike six and that will only leave one day.

SHYLOCK: I must hear this nonsense through, I suppose.

RIVKA: Don't be rude to me, Shylock! You have a friend. Good. A Gentile and gentle man. Good. You made some peace for yourself. I was happy for you. Good. But could you leave it like that, my wise man, always throwing his voice, his ideas about, on this, on that, here, there, to anyone, could you leave it well alone like that? Oh Shylock, my young brother. I've watched you, wandering away from Jewish circles, putting your nose out in alien places. I've watched you be restless and pretend you can walk in anybody's streets. Don't think I've not understood you; suffocating in this little yard, waiting for your very own scholar to arrive. It made me ache to watch you, looking for moral problems to sharpen your mind, for disputations – as if there weren't enough troubles inside these peeling walls. But you *can't* pretend you're educated, just as you can't pretend you're not an alien or that this Ghetto has no walls. Pretend, pretend, pretend! All your life! Wanting to be what you're not. Imagining the world as you want. And now, again, as always, against all reason, this mad pretence that Antonio's ships will come in safe. [*Pause*]. You've mocked their law.

SHYLOCK: Which mocked at us.

RIVKA: A hero! Shylock to the defence of his people. Can't you see what you've done?

SHYLOCK: Asserted dignity, that's what I've done.

RIVKA: That? That's what you've done? Nothing else? [*Pause*.] To assert the dignity of your mocked people you have chained your friend's life to a mocking bond, *that's* what you've done.

SHYLOCK: Go to your room, Rivka, you're becoming excited.

RIVKA: Shylock! Go and find the money! Knock on every Ghetto door, beg, plead, bully – but get it. Now. Before it's too late.

SHYLOCK: Foolish woman. Do you think I haven't tried. The Ghetto is drained. The last tax emptied every purse.

RIVKA: Then let him borrow from his friends.

SHYLOCK: They don't trust his future now.

RIVKA: Then plead with the court to bend the law and relieve you of your bond.

SHYLOCK: Tomorrow. Tomorrow we'll talk about it.

RIVKA: But not everyone in the Ghetto will agree to the bending of the law, will they?

SHYLOCK: Please, Rivka.

RIVKA: Having bent the law for us, they'll say, how often will the Venetians bend it for themselves, and then we'll live in even greater uncertainties than before. They'll be divided, as you are, my clever brother. Who to save – your poor people or your poor friend?

SHYLOCK: We'll talk about it tomorrow.

RIVKA: You want moral problems to sharpen your mind?

SHYLOCK: Tomorrow, tomorrow.

RIVKA: And who *will* you save? The one foreign friend you love or the families of your blood you barely know? [*Pause.*] Well, am I a fool or not? Are there to be jokes or not? Have you a problem or not?

SHYLOCK: Tomorrow, tomorrow. We'll talk about it tomorrow.

RIVKA: Tomorrow! Tomorrow! *What* tomorrow? The clocks will soon strike six and it will be tomorrow. [*Long pause. She rises to leave.*] Me you can get out of the way, your problem – not! [*She leaves.*]

[SHYLOCK *turns to his letter.*]

SHYLOCK [*aloud*]: 'Reflect on our quarrels. They have said all. Your daughter, Jessica.' [*It is as though he has not understood.*] 'Our quarrels.' What quarrels? How could she have called them quarrels? *Enemies* quarrel. 'I am not what you would like me to be.' *What* did I want you to be, Jessica? My prop, my friend, my love, my pride? Not painful things, those. Are they?

Oh, Jessica. What wretched, alien philosophy has taken up your mind, muddied it with strange fervours? Where are you now? Oh, vulnerable youth. You must be so lonely. So lost and lonely. So amazed and lost and lonely. Oh daughter, daughter, daughter.

[ANTONIO *enters. He too appears burdened with worries. They confront each other in silent and all-knowing commiseration, then embrace.*

SHYLOCK *at once begins to fuss over his friend, sitting him down, pouring wine.*]

SHYLOCK: It'll be all right. Your ships will find their harbour and my daughter will find her home.

ANTONIO: But whose harbour and whose home and when?

SHYLOCK: Ah! I see you're gloomy.

ANTONIO: And I see you pretend you're not.

SHYLOCK: And supposing you lose your ships, what? You've no credit, no friends? What?

ANTONIO: I'm in debt to all Venice.

SHYLOCK: No skills to start again?

ANTONIO: Shylock, your own loss has stupefied you. Can you see me starting again? Wanting to? I've lived too long cushioned by huge sums, I'm not only naked without them, but my judgement's been flabbied by them.

SHYLOCK: Oh, now –

ANTONIO: Don't protest. You're evading the implications.

SHYLOCK: What, of a ship sinking or a daughter fleeing?

ANTONIO: Jessica's disappearance is a sad and awful thing, but other threats press.

SHYLOCK: Drink! I think we both need a little, little helpful drink.

ANTONIO: The implications must be faced and talked about.

SHYLOCK: Nothing presses, nothing threatens, – drink.

ANTONIO: We've signed a foolish bond.

SHYLOCK: The bond will not be called upon – drink.

ANTONIO: It's known the ships were attacked, and my entire fortune staked in a single convoy. We've signed a foolish bond.

SHYLOCK: The storm will drop.

ANTONIO: We've signed a foolish bond, whose forfeiture is due.

SHYLOCK: The maritime office's fleet will sail – drink.

ANTONIO: At six o'clock there will be only twenty-four more hours to go.

SHYLOCK: Perhaps the days have been miscounted.

ANTONIO: SHYLOCK! [*Pause.*] What will you do with a knife in your hand and my flesh to weigh?

    [*Long pause.*]

    [SOLOMON USQUE *and* REBECCA *arrive.*]

REBECCA: Signor Shylock, is it true? We heard that your daughter is missing.

SHYLOCK: No commiserations, please. You're welcome. I love my friends around me, but there's been no death in my family, simply – a holiday. Every young person must have a holiday from home. Sit. I'll pour drink for you. Are you hungry? Tell me news.

REBECCA: Little change, families wanting passage to Constantinople, old men waiting for our funds for their voyage to Jerusalem, but your daughter, Signor.

SHYLOCK: Who can write plays in such misery, eh, Signor Usque?

USQUE: Who is there *great* enough to write plays in such misery!

SHYLOCK: Ah ha! Who is there great enough to write plays in such misery!

[TUBAL *and a crestfallen* RODERIGUES *arrive.* SHYLOCK *looks to them expectantly.*]

RODERIGUES: I told you! I warned! [TUBAL *stays him.*]

TUBAL: She has joined the man called Pisani.

SHYLOCK: Pisani?

TUBAL: They left last night for an estate named Belmont.

SHYLOCK: Lorenzo Pisani? A nothing! A man of whom it can only be said, 'He's there!'

A sour, silly young man with little talent but that of envy, who confuses complaint for protestation, and even that betrays with a lazy mind. Jessica! you have been grabbed by air!

[GRAZIANO *enters. Everyone knows what he has come to announce. They wait. He's terrified both of such an audience and the news he brings. He wants to hand the list to* ANTONIO.]

ANTONIO: Read me the list. [*Pause.*] Yes, here.

GRAZIANO: A ship carrying raisins from the Island of Zante, olive oil from Corfu and the cotton from Syria. Another with wine, corn, and cheese from Crete. The Danish ship you chartered for the English cloth and the Spanish wool. The assignment of timber and, the last, from –

ANTONIO: – from the sugar estates of Cyprus. All. They have taken or sunk the consignment I swore would be my last. I do not possess one ducat, Shylock.

[A clock strikes six. TUBAL motions to the others that they
should leave the two friends alone.]

ANTONIO: I cannot raise the money now.

SHYLOCK: I know.

ANTONIO: Nor can you lend it me again.

SHYLOCK: The Ghetto's drained, I know.

[Long pause.]

SHYLOCK: They'll let us drop the bond.

ANTONIO: We cannot, must not.

SHYLOCK: You understand?

ANTONIO: I understand.

SHYLOCK: I'm frightened that you don't.

ANTONIO: I do.

SHYLOCK: I will not bend the law.

ANTONIO: I understand.

SHYLOCK: I must not set a precedent.

ANTONIO: I know.

SHYLOCK: You said. You taught.

ANTONIO: Shylock, Shylock! I'm not afraid.

SHYLOCK: Oh friend! What have I done to you?

[Pause.]

ANTONIO: An act of schoolboy defiance when such times
should be taken seriously.

SHYLOCK: I know.

ANTONIO: Your yellow hat belongs to both of us. We shall
both be put to death.

SHYLOCK: I know.

ANTONIO: I by you. You by them.

SHYLOCK: I know, I know.

ANTONIO: We know, we know! We keep saying we know so
much.

SHYLOCK: Gently, gently, dear friend. I'm not afraid either.

[Pause.]

Just promise me silence in the trial.

ANTONIO: Will we make no explanations? The court must
understand.

SHYLOCK: Understanding is beyond them! I protect my people
and my people's contract. Besides, honour would be accorded

me if I pleaded such explanations. 'He saved his people!' It would be grotesque. Just promise me silence at the trial.

ANTONIO: That's contempt, Shylock. Unworthy of you.

SHYLOCK: You must let my pride have its silence.

ANTONIO: They won't think it's pride, they will mistake your silence for contempt.

SHYLOCK: Perhaps they will be right. I am sometimes horrified by the passion of my contempt for men. Can I be so without pity for their stupidities, compassion for their frailties, excuses for their cruelties? It is as though these books of mine have spoken too much, too long: the massacres by kings, the deathly little spites of serfs, the oppressive jealousies and hurts of scholars, who had more learning than wisdom. Too much, Antonio, too much. Seeing what men have done, I know with great weariness the pattern of what they will do, and I have such contempt, such contempt it bewilders me. Surely, I say to myself, there is much to be loved and cherished. I tell myself, force myself to remember. Surely? Sometimes I succeed and then, ha! I'm a good man to know, such a good man. Children warm to me in the streets. They don't cry out 'Shylock Old Jew' then. No, they skip at my side and hold my hand, and on those days I walk so upright, like a young man, and I feel myself respected and loved. And I love myself also. Why, you rush to ask, if such joy comes to us through praising men, why do we not praise them all the time? You ask! The balance, dear friend, the balance! Take those books, one by one, place on one side those which record men's terrible deeds, and on the other their magnificence. Deed for deed! Healing beside slaughter, building beside destruction, truth beside lie. [Pause.] My contempt, sometimes, knows no bounds. And it has destroyed me.

ANTONIO: Ah, Shylock, Shylock, why didn't we know one another when young?

SHYLOCK [smiling]: I'd have been wiser you mean?

ANTONIO: No, fool! It was myself I was thinking of.

SHYLOCK: I love thee. Antonio.

ANTONIO: And I thee, old man.

SCENE FOUR

[*Belmont. The garden.*
PORTIA. BASSANIO *enters with* LORENZO *and* JESSICA.]

BASSANIO: My dear friends. What a pleasure to meet people you love in new places. Lorenzo, here she is. You've heard her described, now you see her in the flesh. Here, Portia, is the man I spoke to you about – philosopher, prophet, a man who may one day lead Venice – Lorenzo Pisani.

PORTIA: I hope, Signor Lorenzo, you are not as intimidated by what is expected of you as I feel stripped by the words describing me! Nevertheless, says flesh to prophet: welcome!

BASSANIO: And Jessica welcome too. We've not met before and so both Portia and I have this pleasure together.

PORTIA: Oh those sad eyes.

LORENZO: We're honoured and grateful for your hospitality but those sad eyes carry sad news.

BASSANIO: Whose sad news?

LORENZO: Antonio's sad news. The ships are gone. The wreck of one was found and it's assumed the others either shared the same fate or have been taken off for use by the pirates.

PORTIA: But I don't understand the problem. Antonio owes Shylock three thousand ducats. What's that? I'm able to raise that sum and more besides to set him up in trade again.

LORENZO: No good! The hour is up and the Jew has turned mad. He accepts no deviation from his contract and Antonio insists upon sharing responsibility for it. The dilemma for the Doge is unprecedented. 'My people! My bond! My people! My bond!' as though the Jewish population were in threat instead of a poor, beguiled friend of the Jew who must now have the skin of his breast scraped from his bones.

JESSICA: Forgive me, Lorenzo . . . but . . .

LORENZO: You're right. My anger's made me indelicate.

JESSICA: It's not simply that –

BASSANIO: I warned him! A Jew to be trusted?

JESSICA: Please! Gentlemen! Remember me! I'm raw. My

rhythms still belong to the Ghetto. I can't slip so quickly from God to God like a whore.

LORENZO: Jessica!

JESSICA: Yes, I'm also angry. You misrepresent the bond. Whatever else my father's flaws you know the bond had mockery not malice in it.

PORTIA: And that I understand. There's not enough of mockery in Venice. We're a city boasting very little of intelligent self-scrutiny or ridicule. But to mock the law is one thing, to squeeze it of its last punitive drop is another.

JESSICA: He must have his reasons.

PORTIA [warmly]: You must be hungry. Nerissa and I have prepared a light meal. Nothing too heavy.

BASSANIO: And I must prepare my luggage. Antonio will expect me to be near him while the court conducts its inquiries.

LORENZO: I'll join you, there's a principle affecting the future of Venice tied up in this case. Someone must air it.

BASSANIO [leaving]: Forgive me?

PORTIA: The decision is yours. [To LORENZO.] I'll be very happy to look after your Jessica for you. It's a tragic affair but there's nothing we can do in it.

[PORTIA follows BASSANIO off.]

LORENZO: 'Those eyes.' They tell me I'm unworthy of you, that I don't appreciate your sacrifice. I do. Have courage. You've joined the world now.

JESSICA [sardonically]: Is that what I've joined?

LORENZO: Come, lie in my arms these last minutes. You're shocked still. Let me tell you about yourself.

JESSICA [trying to relax]: Oh do, Lorenzo, do tell me about myself, what I've done. Make sense of my actions for me. It seemed such a natural, inevitable thing to do. And now this bond, this wretched stupid bond threatens, threatens.

LORENZO: Hush, then.

JESSICA: I feel so full of discontent.

LORENZO: Quiet, then.

JESSICA: As though it's not in me ever to be happy.

LORENZO: Ssssssh!

JESSICA: I'm frightened and . . .

LORENZO: Sssssssh!

JESSICA: All right. I'm quiet. Look. Start.

LORENZO [after a pause, portentously]: Some families are doomed.

JESSICA: That's not a very joyful start.

LORENZO: You should find all truths joyful.

JESSICA: Oh dear.

LORENZO: Even unhappy ones.

JESSICA: Oh dear, dear.

[He wants to be solemn. She tries to be gay.]

JESSICA: So, some families are doomed.

LORENZO: Parents have ill-chosen one another.

JESSICA: Parents have ill-chosen one another, so?

LORENZO: So, as parents can ill-choose one another, similarly can men ill-choose one another, similarly can men ill-choose their gods.

[JESSICA, slowly realizing with disgust his meaning, rises angrily, and backs away.]

JESSICA: I see.

LORENZO: Not with those reproachful eyes, Jessica. You know that is the truth about yourself. The sadness Portia saw was also of a forsaken race, married to a God they'd thought had chosen them. Doomed!

JESSICA [icily]: You think so?

LORENZO: But there are always survivors. I will make you a wife, a woman and a Christian.

JESSICA [with controlled fury]: Sometimes I think the sadness in my eyes comes from the knowledge that we draw from men their desperate hates. Poisons rise in our presence, idiocies blossom, and angers, and incredible lapses of humanity. That is my doom! to know that secret: that at any time, for any reason, men are capable of such demented acts. So I regard a stranger with dread, reproach, fear. Forever vigilant. That's difficult for him to bear, to be looked at like that, for no reason, to be thought guilty before the act, to be known for the beast in one, the devil in the making. Who can forgive eyes that have such knowledge in them?

LORZENO: I see there's a great deal of unthreading to do.

JESSICA: Yes, I see there is.

[NERISSA *enters.*]

NERISSA: Signor Lorenzo, you must leave at once. The wind is right. I've prepared food for your journey.

LORENZO: There's no better place to be left, Jessica.

[*He embraces her. She cannot respond.*]

Trust me, please.

[LORENZO *leaves.*

JESSICA *looks very much alone.*

PORTIA *enters. At once, women together, they relax.*]

PORTIA: Good, the three of us alone. Talk to me, Jessica. Tell me about the Ghetto. My tutor in Hebrew studies was a strange man called Abraham Cardoso. He came from the Ghetto.

JESSICA: We knew him.

PORTIA: You did? What a coincidence.

JESSICA: Hardly a coincidence, madame, the quarter is so small.

PORTIA: And the buildings. So tightly packed together.

JESSICA: Yes. Always a danger of fire. Last week one young man, a friend in fact, threw himself into the flames attempting to save his mother. [*It's all too much for her. She is weeping. After a moment –*]

PORTIA: Tell me what you love in him.

JESSICA: I loved his questioning the wisdom of age, his clamouring to give youth its voice, his contempt for what men wrote in books. His strength, his seriousness, his devotion. I loved, I suppose, escape from oppressive expectations.

PORTIA: And now?

JESSICA: Now, I'm feeling his strength is arrogance, his seriousness is pedantry, his devotion is frenzy, and I am confused and drained and without ground beneath my feet.

PORTIA: And the truth about the bond?

JESSICA: Antonio asked my father for the loan which he would have given ten times over without a contract.

PORTIA: Shylock didn't want a contract?

JESSICA: Not with his dear friend, no. They almost quarrelled,

till Antonio finally persuaded him – the law must be respected!
The Jews have need of the laws of Venice and so – the bond, in
defiance.

PORTIA: Then I understand nothing.

NERISSA: Why don't *you* attend the court in Venice, madame?

PORTIA: Attend the court in Venice?

NERISSA: Perhaps you'll understand more there.

PORTIA: And having understood, what then?

NERISSA: A word, a thought, have faith in that 'untried intellect'.

PORTIA: Faith in that 'untried intellect' I have, but knowledge
of the law I have none.

NERISSA: Perhaps it isn't law that's needed.

PORTIA: But there's so much work to do here.

NERISSA: Two men's lives are at stake.

PORTIA: But not men I know.

NERISSA: One, her father.

PORTIA: What can I do? I pity men their mad moments but a
bond is a bond. The law demands its forfeitures. A pound of
flesh is a satanic price to conceive, even as a joke but – [*She
becomes a woman struck, as if by revelation. She can't believe
the thought that has come to her. She rejects it but it persists.*]
Holy Mary mother of Christ! I have it! But no. No! No, no, no,
no, it's too simple. The law is complex, devious. This is common
sense. Justice. The law is not to do with justice. No. It *can't* be
applicable. And yet – who could possibly deny . . . the law
may not be just when it demands strict adherence to an
agreement which may cause misery, but it does demand strict
adherence. Then surely . . . dare I? I'm no advocate. My temper's
not for public places . . . and yet . . . a wrong is a wrong . . .

JESSICA: To whom is she speaking?

PORTIA [*triumphantly*]: Why don't we all three go to Venice
and attend the court? There is a contract I must scrutinize and
a father with whom you should be.

JESSICA: Are women granted entry to the courts?

PORTIA: They'll grant these women entry to the courts!

[*The scene immediately becomes the Courtroom of the Doge's
Palace.*]

SCENE FIVE

[*The women turn and sweep into the Courtroom of the Doge's Palace, Venice.*

PORTIA *and* NERISSA *walk straight up to ask the* DOGE *permission to enter. He grants it.* PORTIA *whispers to him. They leave together.* JESSICA *is embraced by* RIVKA *and* TUBAL, NERISSA *moves to the Christian side where are* BASSANIO, LORENZO *and* GRAZIANO. *Present are* USQUE, REBECCA, RODERIGUES *and* SENATORS.]

[*The* YOUNG MEN *are surprised.*]

BASSANIO: Portia!

LORENZO: Jessica!

BASSANIO: Did the women say they were coming?

LORENZO: On the contrary, Portia felt there was nothing to be done.

BASSANIO: Nor is there. Silence! For two hours this court of inquiry has had nothing but silence from him. Shylock! Will you speak?

[*No response.*]

He says nothing, offers no explanation, simply claims the bond.

JESSICA: Explain it to them, father, explain!

[SHYLOCK *growls and turns away. He hates scorning her, but can't help himself. She retires in distress to the Christian side.*]

BASSANIO: Look at that scowl. Have you ever seen such meanness in a face before? [*To* SHYLOCK.] He was your friend! You boasted a Gentile for a friend!

GRAZIANO: When a man says nothing you can be sure he hides evil and guilt, you can be sure.

BASSANIO: But why hasn't Antonio said something?

GRAZIANO: Well, of course, he wouldn't. Bewitched, wasn't he? Forced into the bond. [*Calling out.*] What did you say, old Jew? Not only would I be your friend, but I have to be your friend. Friendship? Ha!

BASSANIO: Shylock, will you speak?

LORENZO: Perhaps it's not Shylock who should speak but some of our own city councillors. Why were they silent? What Jewish money do they owe? It must be huge if they're prepared to let a fellow citizen be skinned alive. [*Calling out.*] Fellow Venetians, is this city so far gone in its quest for profit and trade that there's no morality left? Usury is a sin against charity. When God had finished his creation he said unto man and unto beasts, and unto fishes, increase and multiply, but did he ever say increase and multiply unto money?

ANTONIO: Profit is the fruit of skill, young man!

JESSICA: And this bond was the fruit of friendship, Lorenzo, not usury, you know it!

TUBAL: Besides, most people at some moments in their life become short of money – illness . . .

USQUE: . . . A bad harvest . . .

RODERIGUES: . . . Domestic misfortune . . .

TUBAL: What shall they do? I mean it's a problem!

LORENZO: I promise you that when the young patricians take their seats there'll be more God than Mammon on our statute books. Usury is a sin against charity. The –

TUBAL: And to deprive the people of an opportunity to obtain help is a sin against humanity!

LORENZO [*ignoring him*]: Usury is a sin against charity. The –

TUBAL: Listen to me!

LORENZO: The people suffer from it!

ANTONIO: The people suffer from ignorance, Lorenzo, believe me. To deprive them of knowledge is the sin.

LORENZO: Knowledge! Knowledge! How Shylock's books have muddied your mind. A man can be strong and happy with no knowledge, no art. Turn to the shepherd and the tiller and the sailor who know of the evils of usury, without books, without art. Real knowledge, simple knowledge is in the wind and seasons and the labouring men do.

ANTONIO: You say a man is happy with no knowledge or art? There is wisdom in the wind, you say? The seasons tell all there is to know of living and dying? I wonder? Is it really understanding we see in the shepherd's eye? Is the tiller told more than the thinker? I used to think so, sitting with sailors roughened by salt, listening to their intelligence. They perceive much, I'd say to myself. But as I sat a day here, a day there, through the years, their intelligence wearied me. It repeated itself, spent itself upon the same complaints, but with no real curiosity. How alive is a man with muscles but no curiosity? You wonder why I bind my fate to Shylock, what I see in him? Curiosity! *There* is a driven man. Exhilarating! I thank the shepherd for my clothes and the tiller for my food, good men. Blessed. Let them be paid well and honoured. But they know, I, we know: there is a variousness to be had in life. Why else does the labourer send his sons to schools when he can? He knows what self-respect knowledge commands. All men do, wanting for their children what fate denied them, living without meat and keeping warm with mere sticks to do it. I'd have died before now if no man had kindled my soul with his music or wasn't there with his bright thoughts keeping me turning and taught about myself. Yes. Even at such an hour, I remember these things. Don't talk to me about the simple wisdom of the people, Lorenzo. Their simple wisdom is no more than the ignorance we choose to keep them in.

[*Silence.*]

GRAZIANO: As I thought. Bewitched. A knife hangs over him and he defends the man who holds it.

LORENZO: Be quiet, Graziano.

GRAZIANO: Lorenzo!

LORENZO: Stop meddling. You're a fool! The situation is too complex for you and I've not time for your tavern tattle.

BASSANIO: Quiet now. The Doge is ready.

[*The* DOGE *returns to the official proceeding leaving* PORTIA *to continue perusing papers.*]

DOGE: Antonio Querini?

ANTONIO [*stepping forward*]: Most serene Prince.

DOGE: Shylock Kolner?

SHYLOCK: Most serene Prince.

DOGE: This court has never had before it such a case. The issue's clear, the resolution not. We must retrace and nag at it again. Signor Shylock, are you fully aware that the court is prepared to release both parties from the need to see this contract through?

SHYLOCK: I am, Excellency.

DOGE: Yet you refuse, and state no reason?

SHYLOCK: I refuse and state no reason. Yes.

DOGE: And do you know this man may bleed to death?

SHYLOCK: I have our greatest doctors standing by.

DOGE: To do what? What can even Jewish doctors do to stem such awful draining of a man's life-blood? A strange perverted charity is that. You, Querini, dear fellow patrician, we beg you break your silence, or does this man have some hold over you? We've noticed your absence from the Council's meetings. You once enjoyed the affairs of running our city. Tell the court. Don't be afraid. What has happened?

ANTONIO [*impatiently*]: Nothing has happened, Excellency, more than I've lost my appetite for the intrigues and boredom of administration, but this has nothing to do with our humiliation in this court. Please, may we proceed.

DOGE: Then *you* say why we're here humiliated in this court. Say why you shared the madness of a bond which twice endangers you: from a man insisting that you pay a forfeiture of flesh, and from the law which must punish you for mocking it.

   [*No response.*]

   Your silence does not help.

GRAZIANO: I knew it! I told it! I warned it!

ANTONIO: Graziano, be quiet!

GRAZIANO: A plot! A plot! A Jewish plot!

ANTONIO: Be quiet, I say.

GRAZIANO: I can't be quiet, I love you.

ANTONIO: You love no one and nothing but a safe place with the multitude. Now be quiet.

DOGE: Why do you attack your friends, Antonio? These men who've come to speak for you? And why are you not speaking for yourself?

   [*Pause.*]

LORENZO: Incredible! The man has even chained his victim to silence. Most serene Prince, I beg you –

DOGE: Be careful!

LORENZO: – the reason for humiliation in this court is linked with principles which go beyond this case.

DOGE: Do not attempt to make capital!

LORENZO: We should not be inquiring into silence but questioning if Jews and usury, no matter what the bond, should be permitted to pollute the fabric of our city's life. The real question is –

TUBAL: Do you think we enjoy lending to your poor at the high rate your city imposes . . .?

LORENZO: . . . the real question is . . .

RODERIGUES: Collect for your poor among yourselves!

LORENZO: . . . the real question is . . .

USQUE: You have pious fraternities, collect from them for your poor!

TUBAL: Or use taxes!

LORENZO: . . . THE REAL QUESTION IS . . .

DOGE: The question of the city's contracts with the Jews is a matter for the Council. The laws of Venice are very clear and precise and cannot be twisted this way and that for political significance or gain, nor denied to foreigners, otherwise justice will not obtain. And the principal foundation of our city is justice. The people of Venice must have justice.

ANTONIO [*finally angry*]: Justice? For the people of Venice? The people? When political power rests quite firmly in the hands of two hundred families? That, though he talks of principle, is what Lorenzo is impatient for, to share that power. You use the people's name for through their grievances you'll come to power. One of their grievances is what you call usury. The usurer's a Jew, and the Jew the people's favourite villain. Convenient! Easy! But usury *must* exist in our city. We have many poor and our economy can't turn without it. The Jew practises what he hates because we have forbidden him rights to practise other professions. *He* relieves *us* of the sin. Do we condemn the Jew for doing what our system has *required* him to do? Then if we do, let's swear, upon the cross, that among us we know of no Christian, no patrician, no duke, bishop or merchant who, in his secret chambers, does not lend at interest, for that is what usury is. Swear it! On the cross! No one, we know no one! [*Pause.*] Who's silent now? [*Pause.*] You will inflame the people's grievances in order to achieve power, Lorenzo, but once there you'll sing such different songs I think.

DOGE: You do not make inquiry easy for this court, Signor.

BASSANIO: How can you make inquiries into silence, most serene Prince, the inhuman silence of an arrogant chosen people. Heretical! They still refuse to acknowledge that they are no *longer* the chosen people.

SHYLOCK: Oh horror of horrors! Oh heresy of heresies! Oh sweat! Oh flutter! Oh butterflies, gooseflesh, hair-on-end! Oh windbag of windbags! And *you* I suppose, have been chosen instead?

LORENZO [*flooding the proceedings with conciliatory warmth and charm*]: Most serene Prince. If my friend misapplies the word inhuman, we can perhaps understand. But I must pursue my original plea and ask the court to remember this: the Signor Shylock is not here because he is a Jew. The patricians of Venice are good men and justly fear being accused of such prejudice. No! What is on trial in this court is, I insist, the principle of usury whose evil this bond so tragically exemplifies, and from whose consideration we should not be distracted. The *bond* is inhuman, not the man.

USQUE: Then put Venetian law on trial. The law gave birth to this bond.

LORENZO [*ignoring that*]: The bond is inhuman, not the man. No one doubts the Jew is human. After all, has not a Jew eyes?

SHYLOCK: What is *that* fool attempting now?

LORENZO: Has not a Jew hands?

SHYLOCK: Is he presuming explanations on *my* behalf?

LORENZO: Has not a Jew organs, dimensions, senses, affections, passions?

SHYLOCK [*with incredulity*]: Oh no!

LORENZO: Is not the Jew fed with the same food, hurt with the same weapons, subject to the same diseases, healed by the same means, warmed and cooled by the same winter and summer as a Christian is?

SHYLOCK: No, no!

LORENZO: If you prick him, does he not bleed?

SHYLOCK: No, no, NO! I will not have it. [*Outraged but controlled.*] I do not want apologies for my humanity. Plead for me no special pleas. I will not have my humanity mocked and apologized for. If I am unexceptionally like any man then I need no exceptional portraiture. I merit no special pleas, no special cautions, no special gratitudes. My humanity is my right, not your bestowed and gracious privilege.

GRAZIANO: See how ungrateful the Jew is? I knew it! I told it! I warned it! The Jew was silent because he knew that the moment he opened his mouth he'd hang himself with his arrogance. The Jew . . .

SHYLOCK [*furious but low and dangerous, building*]: Jew! Jew, Jew, Jew! I hear the name around and everywhere. Your wars go wrong, the Jew must be the cause of it; your economic systems crumble, there the Jew must be; your wives get sick of you – a Jew will be an easy target for your sour frustrations. Failed university, professional blunderings, self-loathing – the Jew, the Jew, the cause the Jew. And when will you cease? When, when, when will your hatreds dry up? There's nothing we can do is right. Admit it! You will have us all ways won't you? For our prophecies, our belief in universal morality, our scholarship, our command of trade, even our ability to survive. If we are silent we must be scheming, if we talk we are insolent. When we come we are strangers, when we go we are traitors. In tolerating persecution we are despised, but were we to take up arms we'd be the world's marauders, for sure. Nothing will please you. Well, damn you then! [*Drawing knife.*] I'll have my pound of flesh and not feel obliged to explain my whys and wherefores. Think what you will, you will think that in any case. I'll say it is my bond. The law is the law. You need no other reason, nor shall you get it – from me.

[*He turns to the* DOGE, *justice must be done.* ANTONIO *joins him on the other side of the* DOGE. *They turn to face one another – doomed friends. Though no Jew must take another's life yet* SHYLOCK *has made the decision to damn his soul for the community which he feels is threatened.*]

PORTIA: Most serene Prince, I have read the documents.

[*Pause.*] Your Excellency, forgive my presumption, I know nothing of the law, but I cannot see that there is sufficient detail in this contract to make it legally valid.

[*Murmurs in court.*]

And if not valid, then not binding.

[*Excitement grows.*]

But I'm anxious in case my intelligence is merely foolish faith in little more than a hair of the law.

DOGE: The courts of Venice are open to justice no matter how tenuous a hair binds it to the law.

PORTIA: Then it seems to me this contract contains nothing but contradictions.

[*Tense silence.*]

There is in this bond a call for flesh but none for blood.

[*Noise in court.*]

There is in this bond a call for a precise pound weight but none for more or less.

[*Growing noise.*]

It cannot be executed because torn flesh draws blood.

[*Still growing noise.*]

It cannot be executed because precise weight cannot be achieved.

[*Yet more noise.*]

This contract is not binding because – impossible.

[*A swift silence in court.*]

SHYLOCK [*stunned, moves first to embrace* ANTONIO]: Thank God! Thank God! Of course! Idiots! Cut flesh draws blood. No blood, no flesh. Oh, Antonio, how could such a simple fact escape us? Pedants of the law! Shame on you, a disgrace to your tribe. Go down Shylock, to the bottom of the class. Oh, Tubal, what a fool you've had for a partner. No wonder we never owned the really big warehouses.

[*Offering knife to the three men.*] There! For you! *You* need it. You've no wit to draw blood with your brains or tongue, take this. Cruder, but guaranteed. Ha ha! No blood, no flesh. I love the lady. Young lady I love you. You have a future, I see it, a great future.

PORTIA [*with sadness*]: But not you, old Shylock.

SHYLOCK: Not I? Are you mad? I've been delivered of murder – I've got a clean and honest life to continue. Oh, not for a hundred years, I know, and it's a pity because today, TODAY I feel I want to go on living for ever and ever. There's such wisdom in the world, such beauty in this life. Ha! Not I, young lady? Oh yes, I! I, I, I! A great future, also. Back to my books.

DOGE: No, Shylock, no books.

SHYLOCK: No books? Will you take my books?

ANTONIO: You take his life when you take his books.

SHYLOCK: What nonsense now?

DOGE: No nonsense, I'm afraid, Shylock. An old Venetian law condemns to death and confiscation of his goods the alien who plots against the life of a citizen of Venice.

SHYLOCK: I? Plot? Against a citizen of Venice? Who? Antonio?

DOGE: You pursued that which would end a man's life.

SHYLOCK: But was 'that' which I pursued 'plot'? Plot? Malice aforethought?

DOGE: Malice aforethought or not, the end was a citizen's death.

ANTONIO: However –

SHYLOCK: But there's no perception, no wisdom there –

ANTONIO: However –

SHYLOCK: – no pity there.

GRAZIANO: Pity's called for now!

ANTONIO: HOWEVER! The law also says the offender's life is at the mercy of the Doge –

DOGE: Which mercy I make no delay in offering you. But the State must take your goods. The people of Venice would not understand it if –

SHYLOCK: Oh! The people of Venice, of course.

LORENZO: See what contempt he has.

SHYLOCK: The people again. What strange things happen behind the poor people's name.

DOGE: – The people of Venice would not understand it if the law exacted no punishment at all for such a bond.

SHYLOCK: Of course.

ANTONIO: And I? What punishment do the people of Venice exact of me?

DOGE: Your foolishness, Signor, was punished by the pain of threatened death. Enough!

ANTONIO: The wisdom of patrician privilege, of course.

DOGE: But do not strain it, friend. Do not.

ANTONIO [*bowing*]: I thank you.

> [*The* DOGE *and all leave, except* SHYLOCK, ANTONIO, PORTIA, JESSICA.]

SHYLOCK [*turning to* PORTIA]: And the lady, where is the lovely lady, what does she say to all this?

PORTIA [*raging at the departed* DOGE]: I would not carry a sword in one hand and scales in the other. That image always seemed to me ambiguous. Is my sword held high to defend the justice my left hand weighs? Or is it poised threateningly to enforce my left hand's obduracy?

SHYLOCK: Impartial justice, lovely lady, impartial justice.

PORTIA: Impartial? How? *I* am not a thing of the wind, but an intelligence informed by other men informed by other men informed! *I* grow. Why can't they? What *I* thought yesterday might be wrong today. What should I do? Stand by my yesterdays because *I* have made them? I made today as well! And tomorrow, that I'll make too, and all my days, as my intelligence demands. I was born in a city built upon the wisdom of Solon, Numa Pompilius, Moses!

> [*They exchange sad smiles.*]

SHYLOCK [*shrugs*]: What can one do?

PORTIA: Wisdom, inconsiderately, does not translate in a moment.

> [*They exchange another smile.*]

SHYLOCK [*with sad pleasure, taking her hand, still as to a daughter*]: You have a future, young lady, I tell you, a great future.

> [JESSICA *finds this tender moment between her father and another young woman unbearable and flees.*]

ANTONIO: Shylock! Explain to the court you did not want to set a precedent in law. You'll save your books.

SHYLOCK [*sardonically and with finality*]: No. Take my books. The law must be observed. We have need of the law, what need do we have of books? Distressing, disturbing things, besides. Why, dear friend, they'd even make us question laws. Ha! And who in his right mind would want to do that? Certainly not old Shylock. Take my books. Take everything. I do not want the law departed from, not one letter departed from.

[*Sound of song.*]

Perhaps now is the time to make that journey to Jerusalem. Join those other old men on the quayside, waiting to make a pilgrimage, to be buried there – ach! What do I care! My heart will not follow me, wherever it is. My appetites are dying, dear friend, for anything in this world. I am so tired of men.

[SHYLOCK *moves away, a bitter man. Everyone has left except* PORTIA. *The scene has changed to Belmont. We hear the distant sad singing of a woman. The song is 'Adiós querida', a Sephardic song.**]

SCENE SIX

[*Belmont. The garden. A warm, heavy, melancholy evening.* PORTIA *strolling,* JESSICA *stands aside. The woman singing in the distance. The air is broken by the sound of raucous laughter.*
BASSANIO, LORENZO *and* GRAZIANO *enter carrying food.*
NERISSA *follows them. A picnic is prepared. They talk, spread a rug, light candles while* NERISSA *prepares platters of food.*]

BASSANIO: A farewell supper! Our friends are leaving, Portia. Tonight must be made memorable.

LORENZO: Jessica! Food!

[*But* PORTIA *and* JESSICA *seem reluctant to join the three young men.* LORENZO *alone notes the indifference, especially of* JESSICA.]

GRAZIANO: It's a splendid house. The most beautiful I've seen. Really, Signorina Contarini, splendid. And what a library! It made me pick up a book for the first time in years.

LORENZO [*acidly*]: Which book?

* See EMI label ASD2649, sung by Victoria de los Angeles.

GRAZIANO: No, no, Lorenzo. You can't keep getting at me. We've been through a lot together now and you know me to be your faithful admirer. I know my limitations and I'm happy to be factotum to your cause. Or causes. Name them, I'll follow. Plot them, I'll execute them. Don't be ungracious. There's a lot to be said for a sycophant.

[ANTONIO *appears*.]

PORTIA: I'm so grateful you stayed, Signor Querini. These two weeks have been made bearable, and I've found a new friend.

ANTONIO: While I've found a woman who's made me mourn my youth. What mixed blessings in these last years of my life: to meet an acerbic old Jew who disturbed my dull complacency, and you, blossoming with purpose, reminding me of a barren life. An unfair restlessness at this depleted age. [*Pause*.] He will haunt me, that man.

[*Silence but for the singing*.]

What will you do?

PORTIA: Honour my father's wishes, marry the man who chose lead, look to what must be grown. And you?

ANTONIO: Sort out what has been salvaged from my ships. See my friend off to the Holy Land. Visit him, once, perhaps, before I die, and you often, if I may, before I die.

PORTIA: Oh please! I would be so indebted.

ANTONIO: But what will happen to her?

LORENZO [*calling her to eat*]: Jessica!

[*She ignores him. He waits throughout the next exchange for her to turn to him. She does turn, contemptuously, then turns away*.]

PORTIA: I'll look after Jessica. My marriage is a parent's will, not hers, though. Mine can't be held back, hers, I will see, never takes place.

ANTONIO: But *which* place will she take? There's no father's house to return to.

PORTIA: But there is a Jerusalem, where he can be followed.

ANTONIO: I don't think I really fear for Jessica, but you . . .

PORTIA: I! I'll fill my house with poets and philosophers, and politicians who are poets and philosophers. Bassanio will come to know his place, accept it, or leave it. I am to be reckoned with, you know, not merely dutiful. Although, something in me has died struggling to grow up.

[LORENZO *turns angrily away from looking at* JESSICA, *finally understanding that he's lost her.*]

LORENZO: I don't think I shall ever lose the image of that man's scowl from my mind. Remember? And how silent he was, to begin with.

GRAZIANO: To begin with he would be, very silent.

LORENZO: Fortunately the law is a terrifying thing and the courts are an awesome place.

GRAZIANO: Ha! But he was awed.

BASSANIO: 'And you I suppose have been chosen instead!' How he spat the words out. A man full of despite and comtempt.

[PORTIA *and* ANTONIO *move away to different corners of the garden. They, with* JESSICA, *are three lonely points of a triangle which encircles the grating sounds of an inane conversation.*]

LORENZO: Perhaps now they will learn, the elders. Virtue consists in simplicity, suffering, renunciation!

GRAZIANO: But we forget Portia, his wife . . .

BASSANIO: Not yet, not yet!

GRAZIANO: His wife to *be*. Now there's a mind to be careful of. Should we envy him or fear for him?

BASSANIO: It was in my stars to make such a match for my bed.

GRAZIANO: You're mad to think only of bed with an intellect like that at your side.

BASSANIO: It shall be cherished but not spoilt. I shall turn to it but not let it rule! Ah! Here comes Nerissa with drink for the heroes.

NERISSA: And heroes you are, sirs, true. No denying it. True, true, heroes indeed. Heroes!

[*Only the singing now and a fading, warm and sad evening.*]

FOR THE BEST IN PAPERBACKS, LOOK FOR THE 🐧

In every corner of the world, on every subject under the sun, Penguin represents quality and variety – the very best in publishing today.

For complete information about books available from Penguin – including Puffins, Penguin Classics and Arkana – and how to order them, write to us at the appropriate address below. Please note that for copyright reasons the selection of books varies from country to country.

In the United Kingdom: Please write to *Dept E.P., Penguin Books Ltd, Harmondsworth, Middlesex, UB7 0DA.*

If you have any difficulty in obtaining a title, please send your order with the correct money, plus ten per cent for postage and packaging, to *PO Box No 11, West Drayton, Middlesex*

In the United States: Please write to *Dept BA, Penguin, 299 Murray Hill Parkway, East Rutherford, New Jersey 07073*

In Canada: Please write to *Penguin Books Canada Ltd, 2801 John Street, Markham, Ontario L3R 1B4*

In Australia: Please write to the *Marketing Department, Penguin Books Australia Ltd, P.O. Box 257, Ringwood, Victoria 3134*

In New Zealand: Please write to the *Marketing Department, Penguin Books (NZ) Ltd, Private Bag, Takapuna, Auckland 9*

In India: Please write to *Penguin Overseas Ltd, 706 Eros Apartments, 56 Nehru Place, New Delhi, 110019*

In the Netherlands: Please write to *Penguin Books Netherlands B.V., Postbus 195, NL–1380AD Weesp*

In West Germany: Please write to *Penguin Books Ltd, Friedrichstrasse 10–12, D–6000 Frankfurt/Main 1*

In Spain: Please write to *Longman Penguin España, Calle San Nicolas 15, E–28013 Madrid*

In Italy: Please write to *Penguin Italia s.r.l., Via Como 4, I-20096 Pioltello (Milano)*

In France: Please write to *Penguin Books Ltd, 39 Rue de Montmorency, F-75003 Paris*

In Japan: Please write to *Longman Penguin Japan Co Ltd, Yamaguchi Building, 2–12–9 Kanda Jimbocho, Chiyoda-Ku, Tokyo 101*

PLAYS IN PENGUIN

Edward Albee   **Who's Afraid of Virginia Woolf?**

Alan Ayckbourn   **The Norman Conquests**

Bertolt Brecht   **Parables for the Theatre (The Good Woman of Setzuan/The Caucasian Chalk Circle)**

Anton Chekhov   **Plays (The Cherry Orchard/Three Sisters/Ivanov/The Seagull/Uncle Vanya)**

Henrik Ibsen   **Hedda Gabler/The Pillars of the Community/The Wild Duck**

Eugène Ionesco   **Absurd Drama (Rhinoceros/The Chair/The Lesson)**

Ben Jonson   **Three Comedies (Volpone/The Alchemist/Bartholomew Fair)**

D. H. Lawrence   **Three Plays (The Collier's Friday Night/ The Daughter-in-Law/The Widowing of Mrs Holroyd)**

Arthur Miller   **Death of a Salesman**

John Mortimer   **A Voyage Round My Father/What Shall We Tell Caroline?/ The Dock Brief**

J. B. Priestley   **Time and the Conways/I Have Been Here Before/An Inspector Calls/The Linden Tree**

Peter Shaffer   **Lettice and Lovage/Yonadab**

Bernard Shaw   **Plays Pleasant (Arms and the Man/Candida/The Man of Destiny/You Never Can Tell)**

Sophocles   **Three Theban Plays (Oedipus the King/Antigone/Oedipus at Colonus)**

Arnold Wesker   **Plays, Volume 1: The Wesker Trilogy (Chicken Soup with Barley/Roots/I'm Talking about Jerusalem)**

Oscar Wilde   **Plays (Lady Windermere's Fan/A Woman of No Importance/ An Ideal Husband/The Importance of Being Earnest/Salome)**

Thornton Wilder   **Our Town/The Skin of Our Teeth/The Matchmaker**

Tennessee Williams   **Sweet Bird of Youth/A Streetcar Named Desire/The Glass Menagerie**

FOR THE BEST IN PAPERBACKS, LOOK FOR THE 🐧

A SELECTION OF FICTION AND NON-FICTION

Perfume Patrick Süskind

It was after his first murder that Grenouille knew he was a genius. He was to become the greatest perfumer of all time, for he possessed the power to distil the very essence of love itself. 'Witty, stylish and ferociously absorbing' – *Observer*

A Confederacy of Dunces John Kennedy Toole

In this Pulitzer Prize-winning novel, in the bulky figure of Ignatius J. Reilly, an immortal comic character is born. 'I succumbed, stunned and seduced ... a masterwork of comedy' – *The New York Times*

In the Land of Oz Howard Jacobson

'The most successful attempt I know to grip the great dreaming Australian enigma by the throat and make it gargle' – *Evening Standard*. 'Sharp characterization, crunching dialogue and self-parody ... brilliantly funny' – *Literary Review*

Falconer John Cheever

Ezekiel Farragut, fratricide with a heroin habit, comes to Falconer Correctional Facility. His freedom is enclosed, his view curtailed by iron bars. But he is a man, none the less, and the vice, misery and degradation of prison change a man...

The Memory of War and Children in Exile: Poems 1968–83 James Fenton

'James Fenton is a poet I find myself again and again wanting to praise' – *Listener*. 'His assemblages bring with them tragedy, comedy, love of the world's variety, and the sadness of its moral blight' – *Observer*

The Bloody Chamber Angela Carter

In tales that glitter and haunt – strange nuggets from a writer whose wayward pen spills forth stylish, erotic, nightmarish jewels of prose – the old fairy stories live and breathe again, subtly altered, subtly changed.

The Book of Laughter and Forgetting Milan Kundera

'A whirling dance of a book ... a masterpiece full of angels, terror, ostriches and love ... No question about it. The most important novel published in Britain this year' – Salman Rushdie in the *Sunday Times*

Miami Joan Didion

'Joan Didion's Miami is at once an aggressively real city and a legendary domain to which Swift might well have posted Gulliver ... a work that combines intense imaginative vision with extraordinary argumentative force' – Jonathan Raban in the *Observer*

Milk and Honey Elizabeth Jolley

'In a claustrophobic family of Viennese refugees to Australia, the young boarder Jacob studies the cello, and is alternately pampered and terrified until his father dies and leaves him a fortune ... a quirky, brilliantly written study on the amorality of ignoring reality' – *The Times*

Einstein's Monsters Martin Amis

'This collection of five stories and an introductory essay ... announces an obsession with nuclear weapons; it also announces a new tonality in Amis's writing' – John Lanchester in the *London Review of Books*. 'He has never written to better effect' – John Carey in the *Sunday Times*

In the Heart of the Country J. M. Coetzee

In a web of reciprocal oppression in colonial South Africa, a white sheep-farmer makes a bid for salvation in the arms of a black concubine, while his embittered daughter dreams of and executes a bloody revenge. Or does she?

In Custody Anita Desai

Deven, a lecturer in a small town in northern India, is resigned to a life of mediocrity and empty dreams. Asked to interview Delhi's greatest poet, he discovers a new kind of dignity...

Cal Bernard Mac Laverty

Springing out of the fear and violence of Ulster, *Cal* is a haunting love story from a land where tenderness and innocence can only flicker briefly in the dark. 'Mac Laverty describes the sad, straitened, passionate lives of his characters with tremendously moving skill' – *Spectator*

The Rebel Angels Robertson Davies

A glittering extravaganza of wit, scatology, saturnalia, mysticism and erudite vaudeville. 'The kind of writer who makes you want to nag your friends until they read him so that they can share the pleasure' – *Observer*

Stars of the New Curfew Ben Okri

'Anarchical energy with authoritative poise ... an electrifying collection' – Graham Swift. 'Okri's work is obsessive and compelling, spangled with a sense of exotic magic and haunted by shadows ... reality re-dreamt with great conviction' – *Time Out*

The Magic Lantern Ingmar Bergman

'A kaleidoscope of memories intercut as in a film, sharply written and trimmed to the bone' – *Sunday Times*. 'The autobiography is exactly like the films: beautiful and repulsive; truthful and phoney; constantly startling' – *Sunday Telegraph*. 'Unique, reticent, revealing' – Lindsay Anderson

August in July Carlo Gébler

On the eve of the Royal Wedding, as the nation prepares for celebration, August Slemic's world falls apart. 'There is no question but that he must now be considered a novelist of major importance' – *Daily Telegraph*

The News from Ireland William Trevor

'An ability to enchant as much as chill has made Trevor unquestionably one of our greatest short-story writers' – *The Times*. 'A masterly collection' – *Daily Telegraph*

ARNOLD WESKER'S PLAYS IN PENGUIN

Volume 1: **The Wesker Trilogy**

Chicken Soup With Barley/Roots/I'm Talking About Jerusalem

Over 350,000 copies sold!

'A trilogy which will act as a monument to its era' – Robert Muller in the *Daily Mail*

'The passion of Mr Wesker's themes is matched by the living fire in his writing ... its quality is undiminished by the passing years' – Bernard Levin

'This remarkable experiment ... is very funny, very personal, very touching, very bright, very lively, very human and very beautifully written' – *Daily Express*

Volume 2: **The Kitchen and Other Plays**

The Kitchen
'Flashing, illuminating, moving, funny, passionate, authentic' – Bernard Levin in the *Daily Express*

The Four Seasons
'It sings, often beautifully, of how love came, and worked its transfiguration, and then went away' – Harold Hobson in the *Sunday Times*

Their Very Own and Golden City
'It is territory that few playwrights have ventured into and he renders it with beautiful accuracy' – Ronald Bryden in the *Observer*

ARNOLD WESKER'S PLAYS IN PENGUIN

Volume 3: Chips With Everything and Other Plays

Chips With Everything
'A gauntlet of a play has been flung down on the stage . . . furious, compassionate and unforgiving' – *Observer*

The Friends
'This is Wesker's most ambitious play . . . bold and finally beautiful in its dramatic sweep' – *Evening Standard*

The Old Ones
'It works a singular magic through its author's stubborn belief that his bruised people, undefeated in defeat, are worthy of respect' – *Observer*

Love Letters on Blue Paper
'An uncompromising exploration of death . . . deeply moving' – *Yorkshire Post*

also published

Love Letters on Blue Paper and Other Stories

'Integrity and a deep sense of pity are the qualities that emerge from these thoughtful stories' – *Sunday Times*

In these five finely observed stories, originally published individually, Arnold Wesker unflinchingly faces the complexities of life with both irony and generosity and finds cause for celebration in the midst of sadness.

BY THE SAME AUTHOR

ARNOLD WESKER'S PLAYS IN PENGUIN

Volume 5: **One Woman Plays**

Yardsdale/Whatever Happened to Betty Lemon?/Four Portraits – of Mothers/The Mistress/Annie Wobbler

In this cycle of plays Arnold Wesker explores many contrasting facets of womanhood, from defiance and self-assertiveness to despair and self-denial.

'From this earliest plays, Wesker has always delineated women with understanding and sympathy. Both these qualities are present here ... each character convinces one equally of the depth of her suffering and of the resilience of her spirit' – Francis King in the *Sunday Telegraph*

Volume 6: **Lady Othello and Other Plays**

Caritas, Lady Othello and *One More Ride on the Merry-Go-Round*
'... Just when you think you've got him pinned down as a Jew, along he comes with *Caritas*, a story steeped in Christian mysticism. And when you fancy you've got him nailed as a descendant of lofty Victorian teachers ... he throws off the mask of Puritan self-betterment and social responsibility with a sexy, rueful comedy *One More Ride on the Merry-Go-Round* and a heart-stopping account of a New York love affair in his play *Lady Othello*, both filled with awareness of personal and sexual experience beyond the reach of politics' – Michael Kustow in *Time Out*

When God Wanted a Son
Is anti-semitism here to stay? Wesker explores this question through a dissolved mixed marriage.

Bluey
'A High Court judge sitting alone, in anguish and in judgement on himself ... a riveting work' – *Evening Standard*

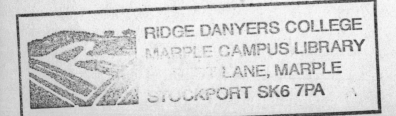